FLANNERY O'CONNOR

Flannery O'Connor:

Voice of the Peacock

KATHLEEN FEELEY, S.S.N.D.

1907

New York
FORDHAM UNIVERSITY PRESS
1982

*To my mother and father
and Flannery's mother*

Acknowledgments

I am grateful to Regina Cline O'Connor, Flannery's mother, for extending hospitality to me twice and for opening Flannery's library to me; to Caroline Gordon Tate, for sharing her memories of Flannery with me; to Leo J. Zuber of Decatur, Georgia, for giving me valuable primary source material; to the staffs of Mary Vinson Library, Milledgeville, and Georgia State College Library at Milledgeville, and to Robert J. Mulligan of Rutgers University Library for their valuable assistance; to Professor David R. Weimer, Rutgers University, for enlightened direction and perceptive criticism; to Sister Maura, S.S.N.D., Chairman and Professor of English, College of Notre Dame of Maryland, and to my colleagues there, for their interest, encouragement, and support; and to Sister Mary Gilbert, S.S.N.D., for typing the manuscript.

Quotations from the works of Flannery O'Connor are used by permission from Harold Matson Company, Inc., for the Estate of Mary Flannery O'Connor; from Flannery O'Connor, *Mystery and Manners*, Occasional Prose, selected and edited by Sally and Robert Fitzgerald, also by permission of Farrar, Straus & Giroux, Inc. Copyright © 1957, 1961, 1963, 1964, 1967, 1969 by the Estate of Mary Flannery O'Connor. Copyright © 1962 by Flannery O'Connor, copyright © 1961 by Farrar, Straus & Cudahy, Inc. Quotations from Carl Jung, *Modern Man in Search of a Soul*, 1933, are used by permission of Harcourt Brace Jovanovich, Inc.

Contents

Foreword

A great deal has been written about the young fiction writer Flannery O'Connor, who died a few years ago. Sister Kathleen Feeley's book is the only one I have read which shows conclusively in what respect her work differs from that of her contemporaries.

Miss O'Connor lived a restricted life because of her invalidism. She died at the age of thirty-nine of a rare form of lupus—the same disease which took her father's life when he was forty. She wrote about people she encountered in her daily life—on her mother's farm, Andalusia, and in her home town, Milledgeville, Georgia—country judges, landowners, farm hands, filling-station operators, Protestant evangelists—both "child" and adult —young men and women who had gone North to college and, in consequence, looked down on their families and neighbors. Many of these people were illiterate. Many of them were religious fanatics. Some of them were freaks. They had one common denominator: violence. It smolders beneath the surface in all her stories and, in the end, frequently erupts in crime.

For most of her early readers violence and the prevalence of the grotesque were the outstanding characteristics of her work. And it is true that at first glance these stories seem to conform to a pattern which of late years has been increasingly popular with Northern readers. The South is commonly regarded as a region which is populated mostly by illiterates, corrupt sheriffs, and freaks. One of her early critics remarked that he could see no difference between a story by Flannery O'Connor and one by another Southern writer, Truman Capote, since they were both "full of freaks."

Miss O'Connor herself dealt with this misconception in an essay: "Some Aspects of the Grotesque in Southern Fiction." She wrote:

> Whenever I'm asked why Southern writers particularly have a penchant for writing about freaks, I say it is because we are still able to recognize one. To be able to recognize a freak, you have to have some conception of the whole man, and in the South the conception of the whole man is still, in the main, theological. . . . I think it is safe to say that while the South is hardly Christ-centered it is most certainly Christ-haunted. The Southerner . . . is very much afraid that he may have been formed in the image . . . of God. Ghosts can be very fierce and instructive. They cast strange shadows . . .

This essay, however, was written near the close of her short life. It took a good many years to reveal the difference between her characters and Truman Capote's, say. His characters are freaks because they embody, along with subterranean upheavals, many of the stresses and anxieties of our times. Miss O'Connor's freaks are seen in a longer perspective. If they are freaks, it is because they have been deprived of the blood of Christ. It is this deprivation which impels them to violence. Haze Motes, an illiterate street preacher in *Wise Blood,* is obsessed by the dogma which theologians describe as the "hypostatic union," the same dogma which held the lifelong attention of the elder Henry James. Henry James, Sr., spoke of it as "the venomous tradition of a disproportion between man and his maker" and attempted to solve his problem by founding his "New Church," of which, as one of his friends wittily remarked, he was "the only member." Haze, less articulate, attempts the same solution. He calls his church the "Church Without Christ" and, finally, unable to perceive any glimmer of light in the dark tunnel of his theological speculations, blinds himself. "The Misfit," an escaped convict in the blood-chilling story "A Good Man is Hard to Find," also wrestles with theological problems—in the intervals of murdering a father, a mother, their three children, and the grandmother of the family. When he has finished his mass murder he pronounces his *Credo,* that if Jesus, who "thown everything off balance," didn't do what He said, then it's nothing for you to do but enjoy the few minutes you got left . . . by killing somebody or burning down his house or doing some other meanness to him.

Sister Mariella Gable, a Benedictine nun, with whom Miss O'Connor frequently corresponded, has pointed out that Flannery O'Connor was writing "ecumenical fiction" before John XXIII sanctioned the "up-dating" of the Roman Catholic Church. One is struck by the fact that most of Flannery O'Connor's characters are Protestants. She once explained to Sister Mariella that she wrote about "Protestant believers" rather than "Catholic believers" not only because she was surrounded by them but because they expressed themselves in "diverse forms of action," that is to say, in actions which were more easily translated into fiction—the kind of fiction she knew she had a gift for writing. For her the Protestant believer is "Christ-haunted."

Miss O'Connor, like one of her masters, Henry James, can be described as Percy Lubbock described James, as a "scholar of the novel." James records his exploration of fictional techniques in his journals. Miss O'Connor has left her record of exploration in the lectures she delivered at various universities and in essays. She came to the conclusion that the fiction writer—the "good fiction writer"—is a "realist of distances." His protagonist, no matter how forthrightly he is portrayed in his mundane surroundings, is always involved in a supranatural experience. The chief concern of the fiction writer, she held, is "with mystery as it is incarnated in human life."

She recognized, of course, that "the realist of distances" is not well thought of in our times, even though he may be in the dominant tradition of American letters:

> Whenever the public is heard from, it is heard demanding a literature which is balanced and which will somehow heal the ravages of our times. In the name of social order, liberal thought, and sometimes even Christianity, the novelist is asked to be the handmaid of his age.

Miss O'Connor, who once blithely remarked that she could wait fifty, indeed a hundred, years to have one of her own stories read right, was convinced that the fiction writer has a higher destiny than the one allotted him by the public. In an essay, "Catholic Novelists and Their Readers," she dismisses the popular notion that the Catholic Church acts as a "restraint on the creativity of the Catholic writer" and maintains that, on the contrary, Christian dogma is an "instrument for penetrating reality":

> The fiction writer is an observer, first, last, and always, but he cannot be an adequate observer unless he is free from uncertainty about what he sees. Those who have no absolute values cannot let the relative remain merely relative; they are always raising it to the level of the absolute.

Christian dogma is also "about the only thing left in the world that surely guards and respects mystery."

I believe that Flannery O'Connor's place in the history of American letters is secure because of the uniqueness of her contribution. She was the first fiction writer of outstanding talent to look at the rural South through the eyes of Roman Catholic orthodoxy. There are many theological implications in her writings, but they lie so far beneath the surface of the literal level that they do not obtrude themselves upon our consciousnesses on a first, sometimes even a second reading. It is not generally known that she was a keen amateur theologian and owned one of the finest private theological libraries in this country.

For this reason I think that, at present, Sister Kathleen's book is the best guide any serious student of Miss O'Connor's work can lay hold of. There have been many books about Flannery O'Connor's work—some excellent, some mediocre. They are, for the most part, critical appraisals of her art. It is time that the bedrock on which her achievement rests is revealed. Sister Kathleen has unusual qualifications for the task. She did not know Flannery O'Connor in life but she is steeped in her writings. And she has spent many hours in her library, reading the books she read, noting the passages she marked. It is our good fortune that she writes on her subject—the theological background of Flannery O'Connor's work—with such lucidity, sympathy, and authority.

CAROLINE GORDON

Preface

Flannery O'Connor evidently took great delight in the reprint of her first novel, *Wise Blood*, ten years after its initial publication. I am equally delighted with this reprinting after ten years. O'Connor stated that her book was written with zest; I will say the same. In this Preface I would like to tell you how the book was written, and respond to critics who have chided me for not doing more than I did in assessing her library holdings, as well as critics who aver that I did too much in trying both to explore the influences on her work and to critique the work.

Recently, I gave a series of lectures on Flannery O'Connor and her place in the American tradition at a number of colleges and universities in Japan. I met with and dialogued with professors of American literature and their students who were quite knowledgeable about Flannery O'Connor and profoundly interested in her. O'Connor's Japanese audience largely regards her as an anti-sentimentalist in American fiction. They bear out a thesis in my book that O'Connor can be read as an exciting and thought-provoking fiction writer by those without knowledge of or interest in the theological base of her writings.

For my Japanese audiences, the theology was an unknown factor. They sensed the presence of mystery in the fiction but could not probe it. In my view, their lack of a fundamental knowledge of Christianity led them to some strange interpretations of her fiction. From their view, each artifact communicated its own integrity; each was a well-wrought story. Critical questions which the stories raised could be answered without any reference to the great event of redemption which each of her stories reflects.

This experience of viewing an author whom I know well

through the eyes of a people who do not share the biblical base
on which her fiction rests or possess a knowledge of Christian
culture leaves me, in Frost's phrase, "only more sure of what I
thought was true." The theological basis of O'Connor's fiction
adds a dimension and subtracts nothing.

O'Connor would have been absolutely delighted at the response her stories evoked. No one asked such questions as
"Why was the farm woman named Mrs. May?" or "What is the
significance of Tarwater's hat?" but rather such questions as "Is
O'Connor's anti-sentimental stance a studied reaction to the
currents in American fiction today, or an expression of her
philosophy of life?" Their comments showed that they recognized the universal quality in O'Connor's characters and
identified with the basic conflict in each story.

In preparing to write *Voice of the Peacock*, I had a rare and
beautiful opportunity to reconstruct mentally an author's
working milieu. In the case of O'Connor, this milieu was
extremely important.

Five years after Flannery O'Connor's death, I visited her
mother. At that time, Mrs. O'Connor was living in the family
home in Milledgeville. The farmhouse where she and Flannery
had lived was still as it had been left after Flannery's death.
During the week I was with Mrs. O'Connor we drove every
morning to the farmhouse. While I worked with the books in
Flannery's bedroom/study and in the living room, Mrs.
O'Connor checked on various aspects of the farm and on the
workers who were putting aluminum siding on the farmhouse.

I saw, immediately, how fortunate I was to be working with
Flannery's materials before any other hand had disturbed
them. It was easy to see from the arrangement of her library
which books were important to her. Two of the large bookcases
in the living room had glass doors and there were a number of
small ornaments in front of the books on various shelves. Other
books were in open cases, obviously more accessible. The books
in her bedroom included an entire set of the monographs
collected under the title of The Twentieth Century Encyclo-
pedia of Catholicism. Near her bed was her breviary and a
Book of Common Prayer. Piled on the floor by her bed were
periodicals: *Thought, Sewanee Review, Southern Literary Review,*
and others. It became apparent to me that I should work in two
concentric circles, one having its mid-point at the large easy

chair by her typewriter in the bedroom/study, and the other in the smaller of the two parlors, which contained the open bookcases.

It was a case of "note now; think later." I started examining the books for dates, inscriptions, and annotations. When I found these I noted the specific edition of the book, the pages and paragraphs annotated or marked, and copied markings and annotations. My object was to find and note the books which seemed to be of most importance to her as evidenced by their markings and their position in her library. I had only a week in which to accomplish this.

I note this procedure to make it clear why I did not list every book in her library. It was obvious to me that some were remnants of a family library and some were review copies of books. I felt that the annotated books, not the compass of the entire library, bore a relationship to the shape of her thinking.

In my recent visits to the fine Flannery O'Connor Room at her *alma mater,* Georgia College at Milledgeville, I have seen almost all of the books I handled, now neatly accessioned and shelved. I realized what a difference it makes to see a library *in situ.* As I look around the room I am now working in, I understand how universally human it is to keep one's favorite and one's most useful books near.

When I returned from my first visit to Flannery O'Connor's home I had—in signs and symbols, in page numbers and line numbers, in phrases and sentences—the heart of the overt literary influence on Flannery O'Connor. You can imagine the zest with which I found the identical books, read the material that was marked, and then—in most cases—read the entire book to put the marked passages into context. A relationship among the books and a pattern of thought emerged. Finally that pattern of thought became a bedrock for her fiction. It was exciting to uncover the connections between abstract ideas and the O'Connor characters and conflicts.

A year later, I returned to Milledgeville for a second visit. This time, Mrs. O'Connor and I lived in the farmhouse—now sparkling with aluminum siding. During this visit I double-checked references and explored the farm more thoroughtly. One afternoon Mrs. O'Connor and I watched a peacock eating the flowers which fringed the house. Mrs. O'Connor quoted Flannery: "Let them alone. The roses are beautiful only for a time and the peacocks are beautiful all year round." It was on this visit that I found the cartoon mentioned in the fourth chapter of my book. I also had more opportunities to meet Flannery O'Connor's friends and the townspeople with whom she interacted. I was able to add a number of personal observations to my accumulation of material. I was able to feel for myself how it was to rise each morning in a small farmhouse in Georgia, to gaze out at the peaceful landscape, to hear the activity of the black farmhands, and to respond to the rhythm of this kind of life. The rhythm was a leisurely one. I remember well the afternoon when I was working intensely in the library and Mrs. O'Connor came in and suggested that we stop for a cool drink on the porch. We sat together on the wide screened porch and I surveyed what Flannery had seen so many times: the wide front yard with peacocks strutting about, the horses in the side pasture, the lake (one of the four artificial lakes to water the animals) barely visible in the distance, and the wall of trees on the horizon. I sensed what a solace this view would be after a morning of intense concentration. I understood how Flannery could call this kind of leisure "recuperating" from the morning's work.

In one of her trenchant answers to a questioner, O'Connor said that she used her eyes on what she was facing. Many times I saw how she used her locale to deepen reality in her stories. On my bus ride to Milledgeville I passed a First Methodist church whose pastor was Dr. Bevel Jones. In one of the small towns there was a tavern sign, "Greenleaf." I saw a new building being erected; a billboard proclaimed that it was the School of Bible Prophesy. In a small town, I passed Chancey's Shoe Store.

Leo Zuber, for whom O'Connor wrote numerous book reviews, wrote me that O'Connor "dropped the comment that one could get some good character leads by reading ads in the *Market Bulletin.*" He sent me several copies, and I saw some of her characters in embryo.

During this visit a certain fusion of elements occurred within my mind. I felt the objective view of O'Connor the author which I had had before I came to Milledgeville merge with the subjective view of O'Connor the writer, the daughter, the friend, the neighbor, the invalid (for example, the electric heater in her bedroom was raised about 18 inches from the floor on cinder blocks because Flannery had difficulty bending down to adjust the gauges), and the raiser of peacocks. I felt in my own being the conflict which she must have felt between what she was reading in theology, philosophy, and psychology and what she saw as she looked at the world around her. Out of that distillation of elements came my reflection and my writing.

Therefore, *Flannery O'Connor: Voice of the Peacock* is a blend of objective research and subjective analysis, which is, I believe, a valid form of literary criticism. I make no apologies for the point of view that O'Connor's belief in the mystery of the Redemption was, to adopt her phraseology, the engine that operated her perception.

In a recent O'Connor study it is noted that one of the books which I mentioned is not currently in the O'Connor library and, therefore, it may have been mentioned in error. I assure you, every book about which I spoke I held in my hands in the O'Connor home. That particular book, *Memoirs of a Tatooist*, elicited from me a cry of delight as I saw a photograph of what was to become in O'Connor's fiction "a moving arabesque of color" on a man's body. In regard to Flannery's total collection, all my sins are those of omission; I committed nothing to my note cards which was not there.

In writing this book, I made some assumptions. When *The Habit of Being* was published I read it with great eagerness and also a sense of concern. Here I would find whether or not my assumptions were correct or, at least, whether some other information would render an assumption invalid. The reading was full of delight. Her letters gave additional depth, breadth, and humor to what I had intuited from her writings and from her life. Nothing she said contradicted my assumptions; rather, her correspondence corroborated and enlarged them.

I have met many people who say that they just do not understand Flannery O'Connor's fiction. I advise them to read the first chapter of my book; read one O'Connor story twice with time intervening; read my analysis of that story in the text; read the story again. In more than half of these encounters, the person returned to say that his or her understanding and appreciation increased. Many readers need a little orientation before they can grapple with the "large and startling figures." I am happy that this book provides such an orientation.

Flannery O'Connor commented that a good story "hangs on and expands in the mind." In several educational, religious, and civic meetings I have attended lately, a wide variety of speakers have alluded to a work by O'Connor to illustrate a point. Also, her foreign audience is growing steadily. All this is a sure sign that she speaks a universal language, even though she does "talk Southern."

College of Notre Dame of Maryland
February 1982

FLANNERY O'CONNOR

CHAPTER I

Carved Wooden Spectacles:

the vision of Flannery O'Connor

"The writer's gaze has to extend
beyond the surface . . . until it
touches that realm of mystery
which is the concern of prophets."
F.O'C.

Near the end of her life, Flannery O'Connor wrote a moving story of a lonely old man living with his daughter in New York who longed to return to Georgia to die. Entitled "Judgement Day," it is the last story in her posthumous collection, *Everything That Rises Must Converge.* In it, a scene which epitomizes O'Connor's vision of reality unfolds as the old man, Tanner, recalls his first meeting with Coleman, the Negro who became his lifelong friend. While supervising a work crew in Georgia, Tanner feels the threat to the morale of his workers which the appearance of a lounging black stranger presents. The stranger, Coleman, seems to be baiting Tanner, the white foreman. His nervous hands whittling a piece of wood, Tanner approaches Coleman. Unaware of the direction in which the knife in his hands is moving, he carves a pair of spectacles, while the Negro watches "as if he saw an invisible power working on the wood." On an impulse, Tanner fastens haywire earpieces on the glasses and hands them to the Negro. Coleman puts them on. Then he "looked directly at Tanner and grinned, or grimaced, Tanner could not tell which, but he had an instant's sensation of seeing before him a negative image of himself, as if clownishness and captivity had been their common lot." *A revelation for the maker of the glasses.*

Then Tanner asked the Negro:
"What you see through those glasses?"
"See a man."
"What kind of a man?"
"See the man make theseyer glasses."
"Is he white or black?"
"He white!" the Negro said as if only at that moment was his vision sufficiently improved to detect it.
"Yessuh, he white!" he said.

Improved vision for one who "can't see so good."
The double epiphany in this scene, which is a modern version of the great restoration-of-sight scenes in Scripture, may well represent the artistic vision of Flannery O'Connor. It is a vision which captures reality accurately, penetrates to its core, and probes its spiritual extensions. Through the carved wooden spectacles of her art, she presents man, distorted, partly grinning,

partly grimacing; partly the clown, living on the surface of life; and partly the captive, under sentence of death and judgment. In this story Tanner's vision of the negative image of himself failed "before he could decipher it." The aura of mystery in which this scene ends is an essential element of Flannery O'Connor's rendering of reality. For her, reality and mystery are inextricably united.

This union of reality and mystery distinguishes Flannery O'Connor's fiction. She once stated, "Fiction should be both canny and uncanny,"[1] and her own work follows this prescription. An example of the power of her fiction to communicate both reality and mystery was once given to me by Caroline Gordon, mentor and friend of the young author. On one occasion when her young friend came North for a visit, Miss Gordon arranged a gathering of her own literary friends whom she wanted Flannery to meet. One of the guests suggested that O'Connor read a story for them. She chose "A Good Man Is Hard to Find." The guests laughed hilariously through the first half of the story; then a strained silence gripped them. (The Misfit, a psychopathic killer, enters the story at its mid-point.) The reading ended in an atmosphere charged with silent response. Miss Gordon remembers that one of the auditors was so moved by the story, whose theological implications he neither believed nor understood, that he spent the next three hours exploring these implications with the hostess. Such was O'Connor's power to combine reality and mystery.

Underlying the penetrating vision of Flannery O'Connor was a deep religious conviction. She stated it simply and matter-of-factly in *The Living Novel,* a symposium edited in 1957 by Granville Hicks:

> I see from the standpoint of Christian orthodoxy. This means that for me the meaning of life is centered in our Redemption by Christ and what I see in the world I see in its relation to that. I don't think that this is a position that can be taken halfway or one that is particularly easy in these times to make transparent in fiction.[2]

To make the mystery of man's Redemption transparent in fiction, Flannery O'Connor grounded her work in reality. She portrayed the visible world by accurate description, making it real—as she said herself—"through what can be seen, heard, smelt, tasted, and touched."[3] She captured people, places, and events in the rural South and, through her art, used them to suggest the life of all mankind. For her, reality did not lead to mystery; it included it. The unseen was as real to her as the visible universe. This belief in spiritual actuality was, in part, a heritage from her deeply Catholic family; her ability to use language effectively to capture reality was an innate talent; her immersion in the cultural world of the rural South was the result of circumstances. These three forces—belief, talent, and environment—worked together in her unique imagination to produce extraordinary fiction.

Basic to a deep exploration of Flannery O'Connor's fiction is an understanding of her absorption in the chief mysteries of Christian life. In answer to a question about her main concerns as a writer, she said, "I will admit to certain pre-occupations: . . . with belief and with death and grace and the devil."[4] She probed these spiritual realities in various ways in her fiction because she believed that they are essential to the fulness of life. But these "pre-occupations" are bound up with Christian theology, not with Catholic doctrine. Therefore, although her fiction communicates deeply spiritual entities, she is far from being a tractarian or a Catholic apologist. In essay after essay in *Mystery and Manners,* a posthumous collection of her occasional writings, she shows only scorn for those who would "use" fiction for any pragmatic purpose, no matter how commendable. Her stories speak of man's alienation from society and from the supernatural world, of his niggardliness with others, of his battle with the forces of darkness, of his acceptance or rejection of grace, because that is what she perceived as she looked around her and looked within her own heart.

O'Connor's belief inspired the basic themes of her fiction; to express them, her talent and imagination led her along the path of comic grotesquery. From childhood, her talent for satirical writing and for cartooning was evident. By the time she was sixteen she had written and illustrated three books, which she designated then as "a novelty type—too old for young children and too young for older people."[5] Her predilection for the unusual, the incongruous, the bizarre had early roots. In an essay on peacock-raising, she tells of her childhood addiction to malformed chickens. "I favored those with one green eye and one orange or with overlong necks and crooked combs. I wanted one with three legs or three wings but nothing in that line turned up."[6] One of her college teachers tells how she fulfilled a final assignment in a required home economics course in high school— "to make an original article of clothing for herself or a child relative." While the other students worked, she seemingly dawdled. Finally the day of reckoning came.

At the end of the week the other projects were laid out on tables ready for the teacher's examination. But no Flannery. The instructor, gradebook in hand, started her inspection of the dainty lace offerings when the door opened and in came the missing student, calm and unhurried, followed by a bantam hen, who frisked along attired in a handmade white pique coat with a belt in the back. (That hen, it turned out, also had an elegant pair of striped trousers.)[7]

The same quiet humor which this action indicates is diffused through the essays and lectures in *Mystery and Manners* and permeates all of her fiction. She linked her innate comic spirit with her religious convictions when she said, "Only if we are secure in our beliefs can we see the comical side of the universe."[8] It was her view of the invisible which allowed her to see the comic aspect of the life around her; always she placed the "seen" in the context of the "unseen." She saw time in the context of eternity, man's struggle against evil as part of the plan for his salvation, the blind malignity of men toward one another as an opening for grace, and flawed and depraved man as the potential "new man" in Christ. Because she envisioned life from its biblical beginnings to its eschatological end, she could smile at what man has made of himself and give him, in her fiction, a glimpse of a new possibility.

O'Connor once said that her reading of *The Humorous Short Stories of Edgar Allen Poe* first inspired her to think of a writing career.[9] Certainly it could have prompted a convergence of her comic spirit and her penchant for the grotesque. Wedged between two larger books in a small bookcase in the dining room of her home, I found that slim volume with its yellowed pages. In it are lesser-known grotesque works of Poe in which the comic element predominates. In such stories as "The System of Dr. Tarr and Professor Fether," Poe bends the grotesquery to achieve a final effect which is almost totally comic. O'Connor uses the same type of grotesquery for a different end. In her essay "The Fiction Writer and His Country," she said:

My own feeling is that writers who see by the light of their Christian faith will have, in these times, the sharpest eyes for the grotesque, for the perverse, and for the unacceptable. . . . The novelist with Christian concerns will find in modern life distortions which are repugnant to him, and his problem will be to make these appear as distortions to an audience which is used to seeing them as natural; and he may well be forced to take ever more violent means to get his vision across to this hostile audience. When you can assume that your audience holds the same beliefs you do, you can relax a little and use more normal means of talking to it; when you have to assume that it does not, then you have to make your vision apparent by shock—to the hard of hearing you shout, and for the almost-blind you draw large and startling figures.[10]

O'Connor's fiction is replete with bizarre situations and grotesque figures that shock one into thought. Never is the grotesque an end in itself. That her use of the grotesque can be misunderstood by those who cannot see the end to which she directed it was made clear to me in a casual conversation with one of the townspeople of Milledgeville, Georgia, O'Connor's home town. A woman told me that she knew Flannery and her mother and often ate at the Sanford House where the O'Connor mother and daughter usually lunched. But she added, "I never went near her because I didn't want her to put me in one of those stories." To her, only the grotesque was visible; its significance was not. In O'Connor's hands, the grotesque became a means to "make new" a reality—natural or supernatural—that the eyes and the mind of man are accustomed to gloss over or ignore. She herself called it "a reasonable use of the unreasonable."[11]

Intrinsic to Flannery O'Connor's communication of reality is the milieu which her fiction evokes—the world of the rural

South. It is the world into which she was born and in which circumstances kept her for almost her entire life. Except for three years of graduate study at the University of Iowa and two years in New York and Connecticut, she spent her entire life of thirty-nine years in Georgia. She was born in Savannah in 1925, and her parents moved to Milledgeville when her father became ill with lupus, a deadly disease of the blood which can affect bone and muscle. He died when Flannery was sixteen. She attended Peabody High School and Georgia State College for Women in Milledgeville and then left Georgia for graduate school and a writing career. When the disease which had killed her father struck her, she was forced to leave the Connecticut home of Robert and Sally Fitzgerald, where she was living and writing, and return to Milledgeville. For the rest of her life she battled with disseminated lupus and the effects of cortisone, the only drug which could keep it under control. Forced at length to use crutches, she left her home in Georgia only for a few trips to speak on college campuses. This circumscribed life could have been a stifling limitation; for her, it became a great strength. She immersed herself so deeply in her region that she could reproduce its authentic voice. Through it, she portrayed the universal in the particular. She found that her imagination was "bound"[12] to this region, and yet she experienced its complete freedom when working in the milieu in which her mind and heart were at home. This immersion in her region makes possible the realistic quality of her fiction. One can truly see the world she describes. Her direct and sharp rendering of the "seen" is deliberate; it makes possible an apprehension of the "unseen." As O'Connor stated it, "I think the more a writer wishes to make the supernatural apparent, the more real he has to be able to make the natural world, for if the readers don't accept the natural world, they'll certainly not accept anything else."[13]

Perhaps because of her intellectual isolation, O'Connor nourished her mind, her spirit, and her imagination by reading. After she became ill, she and her mother moved from their colonial home in Milledgeville to a farm about six miles outside of town. There Flannery devoted herself to her vocation as a writer, and her mother managed the farm. During the thirteen years in which Flannery lived and worked there, she built up a diversified library which reveals many interests, notably Scripture, theology, philosophy, psychology, and art. The books are still there as she left them, dust-edged in spite of the glass doors on the cases. The living room has one large bookcase; the dining room, a large case and a small one; and, in the bedroom-study where O'Connor worked, eight bookcases line the walls. O'Connor marked many of these books, sometimes with marginal emphasis marks, sometimes with underlinings, and sometimes with cryptic marginal notes. These markings reveal her response to great minds of the present and the past. Her interest in Scripture, especially in the prophets of the Old Testament, is apparent in the marked volumes of biblical study and philosophy, chief among which are Claude Tresmontant's *A Study of Hebrew Thought*, Bruce Vawter's *The Conscience of Israel* and Eric Voegelin's *Israel and Revelation*. She read theology, ranging from the works of St. Augustine and St. Thomas Aquinas to those of modern theologians like Karl Rahner and Jean Daniélou. She nourished the life of the spirit by the mystical writings of St. Theresa of Avila and St. Catherine of Siena, the spiritual exercises of St. Ignatius Loyola, and the works of Teilhard de Chardin. She had a special interest in religious men of letters, such as John Henry Cardinal Newman and Baron Friedrich von Hügel. The number of books by and about them on her shelves and her references to them in her lectures indicate that she found them kindred intellectual spirits. O'Connor's interest in philosophy was wide-ranging, including the works of Martin Heidegger, Martin Buber, Jacques Maritain, Henri Bergson, George Santayana, and Edith Stein. The passages which she marked in Carl Jung's *Modern Man in Search of a Soul* show her interest in certain aspects of Jungian psychology. Her library also included a wide range of fiction, so wide that no strong influence is obvious. However, she herself alludes to the influence of Edgar Allan Poe, Nathaniel Hawthorne, Henry James, and Joseph Conrad. The following chapters explore the relationship between Flannery O'Connor's eclectic reading and the ideas which one sees imaginatively expressed in her fiction.

One general impression which her markings give is that she found reassurance in the ideas and observations of other writers which coalesced with her own. Because many of the books are not dated, it is difficult to discern whether other writers inspired ideas in her, or whether their ideas confirmed her own thought. An apt illustration of this convergence of ideas appears in the marked passages which concern the limitations of a writer. O'Connor was acutely conscious of her limitations, both in education and talent, and in the mode of life which her physical condition forced upon her. But she accepted these limitations as factors which sharpened her view of reality. About this she said:

We are limited human beings, and the novel is a product of our best limitations. We write with the whole personality, and any attempt to circumvent it, whether this be an effort to rise above belief or above background, is going to result in a reduced approach to reality.[14]

Because she steadfastly refused to move outside of what she considered her area of competence, she probed deeper and deeper into the mystery of man in the milieu which she could depict. Her markings show that her mind was attuned to other writers who spoke of or showed strength in limitation. In her copy of George Santayana's *Three Philosophical Poets,* she marked in the section on Goethe these lines about Faust:

All experience tempts Faust; he shrinks from nothing that any mortal may have endured; he is ready to undertake everything that any mortal may have done. In all men he would live; and with the last man he will be content to die.

In the margin she wrote: "end result: Dr. Mathew [sic] Mighty-grain-of-salt Dante O'Connor; Teresius." This linking of Djuna Barnes' egotistical protagonist in *Nightwood* with the classical blind seer makes a whimsical comment on the absurdity of unlimited ambition. Further on, Santayana makes his own comment:

Man is constituted by his limitations, by his station contrasted with all other stations and his purposes chosen from amongst all other purposes. Any great scope he can attain must be due to his powers of representation. His understanding may render him universal; his life never can.[15]

O'Connor underlined the last sentence quoted, which seems to accord with her own thought. Considered from an aesthetic viewpoint, a passage from Henry James' *The Future of the Novel* which O'Connor marked points in the same direction. Speaking of Guy de Maupassant, James writes:

> In fine, his readers must be grateful to him for such a passage as that in which he remarks that whereas the public at large very legitimately says to a writer: "Console me, amuse me, terrify me, make me cry, make me dream, or make me think," what the sincere critic says is "Make me something fine in the form that shall suit you best, according to your temperament."[16]

O'Connor paused over a similar idea in David Cecil's *Early Victorian Novelists*. She allied herself with illustrious predecessors when she marked this passage:

> If a writer's creative imagination only works within a limited range, it is clear he ought to stay within it. The great conscious artists—Jane Austen, Flaubert, and Turgenev do; and this is why they are so consistently successful. There is a great deal they cannot write about; but they do not try.[17]

One element in O'Connor's mode of fiction which has been misunderstood is her use of Protestant religious sects to communicate her concerns about Christian life. She writes about backwoods fundamentalists because they are part of the local scene in Georgia and Tennessee, and she knows that their dramatic religious activities are good material for fiction. But she uses the local scene only as a starting place for the transcendent extensions of her thought. As she said to the Georgia Council of Teachers of English, "The Georgia writer's true country is not Georgia, but Georgia is an entrance to it for him."[18] Analogously, she uses Protestant religious activities as an entrance to Christian theology. Some misunderstanding has arisen about this firmly committed Catholic writer's use of her material; I have talked with some of her townspeople who feel that she was ridiculing fanatical Protestant sects. Actually, O'Connor was obeying her own dictum, "The writer uses his eyes on what he happens to be facing,"[19] and exploiting her unique talent: "To some extent a writer can choose his subject, but he can never choose what he can make live. It is characters like the Misfit and the

Bible salesman that I can make live."[20] In a lecture a year before her death, she tried to clarify her intention:

> When you write about backwoods prophets, it is very difficult to get across to the modern reader that you take these people seriously, that you are not making fun of them, but that their concerns are your own, and, in your judgment, central to human life.[21]

O'Connor's stories describe overt religious activities which are signs—even if distorted ones—of the imminence of belief. In this way her stories are truly ecumenical—beyond sects and dogmas, and embracing all mankind.

In her copy of Jung's *Modern Man in Search of a Soul*, O'Connor marked this sentence: "There are hardly any exceptions to the rule that a person must pay dearly for the divine gift of the creative fire."[22] No one will know the terms of her payment, because O'Connor was characteristically silent—or nonchalant—about her crippling disease. To one who asked if her sickness had any effect on her writing, she answered crisply, "The disease is of no consequence to my writing, since for that I use my head and not my feet."[23] She also minimized the cost of discipline, of her three-hour daily stint at the typewriter, where she forged and reforged her fiction:

> Most writers have had many obstacles put in their way. I have had none. . . . There has been no interesting or noble struggle. The only thing I wrestle with is the language and a certain poverty of means in handling it, but this is merely what you have to do to write at all.[24]

In spite of her words to the contrary, all who knew her well affirm that her illness both debilitated the flesh and forged the spirit that was Flannery O'Connor's. Her fiction is the product of that spirit, which, because it was open to spiritual reality, saw all reality more clearly.

In his introduction to *Everything That Rises Must Converge*, Robert Fitzgerald warns against treating O'Connor's stories as "problems for exegesis or texts to preach on."[25] It is a valid caution; such treatment would wrench apart the fictional work, which was conceived as a totality. An understanding of the unity of O'Connor's artifacts is aided by a knowledge of a slim, well-used volume in her library, Jacques Maritain's *Art and Scholasticism.* Among the passages which O'Connor marked is the following:

> Do not make the absurd attempt to sever in yourself the artist and the Christian. They are one, if you really *are* a Christian, and if your art is not isolated from your soul by some aesthetic system. But apply only the artist in you to the work in hand; precisely because they are one, the work will be as wholly of the one as of the other.[26]

Flannery O'Connor, who called herself "a Thomist through and through,"[27] lived by this principle of Thomas's disciple. Because her work is wholly "of the artist," it possesses artistic validity. Because it is also wholly "of the Christian," it has what O'Connor herself called "an added dimension"[28]—an exploration of man's relationship with the divine; a teleological thrust toward the mystery of death; and an anagogical (ultimate spiritual and mystical) level of meaning. It is the movement into this added dimension, or the relationship between natural and supernatural reality, which the following chapters explore.

Through these explorations, it becomes evident that Flannery O'Connor, who was "merely" writing fiction, obeying only the demands of her talent and satisfying only the necessities of art, sensed that she was doing much more. In Jung's *Modern Man in Search of a Soul,* she marked this passage:

> The archetypal image of the wise man, the saviour or redeemer, lies buried and dormant in man's unconscious since the dawn of culture; it is awakened whenever the times are out of joint and a human society is committed to a serious error. When people go astray they feel the need of a guide or teacher or even of a physician. These primordial images are numerous, but do not appear in the dreams of individuals or in works of art until they are called into being by the waywardness of the general outlook. When conscious life is characterized by one-sidedness and by a false attitude, then they are activated—one might say "instinctively"—and come to light in the dreams of individuals and the visions of artists and seers, thus restoring

the psychic equilibrium of the epoch.

> In this way the work of the poet comes to meet the spiritual
> need of the society in which he lives. (P. 171)

This psychological explanation of the role of the artist in society
seemed to strike an answering note in Flannery O'Connor's mind.
However, when she expressed the same idea, she transmuted it to
a spiritual level; she viewed the artist as a healer through his
unique vision. Near the end of her life, she said in a lecture:

> We should realize that if the novelist is a healer at all, it will
> only be through his being a poet. The poet is like the blind
> man cured in the Gospels, who looked then and saw men as if
> they were trees, but walking. This is the beginning of vision.[29]

The following chapters attempt to illuminate the dimensions of
that vision of reality which relate to the deep religious belief
which inspired it. The artistry of her work is apparent; more
subtle are the theological implications which it embodies. A contemporary theologian, Rev. Robert L. Faricy, S.J., commented on
the theology in her work:

> Flannery O'Connor is a theologian as well as a great fiction
> writer. She is both, not less one for being the other. . . . Her
> theological method is to interpret God's message to us in Christ
> by and through her own literary gifts. The result is literature,
> and it is also theology—not a theology that is rationalistic,
> conceptual, or even conceptualizable, but a theology that is
> faithful to its literary form, and one that cannot be separated
> from that literary form.[30]

Only an extraordinary imagination could have effected the fusion
of what Thomistic philosophers call matter and form. The
dynamism of an artist's creative imagination is a mysterious
process which cannot be wholly analyzed. One can only obtain
a glimpse of its power by examining the literature and life on
which it fed and the works which it produced. In her essay
"Toward a Christian Aesthetic," Dorothy L. Sayers discusses the
creative mind in terms which illuminate the source of Flannery
O'Connor's power. She sees the act of creation as threefold, yet
indivisible: experience (analogous to the Father); expression (the

Son, or "Word"); and recognition (the Spirit). Miss Sayers explains that the artist "reveals his experience by expressing it, so that not only he, but we ourselves, recognize that experience as our own." She calls this "the *communication of the image in power,* by which the third person of the poet's trinity brings us, through the incarnate image, into direct knowledge of the in-itself unknowable and unimaginable reality."[31]

This concept of the power of a creative mind describes, in some measure, the power of Flannery O'Connor's fiction. Even when she is communicating what could be termed as "unknowable and unimaginable reality," so powerful is her "imaging-forth" of both the visible and the invisible world that each of us sees as much as his vision can encompass and hears—muffled or clear—an answering echo in his own heart.

Perhaps a single, all-encompassing metaphor for Flannery O'Connor's fiction is the peacock's raucous cry. The O'Connor farm in Milledgeville boasts of a profusion of peacocks, all of them descendants of the pair which Flannery bought from a farm in Florida about ten years before her death. I had read about them before I visited O'Connor's home, but I was unprepared for the splendor of the birds that were parading around the farmyard as Mrs. O'Connor and I drove up the dirt road from the highway. It was springtime, and the cocks were using exhibition techniques to attract the hens. My astonishment at their beauty stilled me completely. After I recovered, I reached for my camera. I remember a cock spreading his tail and then shimmering it with a soft, sexual rustle while he took minute, alluring steps backwards. I thought this was for my benefit until I noticed the hen scratching in the dirt at my feet. The peacocks were not noisy that afternoon—only radiantly beautiful.

Mrs. O'Connor promised me a thrilling sight in the evening when the peacocks roosted. At the end of a long, leisurely supper, I thought she might have forgotten, so I suggested that we go outside before we cleared the table. She smiled at my eagerness, and assured me that we would hear them when they began to roost.

We heard them. Ear-piercing cries penetrated the old farmhouse as the birds flew to various high perches—the barn roof, the water tower, the eaves of the farmhouse, and the nearby trees—and called out to their mates. In her essay on peacocks, O'Connor described what I heard: The cock "appears to receive through his feet some shock from the center of the earth, which travels upward through him and is released: *Eee–oo–ii! Eee–OO–ii!* To the melancholy this sound is melancholy and to the hysterical it is hysterical. To me it has always sounded like a cheer for an invisible parade." Further on in the essay, she says, "In the spring and summer, at short intervals during the day and night, the cock, lowering his neck and throwing back his head, will give out with seven or eight screams in succession as if this message were the one on earth which needed most urgently to be heard."[32]

In describing the cry of the peacock, O'Connor has most aptly described her own writing. She too appears to be expressing "some shock from the center of the earth," which resounds differently on different ears. Most readers attest that her work moves them profoundly—it is hard to ignore her "*Eee–oo–iii! Eee–oo–iii!*"—but critics disagree strongly about how and why they are moved. O'Connor's interpretation of the raucous cry of the bird—"a cheer for an invisible parade"—sounds the note of humor which is an essential characteristic of her writing and speaks of the presence of the unseen which is the hallmark of her fiction.

At the end of her essay, O'Connor writes of her determination to withstand the objections of her "kin" to the increasing number of peacocks on her farm: "I intend to stand firm and let the peacocks multiply, for I am sure that, in the end, the last word will be theirs" (p. 21). Increasing critical appreciation seems to indicate that it will be a long time before the definitive word on Flannery O'Connor will be spoken. It may well be that the "last word" can only be the cry of the peacock: the sound of her fictional voice.

Chapter II

Hulga's Wooden Leg:

the creation of a false self

"The imagination works on what the eye sees, but it molds and directs this to the end of whatever it is making. So my characters are both and at the same time drawn from life and entirely imaginary. Not too many people claim to see themselves in them." F.O'C.

When Flannery O'Connor's first novel, *Wise Blood,* was published, the town of Milledgeville found itself with an author on its hands. The townspeople responded with characteristic Southern graciousness. One thousand formal invitations were dispatched to autograph parties, one at the Ina Dillard Russell Library of Georgia State College for Women from 10 A.M. until noon, on May 15, 1952, and the other at Elizabeth's Bookstore, from 4:30 until 5:30 that afternoon. The master guest list was the Milledgeville telephone directory, with names checked, and, next to some, such marginal notations as "include Aunt Louise." The handwritten list of hostesses for each hour included most of the prominent women of the town. Together with these items in the Flannery O'Connor collection at Georgia College is a photograph of the library autographing party. A long table covered with a white cloth holds stacks of the new book, attractively arranged. Behind the table stand three smiling women; at the end of the table, facing the camera at an angle, sits the scowling author. Years later, Flannery's mother commented laconically about the autograph party: "They never had another one."

One wonders who managed to persuade O'Connor to attend the first; everything about it seems to run contrary to her utterly simple approach to life and her wholly truthful approach to reality. Her position and expression in the photograph express pictorially a bit of dialogue in the story, "Good Country People." After inviting her daughter Hulga to tour the farm with her, Mrs. Hopewell says, "If you can't come pleasantly, I don't want you at all," and the girl replies, "If you want me, here I am— LIKE I AM." In this wry statement one hears a single echo of the leitmotif which dominated Flannery O'Connor's life and which her imagination transformed in various ways in her fiction: truth—or absolute self-integrity and an unflinching view of reality. This concept of "being true" and "seeing truly" is ultimately one, but it can be examined from two aspects.

An honest expression of thought is a sign of one's adherence to truth. The earliest literary expression of Flannery O'Connor's honesty, salted and peppered with courage and independence, appears in the 1945 *Corinthian,* her college literary magazine. As editor, she set forth the staff's policy in the editorial, "Excuse Us While We Don't Apologize." In it she acknowledges that the student writer traditionally has three factions to please—students, faculty, and herself—and she details the interests of those factions. Then she closes with this manifesto:

We on the *Corinthian* staff this year think we will be different. We are agreed that we will be just as bad as all previous staff members—but we will be different. Although the majority of you like the "my love has gone now I shall moan" type of work, we will give you none of it. Although the minority of you prefer consistent punctuation and a smack of literary pretension, we aren't going to worry about giving it to you.

In short, we will write as we feel, preserving a modicum of orthodox English and making a small effort at keeping our originality out of our spelling. Some of us will strive for Art, some of us for free publicity, and some, the wiser of us by far, will not strive.

If you like what we do, that's very nice.

If you don't please remember the paper drive when you dispose of your copy.

—The Editor

This direct approach to truth, sharpened by wry humor, is evident in all of Flannery O'Connor's subsequent statements about the writer and his art.

Questioners frequently tested this truthfulness. During a talk which O'Connor gave at her alma mater after she had become a recognized writer, a student asked: "Miss O'Connor, why do you write?" Her answer was direct: "Because I'm good at it." In a later lecture, she commented that she could feel the unease and displeasure which this answer had aroused. Yet she could not modify it. But she elaborated, with unswerving truth and logic:

There is no excuse for anyone to write fiction for public consumption unless he has been called to do so by the presence of a gift. It is the nature of fiction not to be good for much unless it is good in itself.[1]

In her article about raising peacocks, "The King of the Birds," which first appeared in *Holiday*, she told of another question which received a different type of answer. After describing the glory of her peacocks, she said, "Once or twice I have been asked what the peacock is 'good for'—a question which gets no answer from me because it deserves none."[2] This statement bears out a friend's comment that she did not "bear fools gladly." Interviewers learned to expect only plain language from the shy, soft-spoken Southern girl. They also found that their questions could not lead her where she did not care to go. When C. Ross Mullins interviewed her for *Jubilee,* he asked, "What about the novel today, do you think it's dead, dying, ailing, or what?" She responded characteristically: "The health of the novel is one thing that just doesn't interest me. That's for the English teachers to talk about."[3] A revealing response was elicited by a young student who wrote to O'Connor, suggesting that, in view of their common use of the Southern milieu, she and Carson Mc-Cullers might find conversation stimulating. She replied:

Carson McCullers lives in New York, but I'm sure we would have nothing to say to each other. As a matter of fact, I would rather talk to people who are intelligent in other fields— engineers, doctors, what-have-you. I also like to talk to people who are unintelligent in other fields.[4]

Such straightforward answers are indicative of Flannery O'Connor's integrity. Out of her heart, her mouth spoke.

The young Georgia writer's truthful response to reality is the basis on which all her fiction rests. She saw reality truly because she saw all dimensions of reality, including the invisible. She portrayed it truly, aided, perhaps, by her understanding of the Thomistic philosophy of art. In a lecture on "The Nature and Aim of Fiction," she paraphrases one element of this philosophy: "The basis of art is truth, both in matter and mode. The person who aims after art aims after truth, in an imaginative sense, no more and no less."[5] Because Flannery O'Connor sustained a good deal of criticism from Catholic readers who did not like the "reality" which she portrayed in her fiction, she set about to answer the question of how the Catholic novelist could be "true to time and eternity both, to what he sees and what he believes, to the relative and the absolute," and at the same time be true "to the art of the novel, which demands an illusion of life." In her statement, one can find, in addition to the answer, a basis for the integrity of the person who speaks it; in her, novelist and believer are one.

. . . Dogma is an instrument for penetrating reality. Christian dogma is about the only thing left in the world that surely guards and respects mystery. The fiction writer is an observer, first, last, and always, but he cannot be an adequate observer unless he is free from uncertainty about what he sees. Those who have no absolute values cannot let the relative remain relative; they are always raising it to the level of the absolute. The Catholic fiction writer is entirely free to observe. He feels no call to take on the duties of God or to create a new universe. He feels perfectly free to look at the one we already have and to show exactly what he sees. He feels no need to apologize for the ways of God to man or to avoid looking at the ways of man to God. For him, to "tidy up reality" is certainly to succumb to the sin of pride. Open and free observation is founded on our ultimate faith that the universe is meaningful, as the Church teaches.[6]

Truth in this threefold dimension—to the relative, to the absolute, and to art—was Flannery O'Connor's goal, and she acknowledged that neither the pursuit nor the expression was easy. By seeking "in the object, in the situation, in the sequence, the spirit which makes it itself," she actually sought to "intrude upon the timeless," and found that this could only be accomplished "by the violence of a single-minded respect for truth."[7] It is *that* violence which all her fiction shares.

Perhaps it was her utter truthfulness which, paradoxically, allowed her to imagine and create characters who have destroyed their own integrity to pursue a false good. In a catalog of her freaks, characters who re-create themselves according to a chosen image would mark an extreme position. They are farthest away from grace because they lack the truthful appraisal of reality which grace demands. They have set up a false god—education, or art, or economic security, or comfort—and they falsify their very being in order to pay it homage. A number of Flannery O'Connor's short stories show her imagination working on the idea of falseness in a character. Some of the protagonists in these stories look perfectly normal; others have a physical deformity which is symbolic of a spiritual one. In the course of the action, all are given an opportunity to recognize their self-deception. In the author's vision, this recognition is the first step toward truth, which is, in turn, the necessary condition of Redemption. Conversion—a change of direction—is possible only after one recognizes his perversion.

Comic perversion is a key concept in "Good Country People." Both the girl Joy-Hulga and the Bible salesman have perverted their true selves, and each is revealed in his falsity after the word of God is perverted during a seduction scene—itself a perversion of love. Even the structure of the story appears to be a perversion of a traditional short-story form. Two-thirds of the story elapse before the initial meeting of Joy-Hulga and Manley Pointer, the Bible salesman, occurs. In the first section, Flannery O'Connor sets up a relationship between Mrs. Freeman, the hired man's wife, and Mrs. Hopewell, her employer, and between each of these women and the one-legged protagonist, Joy-Hulga. These relationships structure the story. The opening section also sketches Joy through the eyes of her mother: the hunting accident which destroyed her leg, her immersion in atheistic philosophy, and her attempt, at the age of twenty-one, to rename herself and to redirect her life. With relationships demonstrated, background sketched, and tone established, the first personal encounter of Hulga and her "saviour" takes place. From Manley Pointer's opening question ("You ever ate a chicken that was two days old?") to his final assertion ("I been believing in nothing since I was born") the story moves "like the advance of a heavy truck" to its moment of truth.

That the salesman is peddling Bibles is the central perversion of the story. Flannery O'Connor believed in the power of the word of God. The Bible was for her, as it is for Jews and for Scripture-oriented Christians, the power of God and the wisdom of God. God's scriptural word is not a dead letter; it is a living presence. Reading it does more than enlighten the intellect; it unleashes power that moves the spirit. As a perversion of Christianity has driven Joy to become Hulga, so a perversion of the meaning of Scripture jolts her into self-recognition. In her raging accusation of the deceitful salesman—"You're a fine Christian! You're just like them all—say one thing and do another"—Hulga identifies Christianity with hypocrisy. She adds another indication of the emptiness of the Christianity she sees when, earlier in the story, she cries out to her mother: "Woman, do you ever look inside and see what you are not?" The obvious disparity between what Christians should be and what marks the Christians she knows moves Hulga to embrace Heidegger's emphasis on "being"[8] and his consequent agnosticism. The Bible salesman quoted one verse of Scripture—"He who losest his life shall find it"—to emphasize his desire to be a missionary (one sent). In the climactic scene, this verse is rephrased when Hulga assents to showing Manley Pointer (almost too suggestive a name) her wooden leg. ". . . It was like surrendering to him completely. It was like losing her own life and finding it again, miraculously, in his." This perverse application of Scripture holds an ironic truth: Hulga does lose her life—her self-created being, symbolized by her wooden leg[9] and her new name—by the salesman's deception. Given the structure of the story, there emerges the strong possibility that, having lost her false life, she will see herself (as her cliché-prone mother would say) "without a leg to stand on" and she will hobble toward "home."

Critics of Flannery O'Connor who see only the bleakness of the world she creates comment on her "cold, hard look at humankind."[10] They miss her intimation—often dim and fleeting as this one is—of the discovery of truth which could mean a new life for her characters. The Bible salesman readies Joy-Hulga for grace by his streak of diabolism; in this instance, the devil speaks with the voice of truth. When Hulga asks why he wants to see her leg, the salesman says, "It's what makes you different. You ain't like anybody else." Instinctively she recognizes the truth of his words. Her very deformity is a mark upon her. In *Patterns in Comparative Religion*, Mircea Eliade speaks of the manifestation of the holy which often accompanies the unaccustomed or extraordinary. O'Connor marked this passage in her copy:

> This setting apart sometimes has positive effects; it does not merely isolate, it elevates. Thus ugliness and deformities, while marking out those who possess them, at the same time make them sacred.[11]

By her physical deformity, Joy-Hulga is open to the possibility of hierophany: the sacred may become manifest in her.

This physical deformity is the fulcrum of the plot and the motivating force of Joy-Hulga's character. Evidently her life took a new direction after the accident in her tenth year, and the change was epitomized in her twenty-first year when she changed her name from Joy to Hulga—"the name of her highest creative act. One of her major triumphs was that her mother had not been able to turn her dust into Joy, but the greater one was that she had been able to turn it herself into Hulga." Philosophically, to name a thing is to encompass it, to know it, to control it. To bestow a name indicates power, and to rename shows—biblically —the special call of God. Abram became Abraham to begin the dynasty of God's chosen people; Jacob became Israel to form the Israelite nation; Simon became Peter to head the Church of Christ. God summoned his prophets; Hulga summoned herself to a new life. Her renaming is a comic perversion of God's practice, a self-call to a life of sterile intellectualism.

The residue of "Joy" which remains in Hulga becomes a wry humor, perhaps her saving grace. None of the characters respond to it, but it shows that Hulga has a certain respect for truth. "Get rid of the salt of the earth and let's eat," she advises her mother after overhearing the salesman's line. But her mother responds stolidly, "I can't be rude to anybody." Hulga's humor is also lost on Mrs. Freeman. When the hired woman boasts that her son-in-law is so convinced of the sacredness of marriage that "he wouldn't take five hundred dollars for being married by a preacher," Hulga asks, "How much would he take?" but the quip falls flat. These humorous remarks suggest that Hulga would realize the ridiculousness of her situation at the story's end— deserted in a barn loft far from the house, with her wooden leg stolen—and that she would renew her claim to Joy.

A foil for the self-deluded protagonist is the hired woman, Mrs. Freeman, who is absolutely true to her own myopic vision of the world. Her interaction with Mrs. Hopewell opens and closes the story, framing the encounter between Hulga and Manley Pointer. This interaction shows that Mrs. Hopewell takes refuge in clichés to cloak her inability to deal with Mrs. Freeman and that Mrs. Freeman can cope with anything that crosses her path. The opening description of her "forward" and "reverse" expressions might lead one to suspect that Mrs. Freeman will be the center of the story, especially when she and her husband are designated as "good country people." But once the relationship between Mrs. Freeman and the Hopewells is established, the hired man's wife drops out of the story until the last two paragraphs. Stanley Edgar Hyman calls these two paragraphs "superfluous irony,"[12] but actually they are essential to the structure of the story. For Mrs. Freeman exhibits a quality similar to Joy-Hulga's: she is an all-or-nothing person. She has two expressions which she uses for all human dealings: forward and reverse, and she seldom needs the latter. She admits that "I've always been quick." Hulga's deformity attracts her (Mrs. Freeman and the Bible salesman show an interesting kinship there), and she knows Hulga better than the girl's own mother does. This is evident when she begins to call the girl "Hulga," which Hulga regards as an invasion of her privacy. Mrs. Freeman's statement that "some people are more alike than others" obviously refers to Hulga and the Bible salesman; she senses an affinity between them. Perhaps she suspects that they are both role-playing. One can see that she tends to analyze people and situations; she admits this at the end when she says, answering Mrs. Hopewell's comment about the "simple" (naive, guileless) Bible salesman: "Some can't be that simple; I know I never could." Neither could Hulga be that "simple"; if she could not be Joy, then she had to be Hulga. It was either forward or reverse; there was no in-between. On a more mundane level, Mrs. Freeman reflects Hulga's characteristic mental orientation. And because Hulga has been going in "reverse" of her intrinsic potential for many years, one accepts the possibility that her traumatic experience will thrust her "forward" to the positive pole of her personality.

Concomitant with a respect for truth in Flannery O'Connor's creation of this story is a respect for the mystery of grace. In a lecture on "Some Aspects of the Grotesque in Southern Fiction," she enunciated principles which undergird this story:

> . . . If the writer believes that our life is and will remain essentially mysterious, if he looks upon us as beings existing in a created order to whose laws we freely respond, then what he sees on the surface will be of interest to him only as he can go

through it into an experience of mystery itself. His kind of fiction will always be pushing its own limits outward toward the limits of mystery, because for this kind of writer, the meaning of a story does not begin except at a depth where the adequate motivation and the adequate psychology and the various determinations have been exhausted. Such a writer will be interested in what we don't understand rather than in what we do. He will be interested in possibility rather than in probability. He will be interested in characters who are forced out to meet evil and grace and who act on a trust beyond themselves—whether they know very clearly what it is they act upon or not.[13]

Something within her induces Hulga to make possible her encounter with the salesman. Only this is told: "Joy had been standing in the road, apparently looking at something in the distance, when he came down the steps towards her." Many O'Connor characters gaze at something in the distance, and one feels the presence of mystery. The mystery of grace comes close to the surface of the story in Hulga's expression of her slight hope that there *is* goodness in the world, even though she wants to pervert it. When the salesman presents his unholy trinity of offerings—liquor to dull the mind, pornography to excite the senses, and contraceptives to lock the body—the girl is immobile, mesmerized. Then she speaks in an "almost pleading" voice:

"Aren't you," she murmured, "aren't you just good country people?"

It is the voice of faint hope, evidence of an interior struggle against despair. Near the end of the story, after Manley Pointer has removed Hulga's glasses, the narrator enters her consciousness and she views the world with her eyes: the sky is "hollow"; the trees are "a black ridge"; and the fields are "two green swelling lakes." The whole landscape is "shifty." Her firm world—to which she had formerly paid very little attention—has become as shifting sand to her now, with her sight and mobility impaired. "He who losest his life will find it." And the story closes with "Mrs. Freeman's gaze drove forward."

The difference between the false self which Hulga had created and the histrionic falseness of Tom T. Shiftlet in "The Life You Save May Be Your Own" is the difference between a wooden leg —an artificial likeness of the missing limb—and "half an arm"— a limb obviously incomplete. Hulga believed in her self-created identity; Mr. Shiftlet kept "trying on" roles and poses to hide his essential incompleteness.

Tom Shiftlet arrives on the country scene in a "blinding sunset." Conscious that he is being watched by the old woman and her idiot daughter, Lucynell, whose farm he is approaching, he turns and faces the sun. Then he poses: "he swung both his whole and his short arm up slowly so they indicated an expanse of sky and his figure formed a crooked cross." This silhouette of a crooked cross recurs metaphorically in the action of the story as Mr. Shiftlet twists the key ideas of redemption: the primacy of the spirit over the letter of the law; the freedom of man to use his moral intelligence; and the hard demands of love. In his two-week stay on the Crater farm—he elevates it to a "plantation"— he acquires a wife, a car, and seventeen dollars and fifty cents. As the first, Lucynell, is only a means to the other two, he deposits the idiot girl at a roadside eating place. Then, in a benevolent gesture, he picks up a young boy, who penetrates his paternalistic pose with devastating insight. The story closes in thunder and darkness as "with his stump sticking out the [car] window, he raced the galloping shower into Mobile." References to the sunset, the shower, and the progression of the "fat yellow moon" interlock the regular activity of nature with the devious activity of men.

The falsity of both Mr. Shiftlet and Mrs. Crater is evident by the way each appraises the other for possible gain and acts accordingly. As the story progresses, their two selfish interests converge, resulting in the destruction of the innocent. Mr. Shiftlet's first question, "You ladies drive?" indicates his interest in the car he has just seen in the shed. Mrs. Crater leads quickly to *her* primary question, "Are you married or single?" for she was "ravenous for a son-in-law." Mr. Shiftlet wanted to move as the spirit moved him; in purely practical terms, this demanded a car. Mrs. Crater wanted security: a man around the place who would crank her well winch and keep the farm in repair. For these

interests Mrs. Crater was willing to sell her daughter, and Mr.
Shiftlet to buy her, temporarily. Lucynell, grotesque in her mindless beauty, becomes a salable commodity. But she is much more
than this: in reality, the most innocuous character in the story is
the most dangerous. Mircea Eliade explains:

> Perfection in any sphere is frightening, and this sacred or magic
> quality of perfection may provide an explanation for the fear
> that even the most civilized societies seem to feel when faced
> with a genius or a saint. Perfection is not of this world. It is
> something from somewhere else.
>
> This same fear, this same scrupulous reserve, applies to
> everything alien, strange, new—that such astonishing things
> should be present is a sign of a force that, however much it is
> to be venerated, may be dangerous.[14]

Flannery O'Connor marked this passage and wrote in the margin: "the grotesque is naturally the bearer of mystery; is dangerous." It becomes evident that Lucynell's grotesque incompleteness
is the mysterious force which endangers—in differing measure—
the two warped characters who attempt to use her for their own
ends.

As his histrionic salute to the sunset immediately indicates, Mr.
Shiftlet is a player of roles. He arrives in the role of a tramp,
but soon doffs that for the role of philosopher. After he has
passed silent judgment on the age and make of the car, he begins
to philosophize about the human heart, to demonstrate his absorption in the mystery of fire, and finally to interrogate the old
woman about her philosophy of life. Keeping this role always at
hand for his conversations with Mrs. Crater, the one-armed work-
man becomes restorer of the run-down farm. In a week's time the
steps and the greenhouse roof are patched, the hog pen built, the
fence repaired, and he begins the important work: raising the
car from the dead. He is also a teacher. Lucynell learns her first
word because of his diligence, patience, and "personal interest"
in her. But he realizes that he has played dangerously when he
takes on the role of husband; in some intangible way, it touches
his spirit. As he emerges from the courthouse after his marriage
with Lucynell, he looks "morose and bitter, as if he had been
insulted while someone held him." Depression settles upon him

and continues even after he has rid himself of his idiot bride. In an attempt to lift it, he picks up a hitchhiker, for whom he tries to assume the role of mentor and guide. Forced out of this role, Shiftlet plays the role of a suppliant as the story closes. Particularly in the role of philosopher, the tramp reminds one of a crooked cross. When he speaks to Mrs. Crater of the mystery of the human heart and pictures it lying in a surgeon's hand, he might be paraphrasing the scriptural admonition to "circumcise the heart" by cutting it free from unworthy loves; instead, he is trying to impress an ignorant woman. When he insists upon taking Lucynell on a wedding trip, he appeals for justification to the "spirit" in himself—a parody of the Holy Spirit: "The spirit, Lady, is like an automobile. . . . I got to follow where my spirit says to go"; actually, his intention is simply to get money from Mrs. Crater. When he says, after his marriage, "It's the law that don't satisfy me," he might be echoing St. Paul's praise of Christian freedom; actually he is repudiating his farcical marriage with an idiot. Throughout the story one sees Mrs. Crater's purblind view of Mr. Shiftlet balanced by the narrator's omniscient one. Accompanying Mr. Shiftlet's honeyed words are such descriptions as "a sly look came over his face," and "in the darkness Mr. Shiftlet's smile stretched like a weary snake waking up by a fire." Such contrasting viewpoints illumine Mr. Shiftlet's duplicity.

Although the tramp distorts philosophic ideas about freedom and law and love, he is at least aware of them; he has a certain openness to mystery. Mrs. Crater has none. She is described— not without design—as "the size of a cedar fence post." Anything she cannot touch or taste or see is beyond her ken. Her description of Mr. Shiftlet—"a poor disabled friendless drifting man" —contrasted with his description of himself—"I'm a man . . . even if I ain't a whole one. I got . . . a moral intelligence"— points up the difference in their perceptions. Mrs. Crater does not even realize that she is "using" her daughter to buy her own security, but this does not exonerate her. Rather, it reveals her spiritual obtuseness, which precludes an awareness of grace.

The final scene of the story introduces its only truthful character—a grotesquely honest young boy. The words of the young hitchhiker whom Mr. Shiftlet picks up on his way to Mobile actually express his thoughts. Guessing that the boy is running away from home, Mr. Shiftlet begins a sentimental account of his own mother's influence on his life, which he rejected by running away from her. The boy dismisses Mr. Shiftlet's hypocrisy abruptly and jolts the tramp into an awareness of his falseness. But only momentarily. The tramp recovers, and the story ends with a histrionic gesture with which he evidently tries to impress the Lord himself:

> He raised his arm and let it fall again to his breast. "Oh, Lord!" he prayed, "break forth and wash the slime from this earth!"

Then, unruffled, Mr. Shiftlet continues on his way to Mobile— a fitting destination. The end of the story was changed when it was produced as a television play, "The Life You Save."[15] Flannery O'Connor had sentiments "not suitable for public utterance"[16] about the script writer who ended her story with the tramp returning, conscience-stricken, to reclaim the idiot and return to the farm.

Stories such as this one which present truth only in a distorted form sometimes puzzle those who confuse what is true with what is right. For instance, O'Connor tells of being approached the morning after the telecast which had distorted her story by an acquaintance who had never before indicated the slightest awareness of her fiction. "Why Mary Flannery," the woman said to her, "I do declare, I never dreamed you could do such nice work."[17] The woman obviously would not have thought the story "nice work" if it had been produced as it was written. To clarify such misconceptions, O'Connor made this statement during an interview at Spring Hill College:

> All fiction is about human nature. What kind of human nature you write about depends on the amount and kind of your talent, not on what you may consider correct behavior to be. The best forms of behavior are not more desirable than the worst for fiction, if the writer sees the situation he is creating under the aspect of truth and follows the necessities of his art.[18]

The necessities of art led Flannery O'Connor into caricature in "The Comforts of Home," a story which explores two modes of falseness: sterile rationality and sticky sentimentality. Both Thomas, a middle-aged bachelor and local historian, and his mother, a mindlessly benevolent woman, are overdrawn figures of comedy in a story which ends in melodrama. Cartooning was O'Connor's hobby as a child, and she became expert in it as she grew older. Her sharp, satiric cartoons in her high school and college newspaper achieved local renown. Her college linoleum block cuts show the deft strokes which exaggerate one feature of a character to suggest an identity. O'Connor stopped cartooning when she began writing fiction, but one can see the mind of the cartoonist working in some of her fiction, notably this story. Thomas is large, overbearing, and indecisive; his mother is small, round, and resembles a sibyl. Thomas's procrastination is caught aptly by the narrator's comment: "His plan for all practical action was to wait and see what developed." His mother's right- eous benevolence echoes in her statement, "We are not the kind of people who hate," delivered as positively "as if this were an imperfection that had been bred out of them generations ago." Throughout his thirty-five years, Thomas's plan of action has accomplished his goals; through her lifetime his mother's "box of candy" benevolence has nourished her sense of being good to the world. But the advent of Sarah Ham, a nymphomaniac, into their lives precipitates Thomas into action to curb his mother's sentimentality, which was destroying "the comforts of home" for him. Their encounter with Sarah, alias Star Drake, illumines the false premises on which they have based their lives, and the story's pervading horror is that they do not recognize that false- ness.

Early in Flannery O'Connor's writing career, Caroline Gordon advised her to read Cyril of Jerusalem, a fourth-century doctor of the Church. Miss Gordon was later gratified to see a significant quotation from Cyril used as the epigraph for *A Good Man Is Hard to Find.*[19] O'Connor also used this quotation in several lectures, and, in her essay "The Fiction Writer and His Country," she commented on its significance to her:

St. Cyril of Jerusalem, in instructing catechumens, wrote: "The dragon sits by the side of the road, watching those who pass.

Beware lest he devour you. We go to the Father of Souls, but
it is necessary to pass by the dragon." No matter what form the
dragon may take, it is of this mysterious passage past him, or
into his jaws, that stories of any depth will always be concerned to tell.[20]

In "The Comforts of Home" mother and son fall into the
dragon's jaws. Under the temptation to rehabilitate Star Drake,
the mother lets her "hazy charity" degenerate into sentimentality.
Obeying the diabolical promptings of his dead father, Thomas
tries to preserve the peace of his home by framing the young
girl and, that having failed, by shooting her. That he kills his
mother instead is, some critics believe, her salvation and his
awakening,[21] but the story does not effectively compel the reader
to accept the notion of grace offered and accepted. The whole
story points, instead, to a shallowness of character which would,
in the absence of any signs to the contrary, preclude an openness
to grace.

Thomas's mother—nameless, perhaps to suggest her ubiquity—
exhibits a certain tendency in all her actions. She seems "with
the best intentions in the world, to make a mockery of virtue, to
pursue it with such a mindless intensity that everyone involved
was made a fool of and virtue itself became ridiculous." This
perversion of virtue is exemplified when she uses her son as the
touchstone of all her actions. "It might be you," she tremulously
repeats to Thomas as her motive for helping Star beyond the
limits of reason. Clearly Thomas's mother is a victim of sentimentality.

Flannery O'Connor despised sentimentality, a quality which
has been defined as "giving to any creature more love than God
gives it." She saw sentimentality as an attempted short cut to the
grace of Redemption which overlooks its price. She saw its ener-
vating effect in every aspect of life. In a book on communication,
The Image Industries, she marked this passage in which William
Lynch defines sentimentality:

It is that kind of identification of the solemn levels of human
feeling with anything and everything which produces tawdri-
ness and stupidity. It is a form of judging which corrupts the

very deepest fibres of judgment and leaves the soul open to anything and everything—except reality.[22]

She equated sentimentality with false compassion. In a lecture
entitled "The Grotesque in Southern Fiction," she speaks of compassion in a writer:

> Compassion is a word that sounds good in anybody's mouth,
> and which no book jacket can do without. It is a quality
> which no one can put his finger on in any exact critical sense,
> so it is always safe for anybody to use. Usually I think what is
> meant by it is that the writer excuses all human weakness
> because human weakness is human.[23]

Thomas's mother has evidently made such excuses for Thomas
all his life; by no other means could he have become so grounded
in his selfishness. But there are other consequences of her love
which are more mysterious to her son:

> . . . There were times when he could not endure her love for
> him. There were times when it became nothing but pure idiot
> mystery and he sensed about him forces, invisible currents
> entirely out of his control.

Further in the story he muses:

> . . . But when virtue got out of hand with her, as now, a sense
> of devils grew upon him, and these were not mental quirks in
> himself or the old lady, they were denizens with personalities,
> present though not visible, who might any moment be expected
> to shriek or rattle a pot.

Thomas tells his mother that the power of good stimulates the
devil to act, so he opts for the truce of mediocrity. The story
negates this specious reasoning by demonstrating that it is rather
a corruption of good (his mother's sentimentality masquerading
as charity) which creates an evil counteraction. The mother's
"out of hand" virtue really threatens the comfort of her son for
the first time; this threat causes his father's unconscious influence,
dormant until now, to come alive in his mind. His father's spirit

does not rattle a pot; he squats in the historian's mind to suggest devious and finally criminal ways to remove Star Drake from the once-peaceful home. Thomas sees Star as the devil, unrecognized by his mother, with whom she is enmeshed in a "most foolhardy engagement." But he finds the nymphomaniac, at the same time, "blameless corruption" and "the most unendurable form of innocence" because she is not morally responsible. Because he really does not believe in the devil, he fails to recognize his responsibility for the real devil of the story, the devil in his mind, speaking to him in his father's characteristic position and tone. An unseen power in the story, the father is introduced into Thomas's thoughts gradually, almost casually; at the story's end, his influence is so strong that his commands to Thomas receive instant response. Thomas believes that he has inherited his father's reason without his ruthlessness, and his mother believes that her son has "no bad inclinations, nothing bad you were born with." This unthinking denial that Thomas had inherited what theologians term original sin, together with her using her love for her son to measure all her dealings with others, shows that the mother's "virtue" is mere sentimentality. The final evidence lies in her reaction to Star's suicide hoax:

> Some new weight of sorrow seemed to have been thrown across her shoulders, and not only Thomas, but Sarah Ham was infuriated by this, for it appeared to be a general sorrow that would have found another object no matter what good fortune came to either of them. The experience of Sarah Ham had plunged the old lady into mourning for the world.

Such sentimentality as this is a perversion of love. On the other hand, Thomas's ruthless measures to regain the comforts of home show how selfish reasonableness can quickly degenerate into crime. Both characters fall into the dragon's jaws.

Yet Thomas's fall is greater, because initially he has the greater respect for truth. Although selfish and indecisive, he is not dishonest. He evidently hated his unscrupulous father and firmly rejects his evil suggestions until his father's influence becomes too strong for him to resist. To make the sketch of the diabolical old man convincing, O'Connor uses a caricaturist's device: she describes a characteristic view of him, and lets it suggest the lie that was his life.

> . . . His father took up a squatting position in his [Thomas's] mind. The old man had the countryman's ability to converse squatting, though he was no countryman but had been born and brought up in the city and only moved to a smaller place later to exploit his talents. With steady skill he had made them think him one of them. In the midst of a conversation on the courthouse lawn, he would squat and his two or three companions would squat with him with no break in the surface of the talk. By gesture he had lived his lie; he had never deigned to tell one.

The squatting father, whose voice sometimes hisses in Thomas's ear, is, by his dwarfed position, reminiscent of small-Southern-town officials who still carry on business on the courthouse lawn. Behind him is the dim figure of Milton's Satan, who squatted beside Eve to whisper his temptation. The father "lived his lie" by adopting Southern customs for his own ends; for Flannery O'Connor, this was high treason. The squatting position both expresses the father's cold duplicity and suggests his diabolical influence on his son. The son recognizes the evil inspirations, abhors them, and then knowingly succumbs to them.

In accord with the author's expressed philosophy of fiction, there should be a moment of grace in the story. In speaking of the "tired reader," who needs to be "lifted up," Flannery O'Connor said, "There is something in us, as storytellers and as listeners to stories, that demands the redemptive act, that demands that what falls at least be offered the chance to be restored."[24] In this story there is only the suggestion of the possibility of grace. At the climactic moment, when Thomas is deciding whether or not to plant a gun in the girl's purse, he hears the snores of his mother: "They seemed to mark an order of time that had nothing to do with the instants left to Thomas." Few readers would see in this statement a reference to the Hebrew—or biblical—concept of time, a concept basic to Flannery O'Connor's thought and closely related to her concept of history as a form of order, about which more will be said later. According to Hebrew thought, time is noncyclical; it is a moment-by-moment progression toward a designated end, the Parousia. This concept of time implies that the whole of reality is not yet known, that the world is in a stage of becoming. To look at time in this way suggests a philosophical position which influences one's idea of failure. O'Connor imbibed these ideas from Tresmontant's *A Study of Hebrew Thought*, in which she marked this passage, which is crucial to the end of the story:

> Thus failure, in Hebrew thought with its conception of time-creation, cannot have the same significance as it would in a completed cosmos where time has no function. In a world that is definite and complete, failure is viewed as a thing against which one comes to a halt. But in a world that is being invented, failure is never something static. It is only a moment, a phase in the process of creation, of parturition. . . . Within an evolution failure has a sense.[25]

The story ends in "failure" (although the grotesque sheriff would count the accidental murder a success), but in the biblical framework such failure contains the possibility of reversing itself. That the mother's attempt to protect the girl was an act of pure selflessness and counteracted her lifelong sentimentality is a distinct possibility. That Thomas will become as aware of his own shortcomings as he has been of his mother's is another possibility. With these intimations of the power of Redemption in the lives of unbelievers, the story is content to rest.

"The Comforts of Home" is an anomaly in Flannery O'Connor's imaginative excursions into the theme of truth. Its characters seem to be consciously overdrawn, and the story does not have in it the strong sense of "place" which characterizes the author's best work. Although the importance of setting will be developed in a subsequent chapter, it should be noted here that because the characters seem detached from their surroundings, the story veers into melodrama. In Richard Chase's *The American Novel and Its Tradition*, O'Connor marked his definition of melodrama: "tragedy in a vacuum."[26] Unwittingly, she seems to have illustrated this concept. The only scene in the story which anchors it firmly in a small Southern town (a placement which is Flannery O'Connor's strength) is the scene between Thomas and Farebrother, the sheriff, which takes place on the courthouse lawn. Infused with Southern scenery and mores, this brief scene is strong enough to create the character of Farebrother, which substantiates the references Thomas has made to him. A clue to the authenticity of such scenes as this was supplied by one of O'Connor's friends, Leo J. Zuber, book editor for *The Bulletin*, Savannah-Atlanta diocesan newspaper, and later for *The Southern Cross*, Savannah diocesan weekly. O'Connor wrote reviews for Mr. Zuber's book section. About the various springs which fed her imagination, Mr. Zuber wrote:

> She could not get around very well on foot but would sit in the car while her mother shopped or did other business in town; one can observe a great deal just sitting in a car on the square in a Southern town; the whole local universe passes by.[27]

More of the "local universe" would have rendered this conflict between sentimentality and rationality more persuasive, but the story does succeed in illuminating a perversion of truth by excess —too much "love"; too much "reason."

Much closer than "The Comforts of Home" to Flannery O'Connor's strongest beliefs about the integrity of self, "here I am—LIKE I AM," are two stories which explore man's obligation to be true to the talents which have been given him. In both "The Enduring Chill" and "The Partridge Festival," she narrows this idea to one particular talent—writing. In her lectures to college students, O'Connor spoke frequently about the danger—and ultimately the uselessness—of trying to substitute craft, or cleverness, or technique, for innate talent. In one such lecture she said:

> The ability to create life with words is essentially a gift. If you have it in the first place, you can develop it; if you don't have it, you might as well forget it.
>
> But I have found that the people who don't have it are frequently the ones hell-bent on writing stories.[28]

In these two artifacts, O'Connor explores imaginatively the lives of two young men who have deluded themselves about their talents and in so doing have created false identities. But although the two stories explore similar situations they are quite unlike. Through its form, each renders a unique meaning.[29]

"The Enduring Chill" presents a young man, Asbury, who is immersed in self-delusion. He believes that he is a writer. However, he seems unable to exercise his talent because of his mother's constricting influence on his life. Even though he goes to New York to shake off that influence, he finds himself unable to produce literary work. Finally, sick with a mysterious disease and depressed in spirit, he returns home to die. The story operates on two levels because Asbury is both flesh and spirit. This distinction, different from the body-soul dialectics which the Greeks introduced, is explained in Tresmontant's *A Study of Hebrew Thought*. O'Connor marked this passage, which illumines the concepts of flesh and spirit, ideas on which this story relies.

> The opposition of flesh to spirit is an opposition between two *orders*. Flesh, we have seen, is man's index of frailty, that frailty that comes of being made of dust. The spirit is man's participation in the supernatural order. The spirit summons him to the destiny of a god according to what is written: "Ye are gods."
>
> The flesh, we said, is all of man. In Hebrew "flesh" and "soul" are synonyms. "All flesh" and "every soul" mean man or humanity. Hence the spirit-flesh opposition does not mark a duality within nature itself as does the dichotomy of body and soul. It is in fact a distinction between the order of nature and the supernatural, which is a revealed order. (Pp. 108–109)

Both levels of the story are developed together. Asbury's relationship with his mother, his sister, and the two Negroes on the farm show the falseness of his "artistic" personality. His encounters with two Jesuits ultimately lead him to the recognition of his spiritual illness: he has cut himself off from the Holy Spirit —the Spirit of Truth. Connecting these two orders (which, of course, are intrinsically united in the spiritual man) is Asbury's visible malady, which he believes to be a physical manifestation of intellectual frustration, and which Dr. Block diagnoses as undulant fever.

All of Asbury's relationships with others show his essential falseness. One can almost feel his mother's genuine concern about him, but he refuses her ministrations, speaks cuttingly to her, and secretly rejoices that she will receive a devastating revelation after his death. For he has written her a letter in which he tells her bluntly that she has destroyed him as a literary artist. He hopes this letter will leave her with "an enduring chill." But the vacuous, cliché-prone mother is depicted sympathetically, and it is soon apparent that Asbury's ego, rather than his mother, is destroying him. In the end, the chill which Asbury's letter was designed to bestow upon his mother falls, transformed, upon himself. The pseudo-artist has completely abandoned communication with his sister, Mary George. Principal of a country elementary school and self-styled intellectual, Mary George realizes Asbury's artistic delusions, but, coldly cynical, sees no possibility of a new life for him. A self-sufficient atheist, "there was nothing she was not an expert on." She diagnoses Asbury's condition clinically: "Asbury can't write so he gets sick. He's going to be an invalid instead of an artist." She represents a perversion of truth called "intellectualism," which will be discussed more fully in the following chapter.

The scenes which show the relationship between Asbury and the Negroes, Morgan and Randall, illuminate Asbury's duplicity and the innate integrity of the black farmhands. The summer before his illness, Asbury tries to fraternize with the Negroes, to establish "moments of communion when the difference between black and white is absorbed into nothing." He does this by offering the Negroes cigarettes and smoking with them in the dairy, where smoking is not allowed; finally he drinks warm unpasteurized milk from their jelly glasses and tries to get them to drink with him. Asbury's insincerity in trying to establish any real equality is revealed when he calls Morgan "boy" while seeking communion with him in a glass of milk. Randall's unlettered integrity becomes evident when Morgan asks him why he lets Asbury break the dairy's strict rule about drinking unpasteurized milk. Randall, "very black and fat," replies, "What he do is him; what I do is me." The Negroes do not see that what Asbury does is not really "him," but rather his concept of the way an artist should express himself. The second scene with the Negroes presents a perfect contrast with the first. It moves the confrontation from barn to bedroom, from the Negroes' territory to Asbury's. Feeling that he is on the verge of death, Asbury summons the Negroes to his room so that he can have "some last meaningful experience." He intends to smoke with them once more, and to tell them good-by. But his mother has evidently told the Negroes not to allude to Asbury's debilitated condition, so they keep repeating, "You looks well," "You looks fine," "I ain't ever seen you looking so well before," and the scene turns into a farce. Not even Asbury, who has prepared himself for this encounter "as a religious man might prepare himself for the last sacrament," can delude himself into thinking he has had "a significant experience."

That the story will have a religious dimension—one which will reveal to Asbury the truth about himself that he does not know—is suggested in the opening lines. As Asbury steps from the train which has brought him home from New York, he notices the heavens.

The sky was a chill gray and a startling white-gold sun, like some strange potentate from the east, was rising beyond the black woods that surrounded Timberboro. It cast a strange light over the single block of one-story brick and wooden shacks. Asbury felt that he was about to witness a majestic transformation, that the flat of roofs might at any moment turn into the mounting turrets of some exotic temple for a god he didn't know.

In her copy of Eliade's *Patterns in Comparative Religion*, O'Connor underlined this sentence: "Let me repeat: even before any religious values have been set upon the sky it reveals its transcendence" (p. 39). When questioned by college students about the frequency of her sun imagery, O'Connor said, concerning the sun: "It's there; it's so obvious. And from time immemorial it's been a god."[30] Even without these statements, the diction and the rhythm of the sentences would suggest an awareness of the supernatural.

The religious implications of the story are developed in two contrasting scenes in which Asbury tries to have a "meaningful encounter" with two Jesuits. While in New York, Asbury attends a lecture on Hindu philosophy, and sees in the audience a Jesuit with a "taciturn superior expression" with whom he senses an immediate kinship. After the lecture, the group with Asbury discuss his imminent death and the meaninglessness of salvation. Questioned about salvation, the sophisticated Jesuit remarks that there is "a real probability of the New Man, assisted, of course, by the Third Person of the Trinity." The group ridicules this answer and Asbury ignores it, but the youth is momentarily captivated by the cool intelligence of the Jesuit. This encounter precipitates another meeting with a very different Jesuit in Timberboro. Once again in search of a significant intellectual experience, Asbury forces his mother to invite a local Jesuit, Father Finn, to visit, so he can "talk to a man of culture" before he dies. The "massive old man," blind in one eye and deaf in one ear, who lumbers into Asbury's room is not the type of Jesuit Asbury had expected. He brushes away queries about James Joyce, and gives, unasked, the same answer to Asbury's problem: the Holy Ghost. Perhaps a little too blatantly, Father Finn summarizes the action of the story when he says: "The Holy Ghost will not come until you see yourself as you are—a lazy, ignorant, conceited youth." The priest pummels Asbury with a theological catechesis, but the boy turns the questioning into a game. The Jesuit tries to shock Asbury and his mother ("I should think you would have taught him to say his daily prayers") out of their complacency, but he cannot open their minds to truth. Grace comes freely; it cannot be forced or earned. Carl Jung could well have been speaking of Asbury's experience of grace when he said, in *Modern Man in Search of a Soul*:

> Theology does not help those who are looking for the key [to the knowledge that God is their father], because theology demands faith, and faith cannot be made: it is in the truest sense a gift of grace. We moderns are faced with the necessity of rediscovering the life of the spirit; we must experience it anew for ourselves. It is the only way in which we can break the spell that binds us to the cycle of biological events.[31]

O'Connor marked this passage in her copy. That this idea of the gratuitousness of grace took strong hold on her imagination is emphasized by another marked section in a book on her theological bookshelf: Karl Barth's *Evangelical Theology*.

The God of whom we speak is no god imagined or devised by men. The grace of the gods who are imagined or devised by men is usually a conditional grace, to be merited and won by men through supposedly good works, and not the true grace which gives itself freely. Instead of being hidden under the form of a contradiction, *sub contrario*, and directed to man through radical endangering and judgment, man's imagined grace is usually directly offered and accessible in some way to him and can be rather conveniently, cheaply, and easily appropriated.[32]

In this story, O'Connor demonstrates "the form of a contradiction" by her depiction of the two Jesuits[33]—one cold and intellectual, the other bumbling and gruff, and by the imagery with which she describes the descent of the Spirit.

The link between the flesh and the spirit is Dr. Block, who diagnoses Asbury's disease and thus helps to free him from his artistic illusions. Throughout the story, in an attempt to discourage his mother from summoning the doctor, Asbury keeps repeating, "What's wrong with me is way beyond Block." Because two things are "wrong" with Asbury—one physical and one spiritual—this statement is paradoxical. By diagnosing the physical illness, Block unwittingly prepares the boy for the advent of the Spirit of Truth. What's wrong with "Azzberry" is and is not "way beyond Block." The symbolic link between the natural and supernatural order is "a fierce bird with spread wings" which a water leak has made on the ceiling of Asbury's bedroom. Always the bird has seemed "poised and waiting" to Asbury; as his illness grows worse, he feels that the bird is there "for some purpose he could not divine." On the day which he thinks is his last, he notices that "the light in the room was beginning to have an odd quality, almost as if it were taking on presence. In a darkened form it entered and seemed to wait." "Waiting" connects the "presence" and the bird. At the story's end, "the fierce bird which through the years of his childhood and the days of his illness had been poised over his head, waiting mysteriously, appeared all at once to be in motion," and the Holy Ghost descends, "emblazoned in ice instead of fire." In this story, Flannery O'Connor has artistically distorted traditional Christian imagery connected with the Holy Spirit—the dove, tongues of fire, and a mighty wind—to renew its meaning for the present generation. The dove becomes a fierce watermark bird with an icicle in his beak, whose descent causes a peculiar chill—"a warm ripple across a deeper sea of cold." Contemporary man, who "plays it cool" by noninvolvement, "keeps his cool" by self-control, and lives constantly in a cold-war climate, is conditioned to respond to such imagery.

The descriptions of nature which open and close the story do more than suggest its spiritual dimension; they underline the theme. The unactualized splendor in matter, which the opening description suggests, corresponds symbolically to the unactualized spirituality in Asbury. In George Lawler's *The Christian Imagination*, O'Connor marked a passage which may have been an element in the genesis of this story.

> . . . Just as in man there must be intelligence before there can be faith, just as the gifts of the Holy Spirit must be present in a vague, passive manner in the soul before there can be true contemplation, so it is fitting that there be in matter, before it can be ennobled in the last day, a certain unactualized splendor which renders possible this future reception of excellence.[34]

This potential splendor of matter, which Asbury perceives at the opening of the story, is one of the bonds between man and nature which the story illustrates. However, the allusions to nature are too slight to sustain the weight of the comparison. Another allusion in the center of the story, illuminating "the created universe wait[ing] with eager expectation for God's sons to be revealed" (Romans 8:19), would be necessary to strengthen the connection between man's and nature's potential for glory. Real rather than potential and debilitating rather than exalting, another bond which connects man and nature in the story is undulant fever, which is known as Bang's disease in a cow. This link is suggested in the beginning of the story when a "walleyed Guernsey" stares at Asbury "as if she senses some bond between them." This story suggests that, for better or worse, man is a creature of flesh and spirit, participating in both orders of nature.

Of all Flannery O'Connor's works which depict man as untrue

to himself and therefore false to others, "The Enduring Chill" is the least subtle. Compared with those discussed previously, the spiritual lines are heavier, the advent of grace more marked, the hierophany more overt. One *knows* that Asbury has been readied by bodily suffering and spiritual emptying for the coming of the Spirit, and he *knows* the moment of the descent. But balancing this spiritual weight is the comic tone. At one of the Wednesday evening literary gatherings at her home, O'Connor read "The Enduring Chill" to her friends. One of the auditors, James O. Tate, a Milledgeville businessman who has written a reminiscence of O'Connor, called her reading "a magnificent event." He observed, "She brought out all the comic flavor; her intonation and inflection were perfect. It was by far my most enjoyable time."[35] This heady mixture of high spirituality and low comedy may have been this story's special device to reach the "monstrous reader" of whom O'Connor spoke in an address at her alma mater. In 1960, she told the students at Georgia State College:

> When I sit down to write, a monstrous reader looms up who sits down beside me and continually mutters, "I don't get it, I don't see it, I don't want it." Some writers can ignore this presence, but I have never learned how. I know that I must never let him affect my vision, must never let him gain control over my thinking, must never listen to his demands unless they accord with my conscience; yet I feel I must make him see what I have to show, even if my means of making him see have to be extreme.[36]

By the extremes of low comedy and high seriousness, Flannery O'Connor attempted to show man's return to truth.

Three years after publishing "The Enduring Chill," O'Connor developed the same theme of the artist "hell-bent on writing stories" with different notation in "The Partridge Festival."[37] Asbury is "ignorant"; but Calhoun, the protagonist of "The Partridge Festival," is "innocent"—so much so that "it was impossible for him to believe that every man was not created equally an artist if he could but suffer and achieve it." Asbury believes that he can express himself through writing—a wrongheaded but limited ambition; Calhoun believes that he can right major evils through his projected novel, in which "he would have to show, not say, how primary injustice operated." Asbury is led to face himself by Dr. Block's wise diagnosis; Calhoun is enabled to see himself by an encounter with a madman. Finally, Asbury really believes in his false self; Calhoun has undeniable suspicion that he was his true self when he worked as a salesman. The instrumentation of the two stories supports these differences. The second story has no spiritual dimension, and its low comedy moves at times into farce. While "The Enduring Chill" employs a full range of tones, "The Partridge Festival" is a *tour de force* of consistent tone—detached, amused, almost playful. The story's opening sentence, in which Calhoun emerges from his car "cautiously, looking to the right and left as if he expected the profusion of azalea blossoms to have a lethal effect upon him," sets the comic tone which is maintained steadily to the bizarre end.

Using the journey motif—as old as literature itself—O'Connor tells a tale of self-discovery. Calhoun visits Partridge, his ancestral hometown somewhere in the South, during the Azalea Festival, not only to vindicate the maniacal murderer, Singleton, by writing an exposé of the town's corruption, but also to be inspired by the "singleness" of the mad rebel's life to end the duplicity in his own. His preconceived view of Singleton, largely derived from a newspaper picture showing the murderer's mismatched eyes, conflicts with the varying views which he receives from the townspeople he meets as he walks through the village. He thinks he has found a kindred intellectual spirit in Mary Elizabeth, his great-aunts' neighbor. She instigates their trip to the state hospital to encounter Singleton, whom she sees as a mythical Christ figure. This meeting reveals Calhoun's self-deception and precipitates his self-recognition, which occurs on the road from the hospital.

Several elements of "The Partridge Festival" seem to be imaginative variations of devices which Flannery O'Connor had used in her first story which explored the theme of truth, "Good Country People." In that story, the deceitful Bible salesman brought "Dr." Hulga to self-knowledge; in this, the reverse happens: the "intellectual" Mary Elizabeth forces the encounter which frees the salesman, Calhoun, from his "rebel, artist, mystic" pretensions. In both stories, a single scriptural quotation epitomizes the meaning. Calhoun seemingly reassures his great-aunts and subtly defends his proposed exposé of the town's infamy by saying, fiercely, "Know the truth, and the truth shall make you free." As the story ends, Calhoun, enlightened about himself, accepts the salesmanship which is part of his nature. Both stories also rely on comic perversion. The town of Partridge has perverted aesthetics into economics by all that lies behind its slogan: "Beauty Is Our Money Crop." In the reverse movement, Calhoun has created an artistic spirit to replace his innate economic one; with easy skill and uneasy conscience he sells luxury items in summer to support his artistic life in winter.

The index to the falseness of Calhoun's idea of himself as a literary artist can be found in the overblown diction of the story. When Calhoun grins "sheepishly" at his two great-aunts, and they gently call him "Baby Lamb," no one can take his self-deception too seriously. When the narrator relates of him that Singleton had "captured his imagination like a dark reproachful liberating star," that he left his great-aunts' house "to immerse himself in his material," that when he saw Singleton's outhouse-jail, "the pathos of his friend's situation was borne in on him with a rush of empathy," one can only await the comic pin prick which will end these illusions. This exaggerated rhetoric is not the only means O'Connor uses to undercut the traditionally serious journey motif. The dialogue in this story is different in both amount and kind from her usual trenchant sort. One finds no use of indirect discourse to render the flavor of conversation without recounting it. Each conversation is detailed exactly; each shows Calhoun to be quite like his great-uncle, whose expression was "all innocence and determination." His great-aunts' initial greeting makes it clear that Calhoun is a physical replica of his ancestor, the "master salesman" who composed the town's motto and initiated the Azalea Festival. That he is also of the same temperament becomes evident as the story progresses. The boy himself grasps both resemblances only in the final encounter with his own image in the eyeglasses of his companion.

Of all the incidents which comprise Calhoun's investigation of the town (which he begins by wandering into a drugstore "without set purpose") two reveal best the conflict within him between artist and salesman. The first is his meeting with "a small white girl whose tongue was curled in the mouth of a Coca-cola bottle."

In response to her announcement, delivered with "the certainty of children," that "a bad man" committed the murders, Calhoun launches into a short, impassioned plea for "one of the fundamental rights of man . . .: the right to be yourself." The child is singularly unimpressed and repeats: "He was a bad bad bad man." Calhoun then moves on and enters a barber shop to ask more questions about the town's maniac. The barber tells Calhoun a good bit about Singleton, but one twirl in the chair reveals more about Calhoun.

> [The barber] put the bib on the boy and stood staring at his round head as if it were a pumpkin he was wondering how to slice. Then he twirled the chair so that Calhoun faced the mirror. He was confronted with an image that was round-faced, unremarkable-looking and innocent. The boy's expression turned fierce. "Are you eating up this slop like the rest of them?" he asked belligerently.

In that description, one can see the pumpkin-headed boy recognize himself and reject himself for the person he would rather be—the "fierce" rebel who acted on his convictions (and murdered six men to protest the town ordinance requiring everyone to wear a festival badge). Calhoun imagines that he sees in the mirror his "hidden likeness" to Singleton.

This comic scene anticipates and reverses the recognition scene, in which Calhoun sees his image mirrored in Mary Elizabeth's glasses. "Round, innocent, undistinguished as an iron link, it was the face whose gift of life had pushed straight forward to the future to raise festival after festival." In other words, it was not the maniac rebel, but the image of his great-grandfather which "rose up incorrigibly in her spectacles and fixed him where he was." Stripped of his delusions about Singleton, he is stripped of his delusions about himself. Even as it elaborates the epiphany, the last sentence sustains the comic tone in its comment on the "miniature visage" in the spectacles: "Like a master salesman, it seemed to have been waiting there from all time to claim him."

An interesting and elaborately constructed "twist" in the structure of this story is the false epiphany which precedes the final, true one. Breathless from their flight from the hospital, Calhoun and Mary Elizabeth pull over to the side of the road and look at

each other. "There each saw at once the likeness of their kins-
man, and flinched. They looked away and then back, as if with
concentration they might find a more tolerable image." The false
epiphany is based on a false kinship which has been elaborately
constructed. In the beginning of the story, the boy and the girl
experience an immediate antipathy toward each other. This
grows to "open and intense dislike" until they claim kinship with
Singleton to get passes to see him. They stare at his surname on
their passes and then at each other. "Both appeared to recognize
that in their common kinship with him, a kinship with each
other was unavoidable." When Singleton appears they watch the
bond which they had created with him—and with each other—
crumble under the impact of his "steady monotonous cursing"
and lecherous lunge. They had expected a suffering Christ-figure;
they saw an insane old man. But the ending suggests that a true
bond has been formed by the revelation of each one's falseness.
When, earlier in the story, Calhoun suggests that they seek "an
existential encounter with [Singleton's] personality" he says to
the girl, "You might find your theories enriched by the sight of
him." Actually the sight of him destroys those theories and creates a vacuum, a "nakedness," an opening for truth. In their
being stripped of pretensions by the same encounter lies their
true kinship.

Calhoun's moment of truth is quite different from the enlightenment of the other protagonists in the stories which develop
this theme. He realizes that all his talents point him toward
salesmanship: "In the face of a customer, he was carried outside
himself; his face began to beam and sweat and all complexity
left him; he was in the grip of a drive as strong as the drive of
some men for liquor or a woman; and he was horribly good at
it." He simply does not accept this truth about himself. The
difficulty of this self-acceptance was noted by Jung in *Modern
Man in Search of a Soul*. Flannery O'Connor marked this passage:

But what if I should discover that the least amongst [my
brethren], the poorest of all the beggars, the most impudent of
all the offenders, the very enemy himself—that these are within
me, and that I myself stand in need of the alms of my own

kindness—that I myself am the enemy who must be loved—what then? As a rule, the Christian's attitude is then reversed; there is no longer any question of love or longsuffering; we say to the brother within us "Raca," and condemn and rage against ourselves. We hide it from the world; we refuse to admit ever having met this least among the lowly in ourselves. (P. 235)

The entire story demonstrates Calhoun's attitude toward salesmanship: evidently he considers a salesman the "least among the lowly." Therefore, his acceptance of himself as a salesman is a giant step toward truth.

The writings of St. Augustine, a prototype of the restless inquirer, exerted a profound influence on Flannery O'Connor. She knew his works, and read widely different books about him. She annotated her copy of *Nine Sermons on the Psalms by St. Augustine* and wrote for *The Bulletin* an appreciative review of Romano Guardini's *The Conversion of St. Augustine*. But the book on Augustine which best reveals his influence on her is Jean Guitton's *The Modernity of St. Augustine*. Guitton demonstrates Augustine's contemporaneity by comparing his writings with modern thought, notably the thought of Freud, Proust, Gide, Sartre, Hegel, and Marx. In discussing the timelessness of Augustine's search for truth through the byways of error and sin, Guitton says:

Sometimes by secret stirrings, sometimes by the prompting of circumstance, God recalls the soul to itself. In the most unexpected ways he makes it aware of its wretchedness. . . . His hand is ever present to recreate and restore what he has made. Furthermore, he knows how to make use of the evil that man does, for he does not cease to bring into order what he condemns; though he does not create it, yet he orders it to the good.[38]

Flannery O'Connor marked this passage, and these stories show how deeply the idea embedded itself in her mind. Calhoun—ashamed of the salesman who lurks in the back of his consciousness; Thomas—selfishly absorbed in his own comfort; Asbury—immersed in self-pity; Shiftlet—playing the role of the moment;

Hulga—delivering herself from Joy—all enact the mystery of freedom in a world damaged by sin. In diverse ways, each is offered the chance to accept his true self: here I am—LIKE I AM. Intrinsic to this acceptance is an openness to grace—as real in its subtle presence as an idiot girl sleeping over a plate of grits and as gratuitous as life itself.

CHAPTER III

The "New Jesus":

alienated modern man

"Alienation was once a diagnosis,
but in much of the fiction of our
time it has become an ideal. The
modern hero is the outsider. His
experience is rootless. He can go
anywhere. He belongs nowhere.
Being alien to nothing, he ends up
being alienated from any kind of
community based on common
tastes and interests. The borders
of his country are the sides of his
skull." F.O'C.

Two sheets of scratch paper containing a penciled first draft of a letter of Flannery O'Connor to a young student show how she viewed an ostensible conflict between faith and reason. I found these sheets in one of the books in her library. Omitting the crossed-out sections, the letter reads:

We take in unbelief in the air we breathe and particularly the air of a university. I think this experience you are having of losing your faith, or as you think, of having lost it belongs to faith in the long run, or at least it can belong to faith if faith is still valuable to you. Perhaps I should say I don't know how faith in any age can be without it. Peter said, "Lord, I believe; help my unbelief." It is the most natural and most human and most agonizing prayer in the gospels and until a person begins to experience it in himself his faith cannot begin to take on its deepest dimensions. As a freshman in college you are besieged from all sides with new ideas and new frames of reference, some of it good, more of it bad, most of it seductive. You are not yet in any position to sort it out, however intelligent you are. You are not ready to say you have lost your faith because you don't know what faith is. Right now you are beset with problems that are largely intellectual. One needs the Christian faith in college, if for no other reason than to make one a sceptic—to give pause before the acceptance of everything put on the platter and served.

O'Connor's assertion to the young man that "you don't know what faith is" is based on her total apprehension of reality. For her, reality which the mind could grasp intellectually was part of, and could not contradict, the whole of reality, including its spiritual dimensions, which are the material of supernatural faith. There could be no conflict between faith and reason in the man who acknowledged the limitations of his own mind, who was willing to accept the unseen and incomprehensible part of reality. This total view of reality is characteristic of the people of medieval times. With the advent of rationalism, a sharp division arose between the reality which is accessible to the human intelligence and that which it is unable to comprehend. Slowly a gulf developed between reality and mystery until today they are sometimes seen in opposition to one another rather than as aspects of a single entity.

One can surmise Flannery O'Connor's unified view of all reality because it is the framework for her fiction. One can apprehend this view concretely by noting the ideas which appear frequently in the marked passages in books in her library. In Anton Pegis' foreword to the *Introduction to St. Thomas Aquinas,* she marked the following section:

> The Thomistic man is a knower rather than a thinker and he is a composite being rather than a mind. . . . For what we call the decline of medieval philosophy was really a transition from man as knower to man as thinker—from man knowing the world of sensible things to man thinking abstract thought in separation from existence. What is thinking but dis-existentialized knowing?[1]

In her stories O'Connor sometimes portrays man as "thinker." In her view, this is man alienated from the fullness of reality by refusing to believe anything which his mind cannot encompass. Man as "thinker" is man alienated from that part of reality which is mystery. One can see immediately the hallmark of O'Connor intellectuals: self-sufficient pride. Alexis de Tocqueville, in *Democracy in America,* suggests that this is a national malaise. O'Connor marked this passage in his discussion of the philosophical method of Americans:

> America is therefore one of the countries where the precepts of Descartes are least studied and are best applied. . . . Thus they [the Americans] fall to denying what they cannot comprehend; which leaves them but little faith for whatever is extraordinary and an almost insurmountable distaste for whatever is supernatural.[2]

If one accepts de Tocqueville's designation, one can see from a different angle the universality of Flannery O'Connor's fiction. Even though its locale is limited, it probes a state of mind that is not only a national characteristic but a universal one. As O'Connor herself said, "I'm interested in the old Adam. He just talks Southern because I do."[3] O'Connor also approached the idea of the infinite extensions of reality from a philosophical basis. Her markings in *The World of the Polis*, the second volume of Eric Voegelin's *Order and History*, in which he discusses the philosophical order which the Greeks imposed upon reality, show her interest in Plato's realization that the spiritual order—or the order of unseen reality—must be recognized in any philosophical system. Plato opposed the philosophy of the Sophists because they failed to take spiritual reality into account. O'Connor marked this summary passage:

> Plato opposed his "God is the Measure" deliberately as the counter-formula to the sophist's "Man is the Measure." In sophistic thought . . . there was missing the link between the well-observed and classified phenomena of ethics and politics and the "invisible measure" that radiates order into the soul. The opposition to a world of thought without spiritual order was repeatedly expressed by Plato at critical junctures of his work.[4]

One last direction from which O'Connor evidently viewed the wholeness of natural and supernatural reality can be seen in the aesthetic criteria of Jacques Maritain. In his book *Creative Intuition in Art and Poetry*, O'Connor marked this passage about the philosophical concept of beauty:

> Descartes, with his clear ideas, divorced intelligence from mystery. Modern science is making us aware of his mistake. The Schoolmen, when they defined beauty by the radiance of the form, in reality defined it by the radiance of a mystery.[5]

All these marked passages suggest the extent to which her concept of reality affected other areas of thought.

With this view of the wholeness of reality, Flannery O'Connor wrote movingly of alienated man—man cut off, usually by pride, from a complete apprehension of reality. Sometimes his truncated view of the universe excludes all spiritual reality. Sometimes it ignores social or material reality. Always there is a connection between man's ability to see visible reality truly, and his openness to spiritual reality. O'Connor explored various kinds of alienation from reality in her fiction, but her ultimate concern was man's alienation from the supernatural world. In a lecture at Sweetbriar College in March, 1963, she discussed the connection between literature and theology in what she called an unbelieving but "markedly and lopsidedly spiritual" age. She spoke of three types of alienated man: one who recognizes spirit in himself, but not a spiritual being outside himself whom he can acknowledge as Creator, and who therefore deifies himself; one for whom spirit and matter are separated, who recognizes a divine being but disbelieves in the possibility of apprehending him or communicating with him; and the searcher, "feeling about in all experience for the Lost God," one who can "neither believe nor contain himself in unbelief." She realized that her experience prepared her to write about only these types of alienation because they all presuppose the existence of a personal God. To her Sweetbriar audience she confessed:

> What I say here would be much more in line with the spirit of our times if I could speak to you about the experience of such novelists as Hemingway and Kafka and Gide and Camus, but all my own experience has been that of the writer who believes, again in Pascal's words, in the "God of Abraham, Isaac, and Jacob and not of the philosophers and scholars."

In the last section of her lecture, she explored the question of how to make the experience of man's encounter with the God of Abraham understandable to the modern reader, whose religious feeling had become "if not atrophied, at least vaporous and sentimental."[6]

In her first attempt to depict man deliberately alienating himself from God, O'Connor chose a variation of the genre which Nathaniel Hawthorne had used to explore the same theme more than a century before; her first novel, *Wise Blood*, is a comic romance. Hazel Motes, the protagonist, is a caricature, a sharply drawn figure distorted for comic effect. The world he inhabits has the real-yet-unreal quality which infuses the romance. The novel is a tale of man's attempt to eradicate from his consciousness his belief in Jesus Christ as Saviour. On entering adult life, Hazel tries to rid himself of the faith of his childhood; unable to do this, he envisions a "new jesus" who is not God, so that he can elude spiritual reality. He encounters other characters who are also spiritual "freaks"—persons whose apprehension of God is manifested in twisted and bizarre ways. Through the influence of these characters, he finally returns to the God from whom he has been fleeing. The effective integration of plot and subplot, of surface and symbolic action, of manners and mystery, and of psychological motivations and supernatural grace marks a strong beginning for an author in her early twenties. One finds even at the start a technique which became characteristic of her writing: an attention to concrete detail which establishes the reality of the natural action in order to sustain the thrust into the supernatural realm.

Two "normal" characters frame this story of spiritual "freaks." Flannery O'Connor has her own concept of normalcy and of its deviations. Her normal characters have no conception of the power of Redemption; her freaks, on the other hand, are caught up in this mystery, usually in a distorted way. Mrs. Wally Bee Hitchcock, Hazel Motes's train companion at the opening of the story, looks, speaks, and acts like an average middle-class American grandmother on her way to Florida to visit her daughter's family. Her first statement to Hazel—"I guess you're going home," introduces the theme of the novel. Her second comment, "Well . . . there's no place like home," establishes her cliché-prone mentality, but it does more: it suggests Hazel's spiritual displacement, which the entire story unfolds. The contrast between Mrs. Hitchcock's normal behavior and Hazel's religious fanaticism becomes evident in the following brief exchange. Impelled to concern himself with spiritual reality, Haze (this diminutive is used interchangeably with "Hazel" and suggests cloudy spiritual vision) says abruptly to Mrs. Hitchcock: "I reckon you think you been redeemed." Her response shows her inability to comprehend spiritual matters.

> She blushed. After a second she said yes, life was an inspiration and then she said she was hungry and asked him if he didn't want to go into the diner.

This reaction marks her as "normal." After one last encounter with Haze in the Pullman car, she drops out of the story with a final question which the entire novel answers: "What IS the matter with you?"

Haze's landlady, the second "normal" character, dominates the final chapter and brings the novel to a close. One can see, starkly illumined by the fanatical actions of her boarder, her own common-sense approach to life. Independent and self-possessed, she is in complete control of reality; she can even clear thoughts out of her mind "with no more change of expression than the cat." The tone of the novel, wry and detached throughout, softens in the final chapter when the author moves into the landlady's consciousness and presents Haze's self-blinding and penitential life through her eyes. Slowly she begins to comprehend the meaning of Haze's actions. Her "normal" awareness of life expands to include spiritual reality, although that reality presents itself as mystery. The landlady's final words suggest the fulfillment of Haze's spiritual quest. Gazing at the lifeless body on her bed, Mrs. Flood says, "Well, Mr. Motes . . . I see you've come home."

Both of these women are intrigued by the mystery of Haze's eyes. To Mrs. Hitchcock, "their settings were so deep that they seemed, to her, almost like passages leading somewhere and she leaned halfway across the space that separated the two [train] seats, trying to see into them." Mrs. Flood, the landlady, notices Haze's eyes only after he has blinded himself; then, "if she didn't keep her mind going on something else when he was near her, she would find herself leaning forward, staring into his face as if she expected to see something she hadn't seen before." But the contrast between these two characters' attitudes toward the mystery marks their essential difference. Although Mrs. Hitchcock is immediately attracted to Haze's eyes, she is unwilling to accept their mystery:

> She felt irked and wrenched her attention loose and squinted at the price tag. The suit had cost him $11.98. She felt that that placed him, and looked at his face again as if she were fortified against it now.

Because she had to "place" everything, she cut off any apprehension of that which is beyond man's reason. Mrs. Flood, on the other hand, continued to probe the mystery which Haze's eyes presented to her. Although she reduced it to the question, "What possible reason could a sane person have for wanting to not enjoy himself any more?" she was unable to contain it there. The mystery kept enlarging until she knew that the only way to encompass it was to possess the person who embodied the mystery—her blind boarder. As, sitting beside his body, she "sat staring with her eyes shut into his eyes," she began to see "the pinpoint of light" which, earlier, she had identified with "the star of Bethlehem." This light was leading her past the mystery of Hazel Motes into the heart of the mystery of Redemption.

Framed by these two "normal" characters, the O'Connor freaks enact the major part of the novel. In quick succession they appear: the Jesus-obsessed Hazel Motes; the maternal whore, Leora Watts; the fake blind man, Asa Hawks; his lascivious daughter, Sabbath Lily; the lonely moron, Enoch Emory; the religious "con man," Hoover Shoats; and his decoy, Solace Layfield. Each has a relationship with the divine but in each case it is a distorted one. Hazel flees from and finally grotesquely embraces the Jesus of his childhood; Hawks and Sabbath and Shoats and Layfield all use religion for material ends; Enoch is open only to a diabolical spiritual reality, his "wise blood," which leads him to bestiality. These characters reveal the deepest need of man for a relationship with God, but in their perverse manner of apprehending the divine, they exemplify a distortion of Christianity.

As the novel opens, Hazel Motes has just returned from a four-year stint in the army during which he "reasoned" himself out of his faith. He finds his home in ruins, his family dead, and his village abandoned. Unwillingly, he accepts the circumstances which are existentially analogous to the biblical command, "Leave your people and your father's house and go into a land that I will show you." Such displacement is wrenching to man's nature; "where he wanted to stay was in Eastrod with his two eyes open, and his hands always handling the familiar thing, his feet on the known track, and his tongue not loose." Facing both physical and spiritual rootlessness, he seeks a "place." The novel explores a succession of placements and displacements that culminates in Haze's grim thought:

> Where you come from is gone, and where you thought you were going to never was there, and where you are is no good

unless you can get away from it. Where is there a place for you to be? No place.

His search for place begins in Taulkinham, the only city Hazel knows. After some aimless wandering, he finds, written in a public washroom, the name and address of a prostitute. She welcomes him with the words, "Make yourself at home." In his embrace of sin, awkward as it is, he finds a "place" to be. The next day, at the "altar" of a potato-peeler salesman, he encounters his comic counterpart, Enoch Emory. Together they meet the false blind man and his daughter, who are "hawking" religion. Once again Hazel is unsettled from his placement in sin by what he believes is a true religious conviction as he listens to the blind man say, "You can't run away from Jesus. Jesus is a fact." Although Haze tries to deny his interest in the blind man's message, Hawks, a diabolical discerner of hearts, knows the truth about him. In a passage which appears in the first published version of this chapter, but which was deleted in the final novel, Hawks reveals this knowledge:

> "You got a secret need," the blind man said. "Them that knows Jesus once can't escape Him in the end." "I ain't never known him," Haze said. "You got a least knowledge," the blind man said. "That's enough. You know His name and you're marked. If Jesus has marked you there ain't nothing you can do about it. Them that have knowledge can't swap it for ignorance."[7]

It is not hard to discern why O'Connor deleted this passage: it states the theme too blatantly. The entire novel probes this "secret need" and Haze's recognition and acceptance of it. Haze's security in his placement in sin with Mrs. Watts is shaken by Hawk's preaching. He tries to counteract this displacement by purchasing a car. His final words to the car dealer and his son as they watch him, without license or skill, trying to start the car, signify a new placement: "I wanted this car mostly to be a house for me; I ain't got any place to be." Initially a home, the car becomes his pulpit, from which he preaches the "Church Without Christ." Once again he is "placed"; the car is his security. "No man with a good car needs to be justified." His confidence in the dilapidated car is boundless. But as the car gurgles and groans and develops a tic which takes it six inches forward and four inches back in rapid succession, it becomes obvious that it can only be a temporary security. Soon the car begins to leak oil and water and gas, and it is finally destroyed by a policeman who sees the ramshackle car and its unlicensed driver as a public threat. With the destruction of the car, Hazel is displaced again. But this time, by embracing in a flamboyant act of self-mutilation the Jesus he has been evading, he places himself firmly among the elect and has no more regard for earthly placement. His landlady, attracted by his monthly government check, offers him a place—"a home here with me, a place where you can always stay." Later, drawn by the mysteriousness of his behavior, she offers him marriage: "I got a place for you in my heart." But he ignores her offer, and, in complete disregard for his life, displaces himself by leaving his boarding-house, even while he expresses the conviction that "there's no other house and no other city." He knows only one place of value now—the place of the final meeting with Jesus. By a grotesque death, he reaches that high meeting-place.

Wise Blood is an extreme treatment of alienated man's search for "home." The reality of belief is so strong in Hazel that he is unable to uproot it; therefore, to live comfortably with it, he must transform it into a shadow of reality. He is unable to deny Jesus the divine Redeemer, so he forces himself to create a shadow without substance, a "new jesus" who has only the name and not the power of a Redeemer. Basic to an understanding of Haze's alienation is a true conception of what Redemption means, a conception stated in orthodox terms by St. Paul: "No man is ever justified by doing what the law demands, but only through faith in Christ Jesus" (Gal. II, 15). This essential Christian truth undergoes a significant distortion in Flannery O'Connor's art. She shows, through flashbacks in the novel, that the religious notions of the child Hazel were based on the relationship between personal sin and salvation—that is, that one's personal sin (rather than the sinful condition of mankind) draws down the power of the Redeemer. Haze's grandfather and his mother are his chief religious influences in his youth. The former, with his fanatical preaching about Jesus, who "would die ten million deaths before He would let him [Haze] lose his soul," succeeded only in implanting in the boy the "deep black wordless conviction . . . that the way to avoid Jesus was to avoid sin." His mother, by her extreme piety, inculcated in the boy a "nameless, unplaced guilt" which he could expiate only by "paying." As a child, he walked with rocks in his shoes to pay for looking at a naked woman in a velvet-lined coffin at the circus; after his self-mutilation, he paid for the world's sins in the same way. Haze spent his early years trying to avoid sin, so that he would "owe" nothing to Jesus. In the army he learned that there was no sin and that he had no soul. To convince himself that he believed this, he had to sin deliberately; therefore, free of the army, he headed for the city, to "do some things I never have done before." He fornicates with grim determination, but that does not convince him of "no sin" and "no soul." In some way he must take into account the Jesus of his youth, who is still moving "from tree to tree in the back of his mind, a wild ragged figure motioning him to turn around and come off into the dark where he was not sure of his footing, where he might be walking on the water and not know it and then suddenly know it and drown." So he transforms him into a "new jesus, one that's all man, without blood to waste," one who cannot save and therefore can demand nothing. In a comic parody of all humanistic religions, Haze preaches "the Church Without Christ, the church peaceful and satisfied."

Haze's quest for placement in visible reality forms one narrative line; Enoch Emory's struggle to find friends in the vastness of the city forms another. In the creation of the "new jesus" the two plot lines converge. Enoch Emory enters the story a lonely boy working as a park guard who fastens onto Haze as his only friend. Interspersed between the chapters detailing Haze's flight from Jesus are chapters describing Enoch's pattern of activities in the park, his adoration of a shrunken mummy in the park museum, and finally his murder of the man inside a gorilla costume so that he can *become* Gonga the gorilla. The lives of these two alienated men cross decisively when Enoch hears Haze preaching his new religion and asking for a "new jesus":

> The Church Without Christ don't have a Jesus but it needs one! It needs one . . . that don't look like any other man so

you'll look at him. . . . Give me this new jesus, somebody, so
we'll all be saved by the sight of him.

Immediately Enoch knows that the shrunken mummy whom he
visits daily in the museum is the new jesus. He steals it, hides
it in a gilded cabinet—a grotesque tabernacle—in his bedroom,
and finally delivers it to Hazel's house. Then, in insane jealousy
of a gorilla whose hand people line up to shake, he clothes himself in animal skin, only to find his extended gorilla hand rejected
even more decisively than his human hand had been.

Enoch's odyssey is a comic parody of Hazel's intensely serious
one. By stumbling steps Haze has progressed from his childhood
conviction that he would be a preacher to his fanatical preaching, standing on the hood of his Essex, of the Church Without
Christ. After he realizes that the knowledge in him cannot be
uprooted or disguised, he returns to the service of the stern God
of his youth. Three experiences contribute to his conversion.
The first is Sabbath Lily's facetious question: can a bastard be
saved in the Church Without Christ? Haze answers that there is
no such thing as a bastard in his church, but as he says it he
knows that it is not true. "The thing in his mind said that the
truth didn't contradict itself and that a bastard couldn't be saved
in the Church Without Christ." This is his first realization that
there is a state of sinfulness—analogous to bastardy—that one is
not personally responsible for (in theology this state is called
original sin). Just as, without a savior, "her case was hopeless,"
so is his own case hopeless, even if he had committed no personal
sin, without a savior. This realization opens him to an understanding that faith, and not sinlessness, justifies man. The second
experience in his conversion is Solace Layfield's death. Haze runs
Layfield down with his car because, as he says, "Two things I
can't stand—a man that ain't true and one that mocks what is."
Layfield has been acting as True Prophet for Hoover Shoats, the
easy-money evangelist who took over Haze's Church Without
Christ to make a profit on it. Haze realizes that Layfield is
mouthing words he does not believe, for pay. But as Layfield lies
dying, his true faith in Christ reveals itself. He mumbles his sins
aloud, and ends with "Jesus . . . Jesus hep me." Haze knows that
he has heard only one end of a dialogue and that Layfield's Re-

deemer truly lives. To dismiss the impact of this experience, Haze prepares to preach the Church Without Christ "in the new city." But from his boyhood he had believed in signs (after his penitential walk as a boy "if a stone had fallen he would have taken it as a sign"), and this time the sign is unmistakable: a policeman destroys his car. Frequently, as in this instance, O'Connor characters move from the material to the spiritual realm by looking steadily into space. With his destroyed Essex in the gully below, Haze's "face seemed to reflect the entire distance across the clearing and on beyond, the entire distance that extended from his eyes to the blank gray sky that went on, depth after depth, into space." The policeman tries to get his attention, but "it seemed to be concentrated on space." After his three-hour walk back into the city, he blinds himself. What he had seen in space so filled his eyes that he is compelled to deepen them: "If there's no bottom in your eyes, they hold more."

The final chapter details Haze's life of penance, as grotesque in his embrace of God as his life of flight from God had been. He takes daily walks with rocks in his shoes and wears a barbed wire around his chest. Absorbed in a secret life which his landlady finds mysteriously enticing, he shows no interest in food or comfort or money. Finally Mrs. Flood's overtures of kindness drive him from the house to the place he has been looking for— the place of his meeting with Jesus. He who knows only the stern fundamentalist God of his grandfather dies "under the law." Two policemen, comic in their stupidity, cut the thread of his life with a blow from a billy as they take him back to his boarding-house. Ostensibly he is brought back to pay the money he "owes" the landlady, but really he returns in death to lead her to the "pinpoint of light."

Throughout the story Hazel's laconic assertions about cleanliness epitomize his spiritual condition. Through the opening chapters he asserts periodically, "I am clean." In these words he denies his need for redemption; against this need he unconsciously struggles. After he realizes the meaning of Redemption and embraces a penitential life, he can give as reason for his "monklike" behavior only the statement, "I am not clean." He understands now that no one is clean because the "old" Jesus, the divine Redeemer, lives. He knows that all men are by their nature in need of redemption and can only rely on the mercy of God. Through the story he is constantly moving—by train, by car, and on foot, and finally arrives in a police wagon at the end of the longest spiritual odyssey that man can take.

Through Hoover Shoats and Asa Hawks, Flannery O'Connor parodies nominal Christianity, which makes the perverted but deep Christianity of Hazel Motes seem more desirable. Shoats appeals only to the emotions; he tells the crowd that he "wouldn't have you believe nothing you don't understand and approve of." He promises his listeners that his religion is "based on your own personal interpitation of the Bible, friends. You can sit at home and interpit your own Bible however you feel in your heart it ought to be interpited." Later he comments to Hazel, "If you want to get anywheres in religion, you got to keep it sweet." In return for one dollar, he gives each believer a handshake and the ability to "unlock that little rose of sweetness" inside him. In contrast to Shoats, Asa Hawks uses the negative approach to get money. While handing out "Jesus Calls You" pamphlets, he says, "If you don't repent, give up a nickel." Shoats seems the more perverse, and Hawks the more pitiable character. In his pledge to burn his eyes out to prove his belief, Hawks presumed on supernatural strength, which was denied him. Spurning a harder alternative (admitting his human weakness), he chose the way of deception; any integrity he ever had was washed away in the lime stains on his cheeks.

Enoch Emory exhibits a bizarre kind of alienation from humankind and a diabolical attraction to mystery. He recounts his being "traded" by his father to a "Welfare woman" for an unknown return. He escaped from her and returned home, only to be forced out of the house and into the vastness of the city by his father's new woman. He seems to have no ties with the world of human friendship and concern. His sole allegiance is to the commands of his "wise blood," inherited from his father. Flannery calls him "a moron and chiefly a comic character."[8] His grotesque "way of the cross" (his daily ritual of the Frosty Bottle drink, the visit to the animals, and the adoration of the mummy); his voyeuristic absorption in the activities of the ladies at the swimming pool; his hilarious activity in preparing his room for the "new jesus"; and his automatic responses to communications from his wise blood—all support the author's designation of him as a comic moron. He becomes a foil for Hazel; each is subject to an influence beyond his ken. His descent into animality shows —in caricature—the alternative Hazel could have taken. In Enoch's life, as in Haze's, childhood influence is strong. Enoch's four weeks at the Rodemill Boys' Bible Academy taught him all about Jesus; he rejected Him, and in the novel he seeks another god, someone who communicates with him through his wise blood. In a kind of parody of the "dissociation of sensibility," Enoch thinks of his brain as "divided into two parts. The part in communication with his blood did the figuring but it never said anything in words. The other part was stocked up with all kinds of words and phrases." The mysterious spiritual influence which Enoch terms "wise blood" leads to violence in the two encounters between Hazel and Enoch which the story elaborates. Their initial meeting ends with Enoch boasting of his wise blood; and Hazel responding with force: "he raised his arm and hurled the stack of tracts he had been carrying. It hit Enoch in the chest and knocked his mouth open. He stood looking, with his mouth hanging open, at where it had hit his front, and then he turned and tore off down the street." In their second and last encounter, Enoch shows Haze the "new jesus," and Haze responds again with violence; he hurls a rock which hits Enoch on the forehead, and draws blood—blood which, on the ground, "widened like a little spring." The origin of Enoch's wise blood seems diabolical; it is a negative counterpart of the blood of Redemption.

The theme of alienation is expressed in various ways through the metaphor of vision. Haze's blinded eyes, which give him new sight, become for his landlady "a pinpoint of light," a guide to a higher level of reality. Haze keeps among his possessions his mother's glasses, "in case his vision should ever become dim." In the climactic scene in which Sabbath presents him with the "new jesus," he has just rediscovered and put on these glasses and looked idly into the mirror.

> He saw his mother's face in his, looking at the face in the mirror. He moved back quickly and raised his hand to take off the glasses but the door opened and two more faces floated into his line of vision; one of them [Sabbath holding the mummy] said, "Call me Momma now."

With sharpened vision, he pulls the mummy from Sabbath's arms, bangs it against the wall, and finally drops it through the fire escape door. Useless now, the glasses also crash down to destruction. A perversion of spiritual vision appears in the description of a newspaper picture of Hawks just before he attempted to blind himself: "The mouth had a look that might have been either holy or calculating, but there was a coldness in the eyes that suggested terror." The all-seeing eye of God is grotesquely suggested in the description of a cage at the zoo which attracts Hazel's attention:

> Over in one corner on the floor of the cage, there was an eye. The eye was in the middle of something that looked like a piece of mop sitting on an old rag. . . . [It] was an owl with one eye open. It was looking directly at Hazel Motes.

As if responding to God himself, Hazel answers the look with "I AM clean." The theme of spiritual vision is distorted comically in the description of one of the films which Enoch sees while waiting to meet the gorilla. Called "The Eye," it tells of a mad scientist who performs operations by remote control. "You would wake up in the morning and find a slit in your chest or head or stomach and something you couldn't do without would be gone." In fear, the moronic Enoch slouches down into the seat; "only his eyes looked at the screen." This parody grotesquely suggests its opposite: the bestowal by divine power of "something you couldn't do without"—supernatural grace.

One major symbol epitomizes the concept of spiritual alienation: the shrunken mummy which Enoch gives to Hazel as the "new jesus." It is man without spirit, reduced to a handful of dust. Sabbath suggests the symbolic extensions of the shrunken man when, holding him, she muses that "she had never known anyone who looked like him before, but there was something in him of everyone she had ever known, as if they had all been rolled into one person and killed and shrunk and dried." A final description of the mummy identifies it with alienated man: "His mouth had been knocked a little to one side so that there was just a trace of a grin covering his terrified look." Man trying to cover his terror with a faint grin is man estranged from God.

That Flannery O'Connor chose the romance genre to communi-

cate her theme of alienation indicates the influence of Nathaniel
Hawthorne's work upon her. In her lectures, she spoke of Hawthorne's use of the romance to communicate deep spiritual
realities, and in a letter to a friend she said, "I am one of his
[Hawthorne's] descendants."[9] That she evaluated the potential-
ities of the romance carefully seems evident from her marking
this passage in the introduction to Richard Chase's *The American Novel and Its Tradition*:

> Nevertheless the best American novelists have found uses for
> romance far beyond the escapism, fantasy, and sentimentality
> often associated with it. They have found that in the very
> freedom of romance from the conditions of actuality there are
> certain potential virtues of the mind, which may be suggested
> by such words as rapidity, irony, abstraction, profundity. These
> qualities have made romance a suitable, even, as it seems, an
> inevitable, vehicle for the intellectual and moral ideas of the
> American novelists.[10]

In his discussion (p. 13), Chase lines up the characteristics of romance: characters are two-dimensional without strong relationships to society, each other, or the past; action predominates over
character; action encounters "less resistance from reality" (one
thinks of Shoats' ability to produce, on one day's notice, a True
Prophet who is Haze's double); plot is "highly colored," and its
events have a plausibility that is symbolic rather than realistic
(one thinks of the patrolman's gratuitous destruction of Hazel's
car). *Wise Blood* possesses these characteristics, but they are combined with a comic realism which is traditionally foreign to the
romance. O'Connor herself terms *Wise Blood* "a comic novel."[11]
This mixture of genres blurs the communication; the impact of
Hazel's and Enoch's alienation is weakened because they are both
comic, almost stylized figures. The comic tone which infuses
Wise Blood removes the novel from the romance tradition, even
while its setting, characters, and action place it there. In *The
Violent Bear It Away*, Flannery O'Connor combined these two
disparate genres effectively; she speaks of this combination in a
lecture given in 1960:

> When Hawthorne said that he wrote romances, he was at-
> tempting, in effect, to keep for fiction some of its freedom from

social determinisms, and to steer it in the direction of poetry. I think this tradition of the dark and divisive romance-novel has combined with the comic-grotesque tradition, and with the lessons all writers have learned from the naturalists.[12]

This combination became her great strength, but in *Wise Blood* the two genres are uneasily allied. An example of this misalliance is the chapter which details Enoch's preparations for receiving the "new jesus" into his room. Symbolic, ritualistic—it is the stuff of romance, but the voice is hilariously comic. As he surveys the pictures on his walls, Enoch ruminates on one he hates: a moose standing in a small lake. He counteracts the influence of the moose by unframing it. "Enoch knew the time had come when something had to be done; he didn't know what was going to happen in his room, but when it happened, he didn't want to have the feeling that the moose was running it." Here comedy undercuts romance; laughter wins out.

Flannery O'Connor's ability to deal with mystery (the touchstone of romance) and manners (the raw material of comedy) gives this novel the touch of brilliance that her earliest critics recognized, even though the combination puzzled them. Robert Fitzgerald says about the reaction to that first novel that "the critics didn't know what to make of it," but he adds, significantly, "[Isaac] Rosenfeld and everyone else knew that a strong new writer was at large."[13] In this first major work, O'Connor sought to communicate her vision of alienated man by plunging deeply into two streams of American fiction. Although in time she learned to modulate her comic tone until it encompassed a range which could include the extremes of romance and tragedy, in this work it is brightly comic and unequal to the demands of the theme of alienation.

A romanticist creating her own reality and an agnostic cut off from spiritual reality come into violent conflict in the title story of the first collection of O'Connor short stories, *A Good Man Is Hard to Find*. One of her most perfectly wrought artifacts, it relates the meeting of a vacation-bound grandmother and her family with the Misfit, a psychopathic killer. A piece of comic realism, the story explores the characters' apprehension of reality —both natural and supernatural. The grandmother dominates the first half of the story; through its events one sees that her inability to grasp reality truly alienates her from its spiritual extensions. When the Misfit enters, he brings a different kind of alienation: he has an absolutely honest conception of reality which embodies all reason and no faith. His agnosticism cuts him off from the supernatural world. The violent conflict of these two views marks the advent of grace. About this violence, the author stated:

> I suppose the reasons for the use of so much violence in modern fiction will differ with each writer who uses it, but in my own stories I have found that violence is strangely capable of returning my characters to reality and preparing them to accept their moment of grace. Their heads are so hard that almost nothing else will do the work. This idea, that reality is something to which we must be returned at considerable cost, is one which is seldom understood by the casual reader, but it is one which is implicit in the Christian view of the world.[14]

Violence moves into the story when a grey-haired man with "silver-rimmed spectacles that gave him a scholarly look" slides down the gully to the scene of the family's car accident, and the grandmother shrieks, "You're the Misfit!"

Up to this point, the structure and details of the story have given vivid life to an ordinary family, starting on their annual vacation. Through the action, each member of the family displays his attitude toward reality. A self-centered romantic, the grandmother arranges reality to suit herself when she can, and indulges in fantasy when she cannot. Her false gentility precludes any honest reaction to life: the naked Negro child whom they see in a doorway is "a cute little pickaninny" that she'd like to paint; the tombstones in the cotton field are remnants of a grandiose plantation. To Bailey, her son, bending over the sports section of the paper or over the steering wheel of the car, reality is a heavy weight. The world is real for him—too real. He faces it stolidly until his automobile accident attracts the Misfit. Then, eye-to-gun with his destiny, he can only reiterate, "We're in a predicament." His wife, called "the children's mother" all through the story, is alienated from reality by her passivity. She exhibits no will; she acquiesces to everyone. In the lunchroom,

"June Star said play something she could tap to and the children's mother put in another dime"; in the gully the Misfit asks her if she'd like to join her husband who has just been led away to his death and she replies dazedly, "Yes, thank you." Her one statement of assertion concerning her son's exploring the old house—"We'll all stay in the car"—seems to signal her attitude toward life.

Only the children respond honestly (if brattishly) to reality. They fade out of view when the Misfit takes over the scene with his devastating honesty. But while they, with the grandmother, hold the center of the story, they are foils for her gentle deviousness. They listen to her trying to persuade their parents not to go to Florida. To Bailey she speaks of the danger of meeting the Misfit; to his wife she extols the educational advantages of travelling to new places, and they had all been to Florida. The boy, John Wesley, faces the truth: "If you don't want to go to Florida, why dontcha stay at home?" On the trip, when the grandmother exclaims over the Negro child, June Star comments flatly, "He didn't have any britches on." The story seems to imply that the children instinctively see the visible world truly, and are therefore open to invisible reality.

When the family stops for lunch at The Tower, the scene points up a subtle contrast between man's penchant for closing his eyes to reality (a form of alienation) and an animal's immediate apprehension of it. When the family approaches the lunchroom, the children run toward "a grey monkey about a foot high, chained to a small chinaberry tree." The monkey responds by climbing to the highest limb of the tree. He knows how to deal with the world realistically. During lunch, the grandmother shows her tenuous grasp of reality. As the juke box plays, she pretends that she is dancing in her chair; to Red Sammy, the owner of The Tower, she presents her view that "Europe was entirely to blame for the way things were now." Even though she watches Red Sammy treat his wife as a menial, she calls him "a good man." She seems completely incapable of dealing with the real world. As the group leaves the lunchroom, they notice the monkey dealing effectively with reality; he is "catching fleas in himself and biting each one carefully between his teeth as if it were a delicacy." The two references to the monkey which frame the family's visit to the lunchroom seem to imply a comparison between man's power to deal subjectively with reality, and an animal's instinctive objective response.

As the trip progresses, the pace of the story quickens. The grandmother erroneously remembers an exciting old mansion slightly off their route; the children badger their father to make a detour; clouds of pink dust rise from the dirt road onto which the grandmother directs her son; Pitty Sing, the cat, springs out of the grandmother's hiding place and onto Bailey's shoulder, precipitating the accident. So real are the events of the story that one can accept the metaphysical turn which the story takes when the Misfit enters. With his appearance, two attitudes toward reality converge. The Misfit apprehends visible reality honestly; the grandmother rearranges visible and invisible reality to suit herself. The first conflict concerns the accident: "We turned over twice!" said the grandmother. "Oncet," the Misfit corrected. "We seen it happen." The conflict then moves rapidly to the center of supernatural reality: the Redemption. For the Misfit, it *mattered* whether or not Christ was God: if He was, then all lives were His; if He was not, then life was meaningless. For the grandmother, it really did not matter. She could adjust supernatural reality to her own liking—"Maybe He didn't raise the dead"—just as she could readjust natural reality—"not telling the truth but wishing she were." Although she talked religion— "If you would pray, Jesus would help you"—it is evident that Christ has no reality in her life. The author phrases this ambivalence succinctly: "Finally she found herself saying 'Jesus, Jesus,' meaning Jesus will help you, but the way she was saying it, it sounded as if she might be cursing."

One thing about the grandmother is clear: she believes she is a Southern lady. From her appearance at the beginning of the trip in her navy blue sailor hat to her genteel statement, "I think I have injured an organ" as she sits down in the ditch, the grandmother is a weak, plebeian version of the gentility of the Old South. But as her confrontation with the Misfit becomes more intense, more *real*, the gentility is stripped away. This is symbolized by the fate of her hat, the true sign of a lady: as the Misfit invites Bailey to his death, "the grandmother reached up to adjust her hat brim as if she were going to the woods with him but it came off in her hand. She stood staring at it and after a second she let it fall to the ground." Gradually her concern becomes more oriented to someone other than herself. Although she begins by begging for her life, she ends by pleading with the criminal to save himself. She tells him over and over to pray. It is a strange phenomenon for a person on the edge of death to tell her captor to pray rather than pray herself. Throughout the final dialogue, her concern is obviously with his conversion for her sake. But in a final moment of absolute reality, all pretense is over and vision fills the void: "the grandmother's head cleared for an instant," and her heart embraces the criminal in a movement of perfect charity. The Misfit's comment, "She would of been a good woman . . . if it had been somebody there to shoot her every minute of her life," indicates that he understands the impact of violence which has ended her alienation by returning her to reality and transformed her from a "lady" to a "good woman." The distance which the grandmother travelled after the speedometer registered 55,890 is the distance from her vacuous comment, "look at the cute little pickaninny" to her amazed realization of the bonds of humanity— "Why, you're one of my babies." The story's moment of grace is extended by the description of the dead woman "with her legs crossed under her like a child's [reborn in an act of selfless love] and her face smiling up at the cloudless sky."

The Misfit explains his philosophy clearly, and its echoes can be heard in the voices of Albert Camus, Martin Heidegger, and other alienated agnostics of our time. Because he "wasn't there," and he couldn't "know," he refused to open his mind to belief. Some writers might have made him an existential hero, but Flannery O'Connor portrays the moral sterility of his world. The Misfit describes the world of the agnostic, forced to meaningless suffering in a world beyond his understanding, when he describes the penitentiary: "Turn to the right, it was a wall. . . . Turn to the left, it was a wall. Look up it was a ceiling, look down it was a floor." Symbolic of the Misfit's spiritual condition is the sky which overhangs the scene of the six passionless murders. He calls attention to it as he stands, seemingly embarrassed, in front of his captives. "Ain't a cloud in the sky," he remarked, looking up at it, "Don't see no sun but don't see no cloud either." While describing his walled existence, he looks up again at "the cloud-less sky." As he faces the last of his victims, "there was not a cloud in the sky nor any sun." The sun suggests divinity, and clouds suggest rain, a biblical symbol for grace. The blankness of the sky suggests the Misfit's spiritually unlighted, unnourished world. Yet the Misfit is a "good man" in many respects. The author draws him with compassion and puts him far ahead of Bailey and Red Sammy in gentleness and politeness. With his clear concep-tion of the significance of Redemption, what bars him from belief? The story indicates that pride in his self-sufficiency blocks his apprehension of spiritual reality. An interesting theological corollary of this idea appears in Joseph Peiper's *Belief and Faith*. Peiper quotes from Cardinal Newman, whose influence on Flannery O'Connor seems evident from the number of books concerning him in her library, and her references to him in her essays and lectures. O'Connor marked this passage, in which Pei-per says:

> If a man becomes aware of certain teachings, or of certain data which purport to be the Word of God—then he cannot pos-sibly assume the right to remain "neutral for the present." This is a point to which John Henry Newman repeatedly ad-verts. Men, he says, are greatly inclined to "wait quietly" to see whether proofs of the actuality of revelation will drop into their laps, as though they were in the position of arbitrators and not in that of the needy. "They have decided to test the Almighty in a passionless judicial fashion, with total lack of bias, with sober minds." It is an error as common as it is fatal, says Newman, to think that "truth may be approached *without homage*."[15]

That homage is a mental attitude foreign to the Misfit seems im-mediately evident. His father had said of him when he was a child that he would have to know the "why" of everything. This complete dependence on reason excludes any apprehension of that which the mind of man cannot encompass. Coupled with his complete reliance on reason is the Misfit's self-sufficiency. In a wry repudiation of the crime of theft, he asserts that "nobody had nothing I wanted." That he also repudiates any reaching out toward supernatural reality becomes evident when he answers the grandmother's question, "Why don't you pray?" with the dogmatic assertion, "I don't want no hep; I'm doing all right by myself."

The books in Flannery O'Connor's library give strong evidence of her concern with this type of pride, which is the cause of spiritual alienation. Among her marked or signed books which reflect this interest are James Collins's *The Existentialists*; Martin Heidegger's *Existence and Being*; Gabriel Marcel's *The Mystery of Being*; Henri De Lubac's *The Drama of Atheist Humanism*; Ignace Lepp's *Atheism in Our Time*; and Martin Buber's *The Eclipse of God*. In this last volume, O'Connor marked a passage which seems to explain theologically the Misfit's state of mind:

> All religious reality begins with what Biblical religion calls the "fear of God." It comes when our existence between birth and death becomes incomprehensible and uncanny, when all security is shattered through the mystery. This is not the relative mystery of that which is inaccessible only to the present state of human knowledge and is hence in principle discoverable. It is the essential mystery, the inscrutableness of which belongs to its very nature; it is the unknowable. Through this dark gate (which is only a gate and not, as some theologians believe, a dwelling) the believing man steps forth into the everyday which is henceforth hallowed as the place in which he has to live with the mystery. He steps forth directed and assigned to the concrete, contextual situations of his existence. That he henceforth accepts the situation as given him by the Giver is what Biblical religion calls the "fear of God."[16]

The Misfit is standing in the "dark gate" of the unknowable, and has been standing there during his adult life—a misfit because he belongs neither with the complacent nor with the believers. This gate has become for him "a dwelling" because movement through it demands faith: "the believing man steps forth." Faith implies an acceptance of mystery, which, for the Misfit, is impossible, because he has to know "why." The story leaves open the possibility that the grandmother's mysterious action of love will open the Misfit's mind to the reality of mystery. The grandmother both reaches this gate and steps through it in a single action. Throughout her life she has been estranged from "religious reality" because her existence has never seemed "incomprehensible" or "uncanny" to her. Living only on the surface of life, she is unaware of its depth. She does not discern life's mystery; the Misfit does not accept it. Their conflict brings both face to face with religious reality. The grandmother embraces it, and the Misfit's response is deliberately ambiguous.

In "A Stroke of Good Fortune," Flannery O'Connor explores a different type of alienation—a young woman's alienation from life itself in her unwillingness to become a mother. Ruby Hill, a dull, selfish woman, has as her sole ambition to move to "a subdivision . . . where you had your drugstore and grocery and a picture show right in your own neighborhood." Although happily married to Bill Hill, she does not want children. When she learns that her physical discomfort is probably pregnancy, she moves from unbelief to horror. The story seems to suggest that the new life within her is giving her the possibility of enlarging and enlivening her circumscribed, dull existence. But there is slight indication that the possibility will be realized.

Two factors militate against the successful communication of the alienation theme: the plot, which limits the possibilities of character development severely, and the narrative voice, which fails to give the reader a glimpse of a missing dimension. The entire action of the story centers on the stairway of an apartment house in an unknown city in Tennessee. Ruby progresses from the foot of the stairs to the middle of the third flight, with three stops: on the second floor, Mr. Jaegers calls her into his room to tell her about the discovery of Florida; on the third floor she visits a friend, Laverne, who informs her that her sickness is pregnancy; on her way to the fourth floor, a neighbor's child, Hartley Gilfeet, crashes into her. On the stairs she reflects that she has confidence in the palmist Madame Zoleeda's prediction that her illness will bring her "a stroke of good fortune," and one learns that her determination not to have children stems from her horror at her mother's childbearing, particularly at the birth of her youngest brother, Rufus. As the story closes, Ruby realizes the truth of Laverne's diagnosis.

With such a limited scope of action, something extraordinary is necessary to make so stolid a character come to life. The narrator's voice could have done it, but, unfortunately, after the first paragraph, the author speaks in Ruby's authentically dull voice, which can only further stultify the view of life which the story projects. Twice the author's thought rises above the pettiness of Ruby's musings, but the reflection is intrusive and not true to character. Thinking of her "aliveness" (a beautiful irony) in contrast to the rest of her family, who are "all dried up and puckered up," Ruby reflects on her husband's satisfaction with her, evident even more since she had gained a little weight. Then the sentence: "She felt the wholeness of herself, a whole thing climbing the stairs." Given Ruby's mentality, one doubts her ability to feel anything so abstract as "wholeness." This seems to be rather the author's comment about the completeness of a pregnant woman, which Ruby would never recognize. Later the author describes Ruby's worry about the pain in her stomach.

She had thought the word *cancer* once and dropped it instantly because no horror like that was coming to her because it couldn't. The word came back to her immediately with the pain but she slashed it in two with Madam Zoleeda. It will end in good fortune. She slashed it twice through and then again until there were only pieces of it that couldn't be recognized.

This view of the entity of words was evidently a delight for Flannery O'Connor. It recurs frequently in her stories, but in this one, it seems unsuited to the character who reflects on it. The author's self-imposed limitation of voice narrows both the technique and the vision of the story. If the moment of grace is there (and evidence for it is scanty), Ruby fails to recognize it.

One of Ruby's three interruptions in her journey up the stairs (an obvious if ineffective metaphor for life), her visit with the chiropodist's secretary, illuminates by contrast the lifelessness of the protagonist. From Laverne's initial reaction to Ruby's appearance in her doorway with little Hartley's gun in her hand— "She staggered back to the sofa and fell on it, her legs rising higher than her hips and falling down helplessly with a thud"— the young girl pulses with life. She discerns immediately that Ruby is pregnant and displays it by her pose: "After a second she folded her arms and very pointedly stuck her stomach out and began to sway back and forth." Ruby, alienated, it seems, even from intuition, misses the implication, and Laverne is forced to a more dramatic demonstration to communicate the news to her:

> Laverne began to do a kind of comic dance up and down the room. She took two or three slow steps in one direction with her knees bent and then she came back and kicked her leg slowly and painfully in the other. She began to sing in a loud guttural voice, rolling her eyes, "Put them all together, they spell MOTHER! MOTHER!" and stretching out her arms as if she were on the stage.

Ruby then comes to life to protest life itself:

> Ruby's mouth opened wordlessly and her fierce expression vanished. For a half-second she was motionless; then she sprang from the chair. "Not me" she shouted. "Not me!"

This scene, the most vivid in the story, brings the action to a climax, but instead of a dramatic fall, the action slides slowly to an ambiguous conclusion.

The two encounters which frame this one are less imaginatively conceived, but both highlight Ruby's nonparticipation in (or alienation from) life. She engages in conversation with Mr. Jaegers reluctantly, for she thinks of him as an old person who is out of touch with life. However, their conversation about the fountain of youth reveals that the schoolteacher is more deeply immersed in life than Ruby is. Hartley Gilfeet, the six-year-old boy in the development who gallops past her on the stairway, is the epitome of life; she has only repulsion for him.

Ruby gives only one sign that she is capable of apprehending anything which verges on mystery: she has faith in the fortune teller, Madame Zoleeda, "a stout woman with green eyes that moved in their sockets as if they had been oiled." The palmist predicted that her illness would bring her good fortune, and to Ruby that meant that, to save her health, Bill Hill would consent to move to the subdivision. Even though Hartley Gilfeet has been nicknamed by his mother "Little Mister Good Fortune," she does not make the connection between "good fortune" and "baby." At the end of the story this connection is made for her when she says those words together, as if balancing one against the other, and the echoes "leer" back, uniting them. In her belief in the palmist, Ruby seems to be reaching out—even if in the wrong direction—toward the world of spiritual reality. It is the only sign of hope, even if a distorted one, that she will ever transcend her stolid existence and participate fully in life. Alienation is depicted more effectively in "The Lame Shall Enter First," in which three characters, each alienated from a different aspect of reality, come to a fuller understanding of the world they live in and its spiritual extensions. The title comes from the prophet Isaias and suggests that those who acknowledge that they are spiritually maimed will merit first claim to the grace of Redemption. The story involves the interaction of three persons—a man, a boy, and a child: Sheppard, an intellectual young widower who is too educated to believe in the supernatural world; Rufus Johnson, a crippled juvenile delinquent who has cut himself off from society; and Norton, Sheppard's son, irrevocably cut off from his dead mother, who finds himself becoming alienated from his father. At the story's close, it is clear that the lame boy has opened the eyes of both father and son to an awareness of spiritual reality. Norton embraces death to find his mother, and Sheppard rejects the self-deification which had sustained him. The story develops, in complex unity, three variations of meaning of the scriptural dictum, "The truth shall make you free."

The first section of the tripartite story presents the terms of each character's alienation. Norton fixes an indigestible breakfast for himself, then vomits it, and consoles himself with his jars of nickels, dimes, and quarters. His actions show that he is inconsolable over the death of his mother a year previous and is closing himself into his own world. The child longs to know that his mother is somewhere, and Sheppard refuses to give him this consolation, believing it less than the truth. Instead, Sheppard attempts to impose his own rationalistic view on his son. He tries to set Norton free from grief by the truth: the child's mother is nowhere. He tries to lead him in the path of good works: if Norton did win a thousand dollars, wouldn't he "like to give some swings and trapezes to the orphanage?" Wouldn't he "like to buy poor Rufus Johnson a new shoe?" In so casual a manner, the shoe is introduced; it will grow into the unifying symbol of the story. The obtuse father fits Norton into a conceptual slot in his mind: because he eats cake for breakfast, because he breaks into uncontrollable grief for his mother, because his eyes narrow at the thought of Rufus Johnson using his door key to their house—he is selfish.

Norton's rival for his father's attention is a fourteen-year-old club-footed boy. Raised by his fundamentalist grandfather and nurtured on the Bible, Rufus Johnson refutes Sheppard's clinical diagnosis of his vagrancy with this clear knowledge of himself: "Satan . . . has me in his power." But Satan is only a five-letter word to Sheppard, and he deplores the "elemental warping of nature" which Johnson displays. He had embarked on a year's series of weekly conferences with the boy, in which he attempted to stimulate his 140 I. Q. and rid him of his scriptural delusions. The description of Sheppard's method of "handling" Johnson could have been a sharp parody of a social scientist's technique, but instead it is a portrayal of an intelligent humanist who thinks that education has taught him all there is to know about man. "The case was clear to Sheppard instantly. [Johnson's] mischief was compensation for the foot." As the year progressed, Sheppard had noted a change in Johnson's eyes, which he thought signaled a change in attitude. He believed that he had succeeded in remolding the boy by his eclectic Saturday afternoon discussions, which gave the boy "something to reach for." The author conveys both the genuineness and the obvious error of his belief by the slightly overblown diction: "He watched his eyes and every week he saw something in them crumble. From the boy's face, hard but shocked, braced against the light that was ravaging him, he could see that he was hitting dead center." Later, Sheppard sees the boy rummaging in garbage cans, and, to him, the boy's expression seemed to change when their eyes met: "Something had kindled in the boy's eyes, he was sure of it, some memory of the lost light." The tinge of romanticism renders Sheppard's naive assumptions suspect.

When Johnson enters Sheppard's home, it becomes evident that he has deliberately opted for evil and enjoys deluding Sheppard. The lame boy spends the afternoon tormenting the frightened Norton by desecrating his dead mother's belongings. Even though Sheppard appears to be completely insensitive to his son's misery, the child tries to uphold him when Johnson sneers at

Sheppard's efforts. In spite of his terror, Norton challenges Johnson's denigration of his father: "He's good," he mumbled. "He helps people." Johnson counters this with a key statement:

> "Good!" [he] said savagely. He thrust his head forward. "Listen here," he hissed, "I don't care if he's good or not. He ain't *right!*"

That evening, Sheppard uses what he thinks is his son's problem, selfishness, to induce Rufus to stay with them, in order that he might continue his work in developing the abandoned boy's potential. Even when Norton repeats Johnson's insulting remarks about his father, Sheppard refuses to believe that he has been wrong about the sincerity of the lame boy. Sheppard's reaction to the insults is characteristic: "good" but not "right."

> Sheppard was not put back. These insults were part of the boy's defensive mechanism.

In his best clinical manner, Sheppard attempts to prove to the lame boy that he—Sheppard—is immune to insult from Johnson because he is "above and beyond simple pettiness." This speech of unadulterated righteousness leads to Johnson's final comment to Norton about Sheppard, a remark which shows the extent of Sheppard's alienation from spiritual reality:

> "God, kid," Johnson said in a cracked voice, "how do you stand it?" His face was stiff with outrage. "He thinks he's Jesus Christ!"

The action of the second section of the story shows Johnson becoming more and more alienated from society. He ransacks houses, peers in windows, and lies with consummate skill. Yet he is gentle with Norton, and slowly leads him to an understanding of the spiritual world and to the knowledge that his mother is in heaven. Norton becomes more and more absorbed in the spiritual world. The telescope which Sheppard had bought for Johnson now links Norton to his mother, whom he thinks he sees in the vast regions of space. Sheppard becomes more and more uneasy about the club-footed boy; he is unable to understand his actions and fears that Johnson is using Norton as a weapon against him. His trust in his clinical knowledge weakens, and he becomes vulnerable for the impact of grace.

One of Flannery O'Connor's most moving portrayals of alienation, this story elicits compassion for all three characters. Norton's plight is evident immediately; the "knot of flesh" below his "suddenly distorted mouth," and the sobs for his dead mother which follow show the depth of his suffering. The double view one gets of Sheppard—that which his words and actions present and the view of his thoughts and motivations which the story renders—shows his benighted good will. His awakening is terrible, yet filled with brightness. When he repeats three times, as a summary of his efforts to "save" Johnson, "I did more for him than I did for my own child," and finally hears his voice "as if it were the voice of his accuser," the light is brilliant.

> His heart constricted with a repulsion for himself so clear and intense that he gasped for breath. He had stuffed his own emptiness with good works like a glutton. He had ignored his own child to feed his vision of himself.

Sheppard's misguided estrangement from his own child is symbolic of his greater estrangement from God. As he realizes his error, he runs to embrace his son, only to find that it is too late. Against the stark tragedy of this last moment one must place the revelation which has preceded it to illumine the terrible consequences of alienation from God.

It is more difficult to elicit compassion for Johnson, whose alienation from society jars strangely with his biblical spirituality. He is both angelic and diabolical; he performs the function of a prophet for Norton and Sheppard, yet he calls himself a devil and acts the part. He seems to have a spiritual hold over Sheppard and his child. But he holds Sheppard by his diabolism, which the psychologist does not recognize, and the child by his confident assertion of his beliefs. Devil for one and angel for the other, he leads the older through suffering to truth and the younger to life-in-death. Norton intuitively recognizes Johnson's authority in spiritual matters. When he speaks of souls in hell, he gives the child the intimation that his mother might be *some*-where. After his father tells him again that his mother "doesn't exist," the boy's face contorts as it did in an earlier scene, but—

Instead of howling, the boy wrenched himself away [from his father] and caught Johnson by the sleeve. "Is she there, Rufus?" he said.

Johnson tells the child that his mother is "on high" and in a devilish/angelic manner, he instructs the child about heaven and how to go there. The author characterizes him best as a "clear-eyed sounder of hearts."

Two mealtime scenes illustrate Johnson's double role in the story. He is both child and prophet, both a diabolical figure and a bearer of grace, both an alien figure in civil society and a true citizen—even though an erring one—of the world which the Bible has made real to him. When he comes to Sheppard's home just as a thunderstorm ceases, he is a wet, cold, hungry boy with a streak of the devil in him. He torments Norton, then lies on the boy's bed and orders him to bring him food. Trembling, Norton approaches with a hastily made lunch.

[Johnson] tore into the sandwich and ate steadily until he finished it. Then he took the glass of milk. He held it with both hands like a child and when he lowered it for breath, there was a rim of milk around his mouth.

His last meal in Sheppard's house shows him in the role of prophet. He brings the Bible to the dinner table to continue reading it with Norton. In answer to Sheppard's ridicule of Scripture, Johnson rips a page from the book and eats it.

His eyes widened as if a vision of splendor were opening up before him. "I've eaten it!" he breathed. "I've eaten it like Ezekiel and it was honey to my mouth."

The paradigmatic gesture of Ezekiel in eating the scroll which the Lord gave him symbolizes the prophet's acceptance of the commission of the Lord and its transformation from bitterness to sweetness. Johnson leaves Sheppard's house described as "a small black figure on the threshhold of some dark apocalypse." His final imprecation to Sheppard, "The devil has you in his power," rings with the tone of the prophets and suggests that the boy's own alienation from his "true country" by deliberate evil has ended.

Underlying Flannery O'Connor's presentation of alienated modern man is her concept of man totally integrated into the world of the spirit. Because this concept is clear to her, she can depict its absence in a variety of imaginative ways. Sheppard consciously alienates himself from anything beyond his reason. Ruby's total absorption in self which ignores the "other" and therefore excludes the Divine "other" alienates her from life itself. The Misfit's calm, reasoned agnosticism drives him to spend his life "killing somebody or burning down his house or doing some other meanness to him." Hazel Motes reflects modern man's attempt to come to terms with the reality of belief by remaking the Saviour in his own image. Each of these characters, knowingly or unwittingly, makes himself a "new jesus"—a shrunken, spiritless semblance of man.

Between the pages of Ronald Knox's translation of Scripture, *The New Testament in English*, I found a paper in O'Connor's handwriting. It said:

Faith breeds faith but faith in this age appears as dead as Sara's womb. When we believe today, we believe like Abraham.

Only the faith of Abraham—who believed the word of God when all human reality seemed to negate it—would be strong enough to form the spiritual basis on which these stories rest. Only consummate artistry could have transformed such faith into literature.

CHAPTER IV

The Black Procession:

death in the context of history

"The best American fiction has always been regional. The ascendency passed roughly from New England to the Midwest to the South; it has passed and stayed longest wherever there has been a shared past, a sense of alikeness, and the possibility of reading a small history in a universal light."
F. O'C.

In the climactic scene of "A Late Encounter with the Enemy," Flannery O'Connor describes the death of a wizened Civil War veteran. Sitting on the stage at his granddaughter's commencement exercises, the old man, dressed in his Confederate uniform, sees forming in front of him a black procession, which he imagines is entering a hole in his head—a hole which is slowly deepening and widening. For many years "the past and the future [had been] the same to him, one forgotten and the other not remembered." He had no use for history "because he never expected to meet it again." But at the moment of death, history becomes significant as the past rushes into his mind and forces his vision into the future.

As the music swelled toward him, the entire past opened up on him out of nowhere and he felt his body riddled in a hundred places with sharp stabs of pain and he fell down, returning a curse for every hit. He saw his wife's narrow face looking at him critically through her round gold-rimmed glasses; he saw one of his bald-headed squinting sons; and his mother ran toward him with an anxious look; then a succession of places —Chickamauga, Shiloh, Marthasville—rushed at him as if the past were the only future now and he had to endure it. Then suddenly he saw that the black procession was almost on him. He recognized it, for it had been dogging all his days. He made such a desperate effort to see over it and find out what comes after the past that his hand clenched the sword until the blade touched bone.

The end of the story reveals this "clenching" to be the instant of his death.

This scene exemplifies Flannery O'Connor's earliest imaginative conception of one of the significant ideas in her fiction: that death, the convergence of time and eternity, places the individual's life in the perspective of history—personal, social, and biblical. Concomitant with this idea is one which it includes: that life derives its meaning from the context of history. To appreciate the varied and complex manifestations of this idea in her fiction, it is necessary to view from different perspectives its component parts.

"Death has always been brother to my imagination. I can't imagine a story that doesn't properly end in it or in its foreshadowings,"[1] O'Connor said to an interviewer in 1963. The personal roots of this preoccupation with death are perhaps evident enough. When the disease, lupus, struck her in 1951, she knew that her feet were set on the road which she had watched her father travel to his premature death. But her early fiction gives evidence that death was "brother" to her imagination even before its signs appeared in her flesh. Her one published piece of collegiate fiction, "Home of the Brave," which appeared in the college literary magazine, *The Corinthian*,[2] concerns the sudden and undramatic death of a young soldier, son-in-law of the protagonist. Three of the six stories in her M.F.A. thesis concern death. Two of these, "The Geranium" and "Wildcat," which will be discussed later in this chapter, show old men facing death. The third, "The Train," was reworked into the first chapter of *Wise Blood*, in which Hazel Motes recalls the deaths of his grandmother, mother, father, and brothers as he settles in the coffinlike enclosure of an upper berth.

The request, in 1960, of a group of Catholic sisters that she write the biography of a child with cancer of the face who died in their hospital led Flannery O'Connor to express a deep conviction about the relationship between life and death, between death and human history. Unwilling to write the biography, she suggested that the nuns, Dominican Sisters, Servants of Relief for Incurable Cancer, themselves write the account of the child. She offered to edit the manuscript, and, later, moved by its account of a child who grew into holiness by an acceptance of suffering, she wrote an introduction to the book *A Memoir of Mary Ann*, published in 1961.[3] In the essay she sets Mary Ann's death in the perspective of history. She moves back to Nathaniel Hawthorne (whose daughter, Rose, founded the congregation of sisters who manage the hospital), detailing an incident in which he overcame "ice in the blood" to show compassion which inspired his daughter; she ruminates on the problem that the suffering of children presents; and she rises to a sweeping view of the interconnections of past, present, and future "called by the Church the Communion of Saints." She defines this dogma as "the action by which charity grows invisibly among us, entwining the living and the dead" (p. 228). Reflecting on the impact of the biography which drew her, unwillingly, into "the mystery of Mary Ann," she moves in thought from this specific instance to a universal view of life and death in the context of history:

> The story was as unfinished as the child's face. Both seem to have been left, like creation on the seventh day, to be finished by others. . . .
> [Mary Ann] and the Sisters who had taught her had fashioned from her unfinished face the material of her death. The creative action of the Christian's life is to prepare his death in Christ. It is a continuous action in which this world's goods are utilized to the fullest, both positive gifts and what Père Teilhard de Chardin calls "passive diminishments." (P. 223)

O'Connor closes the introduction with a final statement which crystallizes her idea of the individual life in the perspective of eternity: "I think that for the reader this story will illuminate the lines that join the most diverse lives and that hold us fast in Christ" (p. 228).

Other instances of her concern with death recur throughout her life. In her bookcase I found a penciled cartoon with the notation "age 9" written in an adult hand in the corner. Firm, detailed, and with a keen sense of proportion, the cartoon shows a child walking with her father and mother. In the balloon coming from the mother's mouth are the words, "Hold your head up, Mary Flannery." The child, scuffling along, replies, "I was readin where someone died of holding up their head." In its subject and in its crisp humor, this cartoon exhibits a characteristic bent of mind. In O'Connor's adult fiction, many of her characters meet death. It seems fitting that among the many theological books in her bookcase is Karl Rahner's *On the Theology of Death*.

By her belief that "the creative action of the Christian's life is to prepare his death in Christ," Flannery O'Connor links death with the life which precedes it and consequently with the social milieu in which that life is lived. For her, there is only one vital milieu—the South, with its rich social and literary heritage, its elaborate code of manners, and its distinctive local idiom. Her portrayal of life—and ultimately of death—in her fiction is intrinsically bound up with the South. She spoke frequently of the advantages that this milieu gave to the Southern writer, and perhaps she expressed this idea best in a 1963 lecture, "The Catholic Novelist in the Protestant South." Speaking of this writer, she was, of course, speaking of herself.

The opportunities for the potential Catholic writer in the South are so great as to be intimidating. He lives in a region where there is a thriving literary tradition, and this is always an advantage to the writer, who is initially inspired less by life than by the work of his predecessors. He lives in a region which is struggling, in both good ways and bad, to preserve its identity, and this is an advantage, for his dramatic need is to know manners under stress. He lives in the Bible Belt, where belief can be made believable. He has also here a good view of the modern world. A half-hour's ride in this region will take him from places where the life has a distinctly Old Testament flavor to places where the life might be considered post-Christian. Yet all these varied situations can be seen in one glance and heard in one conversation.[4]

Although this is a relatively late summary of her ideas, these ideas had been in formation during all of her writing career. In the 1963 interview previously mentioned, she answered a question about Southern mores by quoting Marshall McLuhan, but was hazy about where she read him. Her library shows that she read McLuhan's essay "Southern Quality" in *A Southern Vanguard*, edited by Allen Tate and published in 1947. In this book she had encircled the sentence that she later remembered quite accurately: "Formality becomes a condition of survival."[5] McLuhan is speaking of the social code of the South, particularly of the aristocrat's absence of private life because of the constant presence of family and family servants. O'Connor also marked the passage in which McLuhan describes the "life-style" of the South as passionate and tragic and possessing an "ominous sense of fatality." He cites the work of Poe as evidence that this life-style was discernible long before the Civil War, although it was deepened by that conflict. Other sections of the essay suggest ideas which O'Connor would later express in her own terms. McLuhan speaks of the association of thought and feeling which characterizes the South; the integrity of the Southern community where there is no split between the educated and the uneducated; the reason why the Southern novelist is a teller of tales; the use that Southern writers make of external nature as "a major actor or player"; and the reason for the deceptive surface simplicity of Southern fiction (pp. 113–118). All these ideas can be found, deepened and enlarged, in O'Connor's lectures which touch on her homeland.

That Flannery O'Connor immersed herself deeply in her region gives her fiction a social and historical dimension; that she could reproduce to the last nuance the idiom of her people allowed her to place her characters by their speech in the midst of Southern history. Speaking to a Southern Literary Conference, she deplored fiction in which "the characters speak as though they had never heard any kind of language except what came out of a television set." Then she sets forth her credo:

> An idiom characterizes a society, and when you ignore the idiom, you are very likely ignoring the whole social fabric that could make a meaningful character. You can't cut characters off from their society and say much about them as individuals. You can't say anything meaningful about the mystery of a personality unless you put that personality in a believable and significant context. And the best way to do this is through the character's own language.[6]

During her years of graduate study at the University of Iowa, O'Connor wrote a relatively weak story (it was never published, and the idea was never reworked in any way) which shows her imagination working with the idea of the death of an old man in a society uniquely characterized by his language. Entitled "Wildcat," it tells the story of an aged, blind Negro who senses that the wildcat that the boys of the town have gone into the woods to hunt is really after human blood and will, that very evening, claw him to death. The story details his waiting for the approach of death. A flashback to his youth, when an old man in his village was killed by a wildcat, shows the repetitious pattern of life: youth seeks game in the wrong place; the cat finds his prey among the aged. Although the story is imaginatively conceived, it does not possess "felt life." It is filtered through the consciousness of the old man, with both dialogue and narration written in idiomatic language. The story is largely told by dialogue, which makes it difficult to read. Flannery O'Connor never again wrote a story with Negroes as major characters or with dialogue as the chief means of forwarding the plot. Many years later, when an interviewer asked her why Negroes did not figure more prominently in her fiction, she replied:

> I don't understand them the way I do white people. I don't feel capable of entering the mind of a Negro. In my stories they're seen from the outside.[7]

The young writer evidently learned this by writing "Wildcat." She may also have learned by her overuse of dialogue in this story the principle which she stated many years later in advising a neophyte writer:

> Dialogue should be used sparingly, and mostly to reveal character. It follows the law of diminishing returns. The more of it you use, the less its effect.[8]

Although limitations in structure and characterization deprive this story of literary merit, it is of value in revealing the beginning of O'Connor's imaginative vision of death.

Another component of that vision is its biblical dimension. Both her fiction and her essays give evidence that Flannery O'Connor was continually aware of the shaping force of biblical history in the life and death of contemporary man. For her that history was more than a mythical heritage; it was the framework which set in perspective the events of man's life. She knew that she shared the biblical heritage of the majority of Southern people, and she understood the value of that heritage. Commenting on that value, she said, "Behind our own history, deepening it at every point, has been another history."[9] One can see her use of biblical analogues grow as her work matures.

The biblical dimension is noticeably missing, however, in her first published work embodying the theme of death in the context of history. By presenting history as "a black procession" which fills the consciousness of an old man and brings him to death, "A Late Encounter with the Enemy" renders imaginatively the concept of time moving into eternity in the life of one individual who is acting as a representative of history. But, paradoxically, the old man has no consciousness of death ("living had got to be such a habit with him that he couldn't conceive of any other condition") and no interest in history ("what happened then wasn't anything to a man living now and he was living now"). This lack of awareness of Southern history, in which he has played a part, evidently precludes, for him, an awareness of the larger history of salvation which lies behind it.

Within the framework of the story, this omission is necessary, for the narrative suggests Flannery O'Connor's vision of life by presenting the opposite view. Aged George Poker Sash grapples with death in complete unawareness of the meaning of the encounter. The first half of the story explains this lack of perception by showing the old man reacting to life around him only in terms of his ego. Because his memory is as dead as his dangling feet, he accepts and revels in the romanticizing of history which the story illustrates by describing the première of a movie (indubitably "Gone With the Wind") which mythologized the Civil War. Flannery O'Connor underlines the falseness of the "preemy" (the première) by a series of small details, such as the description of Sally Poker's corsage, "made with gladiola petals taken off and painted gold and put back together to look like a rose," which surround the larger deception: "the old man was introduced as General Tennessee Flintrock Sash of the Confederacy, though Sally Poker had told Mr. Govisky that his name was George Poker Sash and that he had only been a major." His appearance at the première as a hero becomes the memory that fills his mind; occasional invitations to "wear his uniform and sit in some conspicuous spot and lend atmosphere to the scene" fill his days. He sums up his philosophy when he muses that "history was connected with processions and life with parades and he liked parades."

Two other aspects of man's relation to history are presented by the old man's granddaughter and her nephew. Sally Poker, age sixty-two, also romanticizes history. She delights in the "preemy" until she realizes, on stage, that below her long black crepe dinner dress with the rhinestone buckle are her work shoes, which she had forgotten to change. Her consternation at this discovery suggests that reality has intruded into her dream. Sally Poker lives in one world and dreams about another. She has spent twenty hot summers obtaining her B.S. degree because, when she started to teach, "everything was normal, but nothing had been normal since she was sixteen." Even though, in retaliation for her education under duress, "she always taught in the exact way she had been taught not to teach," her real moment of triumph would come when, through her grandfather's presence on the stage, she could show her connection with the South's regal past. In the story's final irony, she glances at her grandfather as she receives her diploma and does not realize that he is dead. In contrast to the schoolteacher, John Wesley, the Boy Scout nephew who precipitates the old man's death, has no regard for history. "A fat boy with an executive expression," he has been commissioned by Sally Poker to wheel the General onto the stage, stay with him during the ceremony, and wheel him back to the family group at its close. A member of the new generation, he disregards age, tradition—real or simulated—and instructions in favor of a cold drink on a hot day. Wearing the General's hat, he stops for a Coca-Cola, leaving the old man exposed to the sun. The blazing heat makes the General feel "as if there were a little hole beginning to widen in the top of his head," and death approaches to fill that hole with the black procession of history.

Although the story's diction reflects the limitation of the protagonist's vision, Flannery O'Connor uses symbolic language to describe death as an entrance into an awareness of history. Words such as "Chickamauga, Shiloh, Johnston, Lee" become entities as "a long finger of music in the General's head probed various spots that were words, letting in a little light on the words and helping them to live." Words take forms and come at him "like musket fire." A larger symbolism can be seen in parallel scenes. Twice the General and his granddaughter appear on a stage together. At the première, the General is the romantic figure, and Sally Poker tries to become part of the scene, but for her, as has already been mentioned, romance is undercut by the reality of two brown Girl Scout oxfords protruding from the bottom of her dress. At the graduation, Sally Poker holds her head "a percep-

tible degree higher" as she receives her scroll in the knowledge
that "what all was behind her" is evident to her associates, but
once again reality—death—has intruded. Even in this ultimate
scene, when the rhythm of the sentences and the aptness of the
metaphoric description of death might lead to a certain elevation
of tone, the diction keeps the tone flat, almost banal, as the
opening quotation of this chapter illustrates. In general, the language of the story supports the narrowness of its vision of life in
relation to the past and the future.

Three years after the publication of "A Late Encounter with
the Enemy," Flannery O'Connor explored the same theme again,
this time in a somewhat wider social context in which she probes
the social and economic tensions intrinsic to the Southern
milieu.[10] In "Greenleaf," a double cast of characters, the Mays
and their hired help, the Greenleafs, represent the "old" and the
"new" South. As the narrative develops, Mrs. May looks back on
her fifteen years of handling the Greenleafs and plans for the future, when her two sons, who have no interest in the farm, will
have to deal with them after her death. The shadow of death
darkens the story from the opening words; it takes the form of a
scrub bull belonging to the Greenleaf boys.

The bull is both the central figure in the story and a complex
symbol of the encounter with the divine which is death. The
narrative opens with the bull, having broken out of the pasture,
chewing the bushes outside Mrs. May's bedroom and finally raising its head to stare at her "like an uncouth country suitor." It
closes with the bull's bounding toward her "like a wild tormented
lover" to bring her the embrace of death. Through the story, the
bull instigates all the action. Mrs. May's dawn encounter with it
dominates the breakfast conversation, in which her two sons,
Scofield, an insurance salesman, and Wesley, a teacher, display
their callousness and selfishness. To infuriate his mother, Scofield reveals that the bull belongs to the Greenleaf boys, O.T.
and E.T. This information leads Mrs. May to visit the Greenleaf
farm. Her visit illustrates what the opening section of the story
has intimated: with hard work and government aid, the Greenleaf family—the "new South"—is rising economically, will rise
socially, and will eventually displace the Mays, complacent
middle-class Southerners. The failure of the Greenleaf boys to

claim their bull leads to the climax of the story: Mrs. May forces their father to undertake to kill the bull, but before he can do so, the bull gores Mrs. May to death.

Symbolically, the bull first appears as a god. He stands in the "east," "silvered in the moonlight," and listens "like some patient god come down to woo" Mrs. May. As she slits her blind and the light falls on him, she sees a "wreath across his horns"—part of the hedge which he has ripped loose. Her last view of him before she closes the blind shows her that "the wreath slipped down to the base of his horns where it looked like a menacing prickly crown." To the Christian, this imagery suggests the God-man, Christ, at the hour of his passion and death. Mrs. May's dream, prompted by the bull's "steady, rhythmic chewing," links the bull-as-god with death. She dreams that something is eating her house and property and will continue eating herself, her sons, and everything they own until only the Greenleafs are left. She awakens "when the munching reached her elbow." As soon as Mrs. May learns that the bull belongs to O.T. and E.T., she iden-tifies the bull with the Greenleafs ("That's a Greenleaf bull if I ever saw one") and sees both the bull and its owners as a single menace. The next night her dream is again inspired by the bull crunching underneath her window. This time the death symbo-lism is more complex. A large stone is "grinding a hole on the outside wall of her brain"; she, walking on the inside, watches the sun, "a swollen red ball," and knows that she is safe from destruction by it. But it becomes "narrow and pale until it looked like a bullet. Then suddenly it burst through the treeline and raced down the hill toward her." The dream presages the manner of her death, when the bull, his head lowered, "raced to-ward her."

Her death is foreshadowed more subtly in another scene which links the charging of the bull with the unseen action of grace. Shortly after she had hired the Greenleafs, she found out that Mrs. Greenleaf indulged in "prayer healing." Walking one day on a wooded path through her property, she was startled by a "gutteral agonized voice" groaning "Jesus, Jesus!"

In a second it came again with a terrible urgency. "Jesus! Jesus!"

Mrs. May stopped still, one hand lifted to her throat. The sound was so piercing that she felt as if some violent unleashed force had broken out of the ground and was charging toward her.

She discovered Mrs. Greenleaf "sprawled on her hands and knees on the side of the road," praying for the victims of all the calamities of the day, accounts of which she had cut from the newspapers to bury under her in the dirt. The "violent unleashed force"—which Mrs. Greenleaf was summoning and Mrs. May felt instinctively—was the force of grace, but the imagery of the sentence links it with a charging bull. This similarity suggests the presence of grace when the bull actually charges.

This scene brings face to face the two women in the story who represent two attitudes toward the religious heritage which is a deep and intrinsic part of Southern culture. Mrs. May's reasonableness dominates the story, but Mrs. Greenleaf's religious fanaticism—a grotesque expression of her openness to mystery—permeates it. The year before her death, speaking of the spiritual milieu of the South, Flannery O'Connor defined the Southern "identity" which this story illuminates positively—although distortedly—in Mrs. Greenleaf and negatively in Mrs. May:

What has given the South her identity are those beliefs and qualities which she has absorbed from the Scriptures and from her own history of defeat and violation: a distrust of the abstract, a sense of human dependence on the grace of God, and a knowledge that evil is not simply a problem to be solved, but a mystery to be endured.[11]

Mrs. May has effectively cut herself off from her religious heritage, even though this alienation is not immediately apparent. "She was a good Christian woman with a large respect for religion, though she did not, of course, believe any of it was true." Mrs. Greenleaf embraces in one gesture the suffering world and the source of its healing. Shrieking "Jesus, stab me in the heart," she falls "flat in the dirt, a huge human mound, her legs and arms spread out as if she were trying to wrap them around the earth." Who is to say which woman is more grotesque? O'Connor once said that at least the Southern writer could still recognize a freak when he saw one,[12] and it seems likely from the context of the statement that she meant the Mrs. May type of freak. The story itself gives evidence that a fanatical expression of a true belief in God may be more productive of good than a complacent self-deification which cloaks nonbelief. Mrs. May's two sons are selfish bachelors who demean their professions, quarrel with each other, and plague their mother. Wesley "would not milk a cow to save [his mother's] soul from hell," and Scofield "exasperated her beyond endurance." On the other hand, the Greenleaf boys each have a wife and three children, run a flourishing farm, and, according to a Negro helper, "They never quarls; they like one man in two skins." One cannot miss the implication about the mothers: by their fruits you shall know them. As the ultimate insult to Mrs. May and perhaps as a dim yearning for the heritage which is rightfully his, Wesley, aroused by his mother's nagging, fires this question at her:

"Well, why don't you do something practical, Woman? Why don't you pray for me like Mrs. Greenleaf would?"

Her answer is characteristic:

"I don't like to hear you boys make jokes about religion," she had said. "If you would go to church, you would meet some nice girls."

Cut off from her religious heritage, Mrs. May sees her life and death only in terms of the farm: her life has been spent in fighting to make it productive, and her death could not occur until she has solidified her gains to cushion the future of her sons. That this goal is constantly on her mind is suggested by her son's complaint that she is "always yapping about when-you-die." The sons torment her by talking about whom they will marry when she dies. In protest, she mutters, "They needn't think I'm going to die any time soon," and, in one of the story's most chilling lines, "some more defiant voice in her added: I'll die when I get good and ready."

Whether or not she is ready for death when the bull impales her on his horns is a question that the last scene of the story fails to answer. However, all the details which prepare for that last moment make her encounter with the death-bringing bull inevit-

able. The pasture into which she follows Mr. Greenleaf and the
bull is "a green arena, encircled almost entirely by woods," a
symbolic locale which frequently marks the place of spiritual
confrontation in O'Connor stories. She drives the car to the
center of the pasture, a position which precludes any escape. She
sits on the front bumper of the car, forgetful of Mr.
Greenleaf's words about the bull: "He don't like cars and trucks." She finds
herself strangely sleepy, and the red-hot sun which she had
dreamed about penetrates through her closed eyes. She thinks of
time in terms of past and future, and reviews her life with grim
satisfaction: "Before any kind of judgement seat, she would be
able to say: I've worked, I have not wallowed." These details
suggest that subconsciously she realizes that death is approaching,
but when the bull bounds from the woods and races toward her
"she remained perfectly still, not in fright, but in a freezing unbelief." In this attitude of "freezing unbelief" she dies, with "the
look of a person whose sight has been suddenly restored but who
finds the light unbearable." When Mr. Greenleaf reaches her, she
seems to be "bent over whispering some last discovery into the
animal's ear."

The two sentences describing her look and her position produce an unsettling ambiguity in the story's end. The first suggests the illumination of grace and her rejection of it; the second
—softer in diction and tone—may indicate that the "last discovery" unfolded God's ultimate mercy. The story fails to re-
solve this uncertainty, but a resolution can be suggested by
reference to another source. In 1954, two years before this story
was published, O'Connor signed and dated Alexis de Tocqueville's
Democracy in America, and the number of marginal marks indicate that she read it with care. In the chapter "Self-Interest in
Religious Matters," she marked the following lines:

> "To be mistaken in believing that the Christian religion is
> true," says Pascal, "is no great loss to anyone; but how dreadful
> to be mistaken in believing it to be false."[13]

It may well be that this mistake of which Pascal speaks is Mrs.
May's "last discovery." That this undertaking cannot be gained
from the story itself flaws slightly this masterful treatment (it was

a first-prize story, O. Henry Awards, 1956) of the death of a self-sufficient woman.

The biblical dimension of O'Connor's work was obviously deepened by her reading; biblical studies abound in her library.[14] But the book which may have been most influential in extending the biblical basis of her work is a history of philosophy. During 1958 and 1959 O'Connor read three volumes of Eric Voegelin's six-volume work, *Order and History*. From her annotations it becomes clear that she was impressed with this "massive philosophical inquiry concerning the order of human existence in society and history."[15] The first volume, *Israel and Revelation*, seems to have been influential in directing her faith in biblical history into a philosophical framework which shows this history to be a form of order for mankind. In this volume Voegelin first discusses the cosmological order of the ancient Near East; in this system, the cosmos is the ordering principle for mankind. He then moves to a second type of order, the form of history, which the tiny nation of Israel introduced to the world. One of the passages which O'Connor marked summarizes well the basic argument of the volume and points to the influence it would have on her:

> Israel alone constituted itself by recording its own genesis as a people as an event with a special meaning in history, while the other near Eastern societies constituted themselves as analogues of cosmic order. Israel alone had history as an inner form, while the other societies existed in the form of the cosmological myth. History, we therefore conclude, is a symbolic form of existence, of the same class as the cosmological form; and the paradigmatic narrative is, in the historical form, the equivalent of the myth in the cosmological form. (P. 124)

By "paradigmatic narrative" Voegelin means a historical record of events, some of which would be unimportant in themselves, which shows them to be paradigms of God's way with men. In other words, the sacred history of God's dealings with his Chosen People and of Christ's life on earth delineates an order of existence which gives subsequent events a shape and a significance they would not otherwise have. For example, every form of exile attains a deeper significance when placed against the paradigmatic account of God's command to Abraham to leave his people and his father's house and go into the land which would be shown to him. Every death is, as St. Paul puts it, "swallowed up in victory," because Jesus Christ died and lives eternally. Although from the beginning Flannery O'Connor relied strongly on biblical history as a substructure in her fiction, in her works published after 1959, notably *The Violent Bear It Away*, "The Lame Shall Enter First," "Parker's Back" and "Judgement Day," her emphasis on the paradigmatic quality of biblical history is decidedly stronger.

The paradigmatic aspect of biblical history was certainly not a new one for Flannery O'Connor; her faith had made this view her own long before she read Voegelin. But his placing this view in a philosophical framework, his enriching it by contrasting it with the cosmology of the ancients and the philosophy of the Greeks as two other orders of human existence (this makes up the content of the first three volumes of *Order and History*) certainly fed the springs of O'Connor's imagination. All the statements which she made in print about her use of the mythic background of the Bible are subsequent to 1959 and show the influence of Voegelin's thought. Her clearest statement is contained in her talk, "The Catholic Novelist in the Protestant South," which editors Sally and Robert Fitzgerald date in 1963:

> For the purposes of fiction, these guides [archetypes] have to exist in concrete form, known and held sacred by the whole community. They have to exist in the form of stories which affect our image and our judgment of ourselves. Abstractions, formulas, laws will not serve here. We have to have stories in our background. It takes a story to make a story. It takes a story of mythic dimensions, one which belongs to everybody, one in which everybody is able to recognize the hand of God and its descent. In the Protestant South, the Scriptures fill this role.
> ... In the South, the Bible is known by the ignorant as well [as the educated], and it is always that *mythos* which the poor hold in common that is most valuable to the fiction writer. When the poor hold sacred history in common, they have ties

to the universal and the holy, which allows the meaning of their every action to be heightened and seen under the aspect of eternity.[16]

Although O'Connor did not use the word "paradigm," she expressed that concept in her own terms in this statement. Her use of biblical archetypes and paradigms substituted for classical mythology—a knowledge of which her education had denied her.[17] Perhaps she was thinking of her own position when she marked this sentence in the section on Guy de Maupassant in Henry James's *The Future of the Novel*: "A writer is fortunate when his theory and his limitations so exactly correspond."[18]

The view of biblical history as a principle of order is present only by implication in O'Connor's subsequent fictional "wrestling"[19] with the theme of death in a historical perspective. Published first in 1961, "Everything That Rises Must Converge" subsequently became the title-story of her posthumous short-story collection. This story presents a pseudo-aristocratic mother and her son, Julian, both cut off from the society in which they live. Neither has entered into "the world of guilt and sorrow," which, for Flannery O'Connor, is the only world there is. As the story develops, the mother, relying on the "old manners" and the graciousness which are a part of her culture, encounters a hostile reality in the hour of her death, when a huge Negro woman hits her with her large red purse "that bulged throughout as if it were stuffed with rocks." Her son, who prides himself on his acceptance of the "new South," is actually more estranged from society than his mother is. Her death presages and insures his entrance into the world of suffering humanity.

This story presents a timely variation on the theme of death in relation to history; it is O'Connor's only attempt to deal directly with the Southern racial problem. On the question of racial justice in the South, O'Connor wrote in a letter to Sister Bernetta Quinn:

Justice is justice and should not be appealed to along racial lines. The problem is not abstract for the Southerner, it's concrete; he sees it in terms of persons, not races—which way of seeing does away with easy answers. I have tried to touch this subject by way of fiction only once—in a story called "Everything That Rises Must Converge."[20]

She touches the subject only tangentially, however; the focus of the story is on the relationship between Julian and his mother, which reveals each one's larger relationship to the world in which he lives. Each is out of touch with social reality, and a large "overflowing" Negress destroys both of their fantasy worlds.

The mother's unreal world is the cultural world of the Old South. For her, culture is "in the heart . . . and in how you do things, and how you do things is because of who you are." She holds fast to gracious manners even though she unwittingly displays them in a condescending way. Secure in her private stronghold, she can afford to be "adaptable" to present conditions, such as associating at the YWCA with women who are not in her social class. The "laws of her own fantasy world," which Julian misinterprets, are the regal manners which make her look ridiculous to him, but which are innate to her. Giving a penny to a little Negro boy is "as natural to her as breathing." She would have presented it to any little child who played peek-a-boo with her on a bus. But the black woman's reaction to her benevolence demonstrates that Julian's mother is out of touch with the society in which she lives. She is innocent; her "sky-blue" eyes are as "untouched by experience as they must have been when she was ten." Her memories of the past make her the most naive of racists; she is perfectly willing for "them" to rise—"on their own side of the fence." During the bus ride to the Y reducing class, Julian's mother discovers that the fence has been torn down and, more disconcerting, that her son revels in her discomfiture. Her new awareness is revealed in O'Connor's descriptions of her eyes. When her son deliberately sits next to a Negro and stares at his mother, "making his eyes the eyes of a stranger," her eyes take on a "battered look." When a Negro woman wearing a hat exactly like hers enters the bus and sits down across from her, the mother's eyes assume "a look of dull recognition, as if suddenly she had sickened at some awful confrontation." Her son chuckles at this act of "Fate," and she "turned her eyes on him slowly. The blue in them seemed to have turned a bruised purple." But the code of manners by which she lives rescues her, and she smiles at the woman and her child—a smile which Julian terms "a weapon." Completely unaware that her action might be deemed insulting, she tries to give the child a penny, and the blow from the Negress's handbag effects the heart attack toward which she was tending during the traumatic bus ride. The violence of her encounter with contemporary mores brings her to the threshold of death, where she instinctively retreats into the secure world of her youth, in which her son has no place. As he kneels over her crumpled figure, her one eye "fixed on him, raked his face again, found nothing, and closed."

Flannery O'Connor spoke frequently about the manners of the South as one of its greatest strengths. In reply to a question about Southern race relations, she said, in 1963:

When you have a code of manners based on charity, then when charity fails—as it is going to do constantly—you've got those manners there to preserve each race from small intrusions upon the other. . . . The South has survived in the past because its manners, however lopsided or inadequate they may have been, provided enough social discipline to hold us together and give us an identity. Now those old manners are obsolete but the new manners will have to be based on what was best in the old ones—in their real basis of charity and necessity.[21]

"Everything That Rises Must Converge" witnesses the obsolescence of the "old manners" and the failure of the new ones, which are based, not on charity, but on justice—a virtue of the mind.

Julian believes that "true culture is in the mind." His separation from the society in which he lives is quite deliberate. As his mother is too "innocent" to relate significantly to the world around her, he is too disillusioned—"as disenchanted with [the world] as a man of fifty." Both are unable to move with the flux of time. His fantasy world is an inner compartment in his mind, "a kind of mental bubble in which he established himself when he could not bear to be a part of what was going on around him." His activity there is significant: "he could see out and judge." The story is filtered through Julian's eyes, which are never described, and reflects his judgments. His insensitivity toward his mother appears in his harsh misjudgments of her. He indulges in elaborate daydreams about methods of shocking her into an awareness that Negroes are now her social equals. But although his mind has accepted this equality, his reactions betray him. When the Negro woman enters the bus, he hopes she will sit beside his mother. "To his annoyance," she sits beside him. "He saw his mother's face change as the woman settled herself next to him and he realized with satisfaction that this was more objectionable to her than it was to him." Julian's annoyance indicates that a Negro's choosing to sit beside him is "objectionable," although he takes pride in deigning to sit beside a Negro. The next few sentences detail Julian's elaborate misjudgment (to which he connects a "symbolic significance") of his mother's reaction, which is obviously a reaction to the woman's hat. Julian thus relates to the world around him by cynical misjudgments. Caught between two cultures—the old, inaccessible; the new, undesirable—he effectively withdraws from life.

Connecting the fantasy worlds of mother and son is an old mansion—the mother's ancestral home. The memory of it makes the mother secure in her world of gracious manners; the same memory, both enhanced and diluted by illusion, embitters the son. He deprecates his mother's gentility, never realizing that the same heritage in him has soured into cynicism. His conflicting emotions about the past and the present are expressed in his ambivalent view of the Godhigh mansion: "He never spoke of it without contempt or thought of it without longing." Besides being actual property belonging to the family of Julian and his mother, the "decayed mansion" is a symbol of the old culture of the South, which is no longer inclusive enough to embrace the new relationships which Southern industrialization has brought about.[22] Symbolically, the breakdown of Southern cultural patterns is described in two views of the house: as it was in the mother's childhood and lives in Julian's dreams, with its "wide porch . . . high-ceilinged hall" and parlor of "threadbare elegance" and as Julian viewed it in his childhood—"The double stairways had rotted and been torn down. Negroes were living in it."

Eventually the mother's "culture of the heart" fails because it is unreal; Julian's "culture of the mind" fails because it does not touch his whole being. But the mother accepts her moment of grace when she holds to good manners (the next best thing to Christian charity, in Flannery O'Connor's view)[23] in a moment of psychic confrontation with the new egalitarian culture. Julian moves toward participating in the real world when, at the story's end, he moves toward a new relationship with his mother. Although he had claimed to have "cut himself emotionally free of her," and at one point in the bus ride "he could with pleasure have slapped her as he would have slapped a particularly obnoxious child," he reacts differently when he realizes that he is losing her. He calls out "Mother," and then "Darling, sweetheart," and finally in the anguish of the abandoned, "Mamma, Mamma!" The tide of darkness which was "sweeping her from him" seems, after this filial outcry, to "sweep him back to her." His true relationship to her, newly acknowledged, is the basis of his relationship to society; inevitably he will enter "the world of guilt and sorrow."

The theme of the story is suggested in the statement made by the mother and ridiculed by the son: "If you know who you are, you can go anywhere." Overtly it means that a sense of the value of self sustains one in difficult encounters. But the statement has wider implications. In Flannery O'Connor's view, who-you-are is a creature fallen from grace but redeemed by Christ. It is this truth that guarantees limitless possibilities: "you can go anywhere," even "up." Everything that rises must converge. The story shows the "rising" of Julian's mother, and, by implication, his own. Their convergence—the convergence of heart and mind which they represent—would inaugurate the "new manners" on which Flannery O'Connor relied to save the South. A more complex work than its surface suggests, this story does far more than explore Southern racial tensions. It unites the author's key ideas about personal integrity, man's relationship with society, and the power of death to give life new clarity.

O'Connor reworked the theme of man's death in the context of history for the last time in "Judgement Day." Written during her final illness, it reveals a new depth and complexity in her imaginative vision of death. Actually it is a reworking of an earlier story, "The Geranium," her first published work, which became the title story of her M.F.A. thesis. The basic plot in both stories is similar: an old man, displaced from his native soil, lives with a bluntly benevolent daughter in an apartment in New York and longs for home. To view the two stories together is to see both the continuity of her thought and the development of her imagination.

In "The Geranium," Old Dudley, living in New York, longs to be back in Coa County, somewhere near Atlanta. While sitting at a window in his daughter's apartment, waiting for a pink geranium to be placed on the opposite window sill, he reminisces about his home and evokes in memory the one person he feels most "kin" to—a Negro named Rabie. Through the old widower's reminiscence, one learns about Dudley's skill in fishing and hunting. When his daughter asks him to do an errand, he meets the "Yankee nigger" who lives next door. The black man overtakes him on the stairs, and, at the sight of Dudley shooting imaginary birds, he calls out, "What are you hunting, old timer?" This humiliation hollows the old man's knees, and he slips and falls. The Negro helps him up, and, as Dudley returns, inwardly raging, to his room, he sees the geranium plant lying in the alley six floors below.

Obviously, and so not effectively, the geranium—pale pink with a green paper bow, which "shouldn't have been there" on the window sill and which finally ends in the alley "with its roots in the air"—is both the old man's preoccupation and a symbol of himself. The old man waits for it to appear on the sill, thinks of it twice during the story, and sees it in the alley at the end.

In contrast to this early use of symbolism, Flannery O'Connor deepened every element of "Judgement Day" to make the entire story of the old man's death symbolic of man's universal longing for "home." The same plot elements yield a deeper communication through a complex, imaginative treatment. Tanner, like Old Dudley, lives with his daughter and son-in-law in a New York apartment and spends his time sitting by a window which looks out "on a brick wall and down into an alley full of New York air." But on learning that his daughter intends to break her promise to bury him in Georgia, he determines to return home "dead or alive." After the daughter leaves for the store, he starts with sturdy heart and trembling legs down the apartment stairs and falls. The hands that shake his dying body are those of the Negro actor who lives in the next apartment. Two long flashbacks contrast Tanner's life in Georgia and in New York. One tells of Tanner's association with Coleman, his Negro servant and friend, and of his being forced from their squatter shack by a Negro landowner and delivered into the kindly clutches of his daughter. The other flashback shows him, a few weeks previously, being manhandled by the Negro actor, in response to his friendly overture: "I thought you might know somewhere around here we could find us a pond, Preacher." These scenes suggest the barrenness of the present and the richness of the past to authenticate Tanner's desperate determination to return to his homeland.

"Judgement Day" is infused with biblical overtones. Tanner thinks and speaks in scriptural images and idioms, a fact which suggests that his roots are sunk not only in Georgia soil but also in the religious heritage which that soil has bequeathed to him. His daughter, "enlightened," has cut herself off from this. To her father's anguished cry, "Bury me here and burn in hell," she replies, "And don't throw hell at me. I don't believe in it. That's a lot of hardshell Baptist hooey." She offers him TV for "some inspiration and an out-let," so he will "quit thinking about morbid stuff, death and hell and judgement." But he knows the whore of Babylon. "The Judgement is coming," he mutters to her. "The sheep'll be separated from the goats. Them that kept their promises from them that didn't." His prophetic words apparently make no impression on her, but the story ends in quiet understatement of the effect which the old man's faith had on his daughter:

> She buried him in New York City, but after she had done it she could not sleep at night. Night after night she turned and tossed and very definite lines began to appear in her face, so she had him dug up and shipped the body to Corinth. Now she rests well at night and her good looks have mostly returned.

By her emphasis on homecoming interlocked with judgment day, the day of final return, Flannery O'Connor lifts the story to the level of a paradigm. "It was being there [home] that mattered; the dead or alive did not." In Tanner one can see the expatriates of biblical history returning from cultural and religious exile to their homeland. "The Lord is my shepherd; I shall not want," he murmurs aloud, reassuring himself with the

words of a psalmist in exile as he prepares to descend the stairs.
Tanner's obsession with the place of his burial reflects an ancient
and universal concern with burial rites, for primitive people
commonly believed that their earthly resting place prefigured the
place of eternal rest. One remembers the procession of Israelites
out of Egypt with the bones of Joseph so that he might sleep in
the land of their fathers. Against this larger backdrop of sacred
history, the story achieves added significance.

As Flannery O'Connor's imaginative grasp of the reality of
death developed, she became more sensitive to the presence of
mystery. Rather than diminish the reality of her fiction, this
awareness of mystery increased it. This fact is illustrated well in
the two stories under discussion. One feels the presence of mystery in direct proportion to one's absorption in the reality of the
story. In "The Geranium," reality is muted and mystery is absent.
The scenes of hunting and fishing which define the relationship
between the old man, Dudley, and his Negro friend Rabie are
unconvincing. The bond that links them is not strong enough
to draw Dudley back home "dead or alive"; he returns only in
imagination. Moreover, Dudley left Georgia to live with his
daughter for an unconvincing reason: he wanted to see for himself the city he had seen in a movie. In "Judgement Day," on the
other hand, the situation is both more real and more infused
with mystery. Complex and humorous, the Tanner-Coleman
relationship has a strong psychological basis which supports the
details of the story.

Between the writing of these two stories, O'Connor made a
strong statement about reality in fiction:

> The novelist is required to create the illusion of a whole world
> with believable people in it, and the chief difference between
> the novelist who is an orthodox Christian and the novelist who
> is merely a naturalist is that the Christian novelist lives in a
> larger universe. He believes that the natural world contains
> the supernatural. And this doesn't mean that his obligation to
> portray the natural is less; it means it is greater.[24]

The "larger universe" is present in the meeting of Tanner and
Coleman that leads to the improvement of vision for both maker
and wearer of the "carved wooden spectacles," the incident which

opens this study. Their meeting is as real as their relationship is mysterious.

After Coleman put on the glasses that Tanner had made, he acknowledged that Tanner was a white man, and, mysteriously, from that moment the bond between the two men was so strong that Tanner entrusted himself, alive and dead, to the care of his Negro friend. Also quite believable is the reason that eventually separated them. Tanner went to New York because he could not bear to be "a nigger's white nigger." His and Coleman's shack was found to be on a Negro doctor's property, and he had to either leave or run his still for the benefit—and worse than that, with the permission—of the Negro. It was a realistic situation which drove the old man into exile.

That the aura of mystery which pervades life and death can coexist with comedy seems to be a realization that Flannery O'Connor developed gradually in her imaginative treatment of this theme. "The Geranium" has little comedy; it increases in the works that follow and completely permeates "Judgement Day." The pathos of old age and displacement is both heightened and relieved by comedy. Comparable passages in the two stories reveal that the comic element deepens the penetration of the theme. For example, in each story, the old man wants to show the big city to his Negro alter ego. In "The Geranium," it is told this way:

> Old Dudley would have liked to have explained New York to Rabie. If he could have shown it to Rabie, it wouldn't have been so big—he wouldn't have felt pressed down every time he went out in it. "It ain't so big," he would have said. "Don't let it get you down, Rabie. It's just like any other city and cities ain't all that complicated."

In "Judgement Day," Flannery O'Connor takes the same idea and penetrates it more deeply by heightening the comedy:

> When he was safely back in the apartment again, he had imagined going over it with Coleman. He had to turn his head every few seconds to make sure Coleman was behind him. Keep to the inside or these people'll knock you down, keep right behind me or you'll get left, keep your hat on, you damn

idiot, he had said, and Coleman had come on with his bent running shamble, panting and muttering, What we doing here? Where you get this fool idea coming here? I come to show you it was no kind of place. Now you know you were well off where you were. I knowed it before, Coleman said. Was you didn't know it.

Much of the humor of the second story emanates from the disparity between Tanner's assumptions, so logical to him, and the urban milieu in which he finds himself, in which a different set of assumptions prevails. For instance, Tanner waits in the hall to speak to the Negro next door, and when the man comes out he brushes past Tanner and ignores his greeting. "Could be deaf and dumb, Tanner thought." When Tanner finally gets through to the Negro, his naive assumptions are pitted against a sophisticated world. " 'Good morning, Preacher,' he said. It had been his experience that if a Negro tended to be sullen, this title usually cleared up his expression." The violent reaction of the Negro in this instance foreshadows their last encounter, which ends in Tanner's death.

Perhaps because dreams are an integral part of the small death that is sleep, they are frequently part of Flannery O'Connor's vision of death. In "A Late Encounter with the Enemy," Sally Poker's dream of her grandfather sitting naked (except for his hat) on the stage at her graduation symbolizes the power of death to strip one of illusions. (O'Connor added this dream to the story sometime between its magazine publication and its appearance in her first short story collection.) In "Greenleaf," Mrs. May's two dreams presage her death. The final scene of "Judgement Day," which has no counterpart in "The Geranium," combines death and resurrection by means of a dream. Flannery O'Connor had evidently learned much about dreams between the writing of her first and last works of fiction. Her library contained several books about dreams or with extensive sections on dreams, among which were Bergson's *The World of Dreams,* published in 1958, Pedro Meseguer's *The Secret of Dreams,* signed and dated 1960, Freud's *Basic Writings,* signed and dated 1947, and Jung's *Modern Man in Search of a Soul.* In "Judgement Day," the dream sequence is the creative center of the story. After

Tanner receives his daughter's promise to "ship him back," he dreams of his return to Corinth, and the dream blends the literal return of his body to the land he loves and his resurrection on the last day. He wanted to return "dead or alive"; in the dream, he is both dead and alive, as he arrives in the depot scratching on the inside of his coffin. While enjoying the delights of resurrection, he is also playing a splendid trick on his friend Coleman, who, as his coffin is being opened, would be "jumping up and down, wheezing and panting with excitement." This dream, conceived in the security of his daughter's promise, returns to become confused with reality in the final scene, and he dies with "I'm on my way home" on his lips. In 1957, O'Connor read Raymond Hostie's *Religion and the Psychology of Jung*. She marked these lines: "In Freud's view the dream, as a sign, was a deceptive mask. In Jung's view, on the other hand, as a symbol, it was more like an expressive face."[25] The dreams in all these stories are symbolic, expressing the true face of the dreamer, but perhaps none is more expressive, both in its psychological aptness (one final trick on Coleman) and in its theological meaning (death as an entrance into the homeland of man), than Tanner's dream of life-in-death.

Some years after O'Connor's death, her mother was approached with a suggestion about establishing a memorial for Flannery. She refused. "She has written her own memorial," she replied. "Her work is her memorial." This statement echoes her daughter's conviction that "the creative action of the Christian's life is to prepare his death in Christ." In tracing Flannery O'Connor's imaginative vision of death as she expressed it in her fiction, one is penetrating deeply into the core of her vision of life.

CHAPTER V

The "Artificial Nigger":

the numinous quality of reality

"All novelists are fundamentally
seekers and describers of the real,
but the realism of each novelist
will depend on his view of the ultimate reaches of reality." F. O'C.

Both her life and her fiction give evidence that Flannery O'Connor was deeply aware of the sacredness of reality. She knew that the world was "charged with the grandeur of God" and she renewed her spirit by direct contact with the natural world. On a routine working day, O'Connor would spend the morning writing at her desk in her study-bedroom and the rest of the day recovering from the effort. In the afternoon and evening, she would sit on the wide screened porch at Andalusia, watching the colts romp in the side pasture or the sun glint on the lake just visible through the trees. Sometimes she would walk around the farmyard, feeding peacocks, Chinese geese, pheasants, and ducks. Sometimes she would just look at the peacocks—just look and look. As she said in her essay on peacocks, "The King of the Birds," "As soon as the birds were out of the crate, I sat down on it and began to look at them. I have been looking at them ever since, from one station or another, and always with the same awe as on that first occasion."[1] Her great pleasure in these extraordinarily beautiful birds is significant: for her they represented the essential glory of matter made visible.

O'Connor sometimes spoke of the influence which Joseph Conrad exerted on her, the basis of which seems to be Conrad's reverence for the visible universe. Although the two writers express this reverence in strikingly different ways, both share the ability to penetrate matter to its essential core, which is spiritual. In her essay on "The Nature and Aim of Fiction," O'Connor alludes to Conrad's goals:

> Conrad said that his aim as a fiction writer was to render the highest possible justice to the visible universe. That sounds very grand, but it is really very humble. It means that he subjected himself at all times to the limitations that reality imposed, but that reality for him was not simply coextensive with the visible. He was interested in rendering justice to the visible universe because it suggested an invisible one.[2]

As every reference which O'Connor makes to Conrad has this basis, one can assume that it was an aim she had made her own.

But the roots of O'Connor's reverence for matter go deeper than an artist's reverence for reality; she embraced the Christian concept of the intrinsic sacredness of matter. This basic Christian belief has been clouded at various times in past centuries by heresies which taught that matter is, of itself, evil, and must be sanctified by man. Even St. Augustine himself was, for a time, caught in the meshes of Manicheanism. After he had embraced Christianity, he combated this error effectively by his writing. That O'Connor linked Conrad's artistic aim and an Augustinian belief in the holiness of matter is evident from her annotation of a passage in George Lawlor's *The Christian Imagination*:

> It was a serious error in those of whom Augustine speaks [the adherents of Manicheanism] to assume that it does not matter what men think of the created universe so long as they think rightly concerning God. For error in the matter of the universe means false opinion about God.[3]

In the margin of these lines, O'Connor wrote: "Conrad: highest possible justice to the visible universe." In this instance as in so many others, literary theory and religious belief coalesced.

In Claude Tresmontant's *A Study of Hebrew Thought*, the scriptural basis for the holiness of matter is explicitly detailed, beginning with the Genesis account of creation and its lyrical refrain, "God saw that it was good." Tresmontant explains that, for the Hebrew mind, there is no sharp division between the sensible and the intelligible; rather, "the sensible world is a language." It is "a work of revelation waiting to be grasped" by the intelligence of man.[4] It follows, of course, that evil must have a different source, which can only be the wayward heart of man. O'Connor marked one passage which illuminates not only her belief in the holiness of matter, but also her conviction of the prime importance of truth.

> The Bible . . . proclaims the excellence of the created and the sensible. The origin of evil is to be found elsewhere and the carnal, not being its prime cause, is freed from blame. The cause is spiritual. The typical sin is a lie. (P. 99)

The concept of the holiness of matter which underlies O'Connor's fiction is one example of the theological basis of her work. Caroline Gordon, who was in a position to evaluate O'Connor's strength and weakness, has strong views about the importance of this theological basis. Speaking to me about Flannery's lack of a classical education which, according to Miss Gordon, deprived her of both a mythological substructure and the rhetorical devices necessary to produce an elevated tone, she said, "Flannery would never have made it without her theology. If her work endures—and I think it will—the theology in her work will be the basis of critical appreciation in years to come." That O'Connor grasped this truth about herself seems evident in her comment on her work: "Belief, in my own case anyway, is the engine that makes perception operate."[5] One can see in all her work and particularly in the stories which will be discussed in this chapter that her belief in the intrinsic holiness of matter sharpened her perception to such a degree that she was able at times to "image forth" the holiness at the core of matter.

In *The Sacred and the Profane*, Mircea Eliade names this manifestation of the sacred in matter by a Greek term—hierophany. He calls it a mysterious act, a "manifestation of something of a wholly different order, a reality that does not belong to our world in objects that are an integral part of our natural 'profane' world." He explains the paradoxical quality of the manifestation:

> By manifesting the sacred, any object becomes something else, yet it continues to remain itself, for it continues to participate in its surrounding cosmic milieu. A sacred stone remains a stone; apparently (or, more precisely, from the profane point of view), nothing distinguishes it from all other stones. But for those to whom a stone reveals itself as sacred, its immediate reality is transmuted into a supernatural reality. In other words, for those who have a religious experience all nature is capable of revealing itself as cosmic sacrality. The cosmos in its entirety can become a hierophany.[6]

Eliade deals with the sacredness of matter from a relative viewpoint: his study elucidates what the religious man's "total experience of life proves to be in comparison with the experience of the man without religious feeling, of the man who lives . . . in a desacralized world" (p. 13). For Flannery O'Connor there was only one view of reality—an absolute one, which sees the visible and, as Tresmontant phrases it, "discerns the spiritual sap which courses through it."[7] For her, hierophany is a special manifestation of the numinous quality in matter which can become, for the perceiver, a source of supernatural grace. And the measure of man's openness to that source of grace is the measure of his truthful perception of reality.

Closer to O'Connor's view of reality than Eliade's essentially subjective one is the view of the Jesuit theologian-paleontologist, Pierre Teilhard de Chardin. O'Connor read Teilhard relatively late in her writing career. All the books in her library by or about Teilhard are signed and dated from 1960 to 1962. These include Teilhard's *The Divine Mileu* and *Letters from a Traveller* and books about Teilhard by Nicholas Corte, Oliver Rabut, O.P., Charles E. Raven, and Claude Tresmontant. In 1961 she reviewed *The Phenomenon of Man* for *The American Scholar*. That she also read *Hymn of the Universe* is evident from her comment written to Sister Jean Marie Kann that she found the "Hymn to Matter" to be "the most devastating and enchanting statement of Christian asceticism."[8] Leo J. Zuber, book-review editor for two Georgia diocesan papers, wrote to me that she asked to review "anything and everything I might get" on Teilhard.[9]

It is not surprising that O'Connor should feel an immediate kinship with the scientist-poet-priest, who formulated a highly sophisticated theory of evolution. In this theory he combined the "data" of divine revelation which he had always accepted in faith and the archeological data his explorations in the Far East had uncovered. Teilhard was convinced of the holiness of matter; he believed that the furthest extension of the Divine Spirit permeates the most minute forms of inanimate matter. For him, matter contains a form of life not discernible to the scientist as scientist, but present to the scientist as poet and believer. This divine life in matter is directing an evolution which scientists can see and measure, and it is directing it to an end which can be foreseen: the convergence of all in Christ. The originality of Teilhard's theory inheres in its assertion that the direction of the evolution of matter is contained in matter itself. The spark of divine life in matter and in man will raise both up to a final convergence of all creation at the end of time—the Omega point —in Christ. In his study, *Pierre Teilhard de Chardin: His Thought*, Claude Tresmontant sums up the Jesuit's work in a passage which O'Connor marked: "From a theological point of view Teilhard de Chardin's work can be defined as an effort to shed light on the *natural* conditions and preparations leading to a *supernatural* consummation."[10] With very little change in meaning, this statement could apply to Flannery O'Connor's fiction. The sentence could be a corollary of O'Connor's statement about her work: "When fiction is made according to its nature, it should reinforce our sense of the supernatural by grounding it in concrete observable reality."[11] In the following excerpt from O'Connor's review of Teilhard's *The Phenomenon of Man*, one can sense the convergence of two kindred spirits. She says of Teilhard:

> His is a scientific expression of what the poet attempts to do: penetrate matter until spirit is revealed in it. Teilhard's vision sweeps forward without detaching itself at any point from the earth. . . . The poet, whose sight is essentially prophetic, will at once recognize in Teilhard a kindred intelligence.[12]

The only book on Teilhard which O'Connor marked extensively was Tresmontant's study. As she dated the book 1960, it may have been the first book she read about him. From her markings, it becomes clear that three ideas of Teilhard found an immediate echo in her own thought. One is that the positive direction which Teilhard saw in evolution is a great support to modern man, to help him "escape a feeling of isolation and forlornness."[13] That O'Connor was concerned about this problem seems evident from her marking comparable lines in Carl Jung's *Modern Man in Search of a Soul*. In his chapter on the aim of psychotherapy, he speaks of cases in which rational treatment does not yield satisfactory results. Jung says, "About a third of my cases are suffering from no clinically definable neurosis, but from the senselessness and emptiness of their lives. It seems to me, however, that this can well be described as the general neurosis of our time."[14] Many of O'Connor's stories deal with characters who suffer from such a "general neurosis." Her fiction illuminates an instant of direction in the lives of characters such as Hulga and Julian who are drifting about in an existence empty of purpose.

The second concept in Teilhard's thought which has a corollary in O'Connor's work concerns the use of violence. In Teilhard's theory, once evolution has reached the level of man, it is
dependent upon man's will. From that point on, the only thing
that can thwart evolution is man's ennui. Here Teilhard saw
great danger in philosophies of the absurd, which nourish such
ennui. Tresmontant quotes from a pamphlet of Teilhard's, "La
structure phyletique de group humain," to show the importance
of violence in combatting the apathy of man. Teilhard says:

> I have often said, and I will repeat it: amid heaps of wheat,
> coal, iron, uranium—or under any other kind of demographic
> pressures—the man of tomorrow will go on strike if he ever
> loses the taste for the ultrahuman. And not just an ordinary
> taste for it, but a deep and violent one, a taste which constantly
> rises in him in concomitance with the growth of the power of
> vision and action.[15]

O'Connor marked this passage, and she underlined the phrase, "a
deep and violent one." In her fiction she depicts, not a violent
taste for the ultrahuman, but a violent apprehension of it. She
uses violence to bring her characters to what she calls "the extreme situation that best reveals what we are essentially." Speaking of her use of violence, she insists that it is a means and not
an end; she sees it as "a force which can be used for good or evil,
and among other things taken by it is the kingdom of heaven."[16]
For instance, the Misfit's violence recalls the grandmother to
reality, and Rufus Johnson's violence reveals to Sheppard what
he is essentially.

The third idea, more complex than the other two, concerns
the biblical basis of Teilhard's and O'Connor's thought. Teilhard
unifies two views of the world which often seem disparate—the
reality of creation as we see it, and the scriptural promises of
Christ. He sees creation and revelation in a single vision. He
views as a single entity God's word as it was spoken in matter and
His word as it was transcribed in Scripture. Tresmontant states
that Teilhard found a schism between God's world as he saw it
and "Christianity *as it was and is too often presented.*" To
discern the unity which he knew existed, he went back to the
beginning of Christianity, to the Scriptures, to find "a new type

of sanctity, a new spirituality" which was a "prolongation of Biblical spirituality." This spirituality has deep roots in matter, and consists in man's "participating in the consecration of the world, in sanctifying and supernaturalizing the real which has been given to us by 'working together' with God."[17] That this conception of a biblical spirituality rooted in matter accorded with O'Connor's own ideas about the intrinsic value of matter seems evident in her review of Teilhard's *The Divine Milieu*. Commenting on the sense of expectation which Teilhard has renewed in Christianity, she predicted that his books "will probably have the effect of giving a new face to Christian spirituality." She ended this review with a sweeping declaration of Teilhard's importance: "It is doubtful if any Christian of this century can be fully aware of his religion until he has reseen it in the cosmic light which Teilhard has cast upon it."[18] Accenting another aspect of the Jesuit's work, O'Connor says in her review of Oliver Rabut's study of Teilhard: "He was a scientist who saw deeply certain intellectual and spiritual needs of our times. . . . The discovery that we owe to Teilhard is that vocation of spirit is visible, concrete, and of absorbing interest."[19] The phrase "vocation of spirit" is a puzzling one. A key to her use of it can be found in her essay "The Catholic Novelist in the Protestant South." In discussing the "underground religious affinities" which the Catholic writer has with the "backwoods prophets" and "shouting fundamentalists" of the South, she affirms that the Catholic writer is free to find his subject matter in this "invisible Church" and then adds that "this will be the vocation of many of us brought up in the South."[20] Both Teilhard and O'Connor were called toward a deep penetration of the reality around them, which became both a call to, and a method of, sanctity.

In Tresmontant's study, O'Connor marked a passage which is actually a quotation from Teilhard's work, *The Divine Milieu*. It seems to epitomize the connection between the Georgia writer and the Jesuit scientist:

> By virtue of the creation and still more of the Incarnation, *nothing is profane* here below on earth to him who knows how to see. On the contrary, everything is sacred for him who in every creature distinguishes the particle of the elected being

that is subjected to the attraction of Christ in the process of consummation.[21]

One finds the same idea transmuted into artistic terms when O'Connor says in her lecture "Novelist and Believer" that "the artist penetrates the concrete world in order to find at its depths the image of its source, the image of ultimate reality."[22] It is this penetration of the visible world and consequent revelation of ultimate reality which is the strength of her fiction.

In certain of Flannery O'Connor's stories in which a child is the central figure this penetration of reality is especially poignant because it involves an initial apprehension of the presence of evil in the heart of man. O'Connor never underestimated the awareness of a child. In one of her lectures, speaking of the writer's need to experience life, she said dryly that "anybody who has survived his childhood has enough information about life to last him the rest of his days."[23] The children in her stories undergo an initiation bound up with the sacredness of matter. In some, an older person is part of the initiation scene, ostensibly as teacher, but actually as one whose eyes are opened to reality through the child. These stories show a child in a world of both sacred and secular dimensions. Although all were written before O'Connor read Teilhard de Chardin, they show essentially why his theories became part of her artistic creed. She had already "known" them in her imagination.

"The Artificial Nigger" and "A View of the Woods" present two contrasting views of initiation into reality. In the first, a proud old man, in trying to teach his grandson the evils of the world, becomes aware for the first time of the evil in his own heart and of God's healing mercy, of which he had never before thought himself in need. In the second, a stubborn old man confronts the mystery of reality for the first time when he tries to combat a strange phenomenon beyond his ken—the symbolic reality to which his granddaughter's actions conform. Both stories illuminate the intrinsic holiness of matter by an explicit hierophany, but the effect in each case is different. Both illustrate the dictum that the typical sin is a lie.

In "The Artificial Nigger," the grandfather, Mr. Head, has decided to bring his grandson, Nelson, face to face with the real world. For ten years the boy has lived in the isolation of the country, and, knowing that he will soon yearn for a larger world, Mr. Head intends to give him his fill in one visit to the city. He has planned carefully for this day, with a "moral mission" in mind. He will show him "everything there is to see in a city so that he would be content to stay at home for the rest of his life." But there is an unseen reality of which Mr. Head knows nothing. The opening of the story suggests this spiritual reality by its description of the "miraculous moonlight" which charges the old man's rustic bedroom with grandeur. It transforms the wooden floor boards into silver, the pillow ticking into brocade, the straight chair into an attentive servant, and the slop jar near Nelson's bed into "a small personal angel." The day will unfold to Mr. Head the spiritual reality which silvers all of life: the mercy of God. That same reality will also be grasped—in a measure suited to his capacity—by the boy. But each must be readied; each must be purged of his pride.

Mr. Head has the pride of Adam. He is "entirely confident that he could carry out the moral mission of the coming day." He knows himself to be "a suitable guide for the young." Even when he fails to awaken before his grandson as he had planned, his self-confidence is unshaken. During the train ride to the city, he lords it over Nelson, even to demonstrating the ice water cooler "as if he had invented it." Only after he is in the city for a while and he realizes that he has lost both their lunch sack and the direction back to the station does his confidence weaken. But, gathering his pride, he decides to increase Nelson's dependence on him. He hides while the boy sleeps and then watches Nelson waken alone, terrified, and dash madly down the street and into an old woman carrying groceries. Fear of reprisal for the boy's misdeed grips him—the same fear which forced the apostle Peter to say, "I do not know the man." With his grandson panting against him, he repeats the great denial: "This is not my boy; I never seen him before." An instant later, when he feels "Nelson's fingers fall out of his flesh," he knows for the first time that he is a sinner. He is ready for a revelation of God's mercy.

Nelson has only one cause for pride: he was born in the city. His insistence that this will be his second visit infuriates his grandfather. The old man plans to test the validity of Nelson's

claim by seeing whether he will recognize a "nigger." Nelson fails
the test, and his experiences on the train make him cling to his
grandfather with uncharacteristic dependence. "For the first time
in his life, he understood that his grandfather was indispensable
to him." But during the day's journey, as he becomes aware of
his grandfather's insecurity in the city, his independence reasserts
itself. His grandfather's explanation of the "endless pitchblack
tunnels" which make up the city sewer system (the boy immediately connects them with hell) shakes him momentarily, but
moving away from the dangerous openings at the curb, he still
insists, "This [the city] is where I come from." The scene in
which he sees—really sees for the first time—a woman (the fact
that she is a Negro is essential to the design of the story but not
to Nelson's initiation) teaches him more than his grandfather
had anticipated.

> He stood drinking in every detail of her. His eyes traveled up
> from her great knees to her forehead and then made a triangu-
> lar path from the glistening sweat on her neck down and
> across her tremendous bosom and over her bare arm back to
> where her fingers lay hidden in her hair. He suddenly wanted
> her to reach down and pick him up and draw him against her
> and then he wanted to feel her breath on his face. He wanted
> to look down and down into her eyes while she held him
> tighter and tighter. He had never had such a feeling before.
> He felt as if he were reeling down through a pitchblack tunnel.

This encounter drains all pride from Nelson; in some obscure
way, he realizes what Mr. Head has not learned in sixty years:
that one's moral reactions cannot always be "guided by his will
and strong character," as Mr. Head asserts. His face "burning
with shame," Nelson takes the old man's hand. His trembling
mouth could have told his grandfather that he had seen enough,
even before he voiced his capitulation: "I only said I was born
here and I never had nothing to do with that. I want to go
home." But unaware of the reality called "feelings," the grandfather subjects the boy to one last test, which leads to his denial
of the boy and to Nelson's experience of being betrayed. Then
the boy's humility moves into hatred. He is unable to deal with

this new reality; "this was the first time he had ever had anything to forgive." He, too, is ready for a revelation of what forgiveness means.

The agent of revelation is an "artificial nigger" on a front lawn, which catches Mr. Head's attention "like a cry out of the gathering dusk." The plaster figure of an ageless Negro sitting unsteadily on a wall, "a wild look of misery" in his eyes, draws Mr. Head and Nelson together, and each says in wonder, "An artificial nigger." Then the statue becomes more than it is; reality becomes the bearer of grace. Both the offender and the offended "could feel it dissolving their differences like an action of mercy." Words fail Mr. Head, who all during the day has definitely explained the urban world to Nelson. When he tries "to explain once and for all the mystery of existence," he hears himself saying, "They ain't got enough real ones here. They got to have an artificial one." In some distorted way, this statement attributes value to the Negro race, which, through the day, Mr. Head has been demeaning to Nelson. Earlier, he had showed the boy how "they rope them off" in the train diner; he had pointed out the store "where you walked in and sat on a chair with your feet on two rests and let a Negro polish your shoes"; he had identified the evil of the city with its Negroes, growling from time to time, "Anybody wants to be from this nigger heaven can be from it." But the close of the story indicates that the world is charged with grandeur, even where one least expects to find it—in the statue of a "nigger."

When the travelers return home, the moonlight reappears, silvering the grass, glittering on the clinkers, and turning clouds into lanterns as Mr. Head and Nelson step off the train at the junction. But it falls upon a different grandfather and grandson: each has become aware of a new reality. Mr. Head, "an ancient child," understands the mercy of God; Nelson, "a miniature old man," has experienced a lifetime of emotions—carnal desire and treachery and hate and mercy. Each has led the other to wisdom. Although the opening suggests that this will be Mr. Head's story—his stature and name suggest universal man—as the story proceeds it becomes equally Nelson's story. Both teacher and pupil are initiated into the mystery of spiritual reality. The story closes with its focus on the boy, as he mutters, "I'm glad I've went once, but I'll never go back again."[24] Even on this level, the trip to the city has been successful.

O'Connor called this her favorite story.[25] The terms of its appeal are tenderness, humor, and sensitivity to many levels of reality. Her account of the story's genesis is valuable because it suggests the way in which her imagination penetrated beyond the seen and the known. During a symposium at Vanderbilt University in 1959, she explained the title:

> Well, I never had heard the phrase before, but my mother was out trying to buy a cow, and she rode up the country a-piece. She had the address of a man who was supposed to have a cow for sale, but she couldn't find it, so she stopped in a small town and asked the countryman on the side of the road where the house was, and he said, "Well, you go into this town and you can't miss it 'cause it's the only house in town with a artificial nigger in front of it." So I decided I would have to find a story to fit that. A little lower level than starting with the theme.[26]

The artifact which is the end product of this experience presupposes an artistic vision which sees far beyond the surface. Better than any of her words about reality, this incident illustrates O'Connor's ability to move from the surface of an object into what William Blake called threefold and fourfold vision. She described this vision, which allowed her to move from a plaster-of-Paris hitching-post statue to the depth of the heart of man, when she wrote: "The novelist writes about what he sees on the surface, but his angle of vision is such that he begins to see before he gets to the surface and he continues to see after he has gone past it. He begins to see in the depths of himself."[27] The story illuminates natural and supernatural reality conjoined in the "artificial nigger."

The mysterious power of matter to symbolize a greater reality is likewise captured in "the woods" in the story, "A View of the Woods." Once again an old man, Mark Fortune, attempts to teach a lesson to a child, his granddaughter, Mary Fortune Pitts. But although the old man and the nine-year-old girl look alike and seem to have the same temperament, they view reality differently. The old man grasps it, evaluates it, and uses it for his financial gain. The child penetrates it and realizes its symbolic value.

One is given a clear indication of these opposing views of reality before they collide drastically in a struggle which ends in death for both of them. Mary Fortune, the only member of the Pitts family whom the grandfather accepts as his kin, is his confidante, his miniature alter ego, and will be his sole beneficiary at his death. He despises her parents, humiliates them when he can, and keeps them dependent on him by refusing to sell them the property they are living on. For ten years Mary Fortune's father has been thwarted in his efforts to make a living on the farm by the old man, who, in the name of progress, would do a thing such as sell the field which Pitts had just cleared of bitterweed to make a pasture for his cows. Because the child *is* her grandfather in so many exterior ways, Pitts vents on his daughter the wrath which the old man provokes in him. At times, for no apparent reason, he takes her to the woods and beats her. She goes willingly, and her grandfather notes an expression on her face— "part terror and part respect and part something else, something very like cooperation." It infuriates and puzzles him. Even though the grandfather has witnessed the father beating the child, Mary Fortune denies that she has ever been beaten. Again and again she reiterates the prophetic words: "Nobody's ever beat me in my life and if anybody did, I'd kill him." For in some way that she would be at a loss to explain the child knows that her father is not beating her; he is beating her grandfather's image in her. But the old man cannot grasp this substitution; her strange conduct in this affair is "an ugly mystery" to him.

His incomprehension of this mystery denotes his stolid and literal view of reality. This comes into conflict with Mary Fortune's symbolic view in the incident which causes the story's denouement. Mr. Fortune announces that he intends to sell "the lawn," the lot in front of the house which, empty, affords the family a view of the woods across the road. On it will rise a general store and a filling station, which might form the nucleus of a new town to be named Fortune, Georgia. The lots on the new lake which the electric power company had created would soon have houses, and the city would run a paved road out to the town. Mr. Fortune envisions it all; he believes in progress and, unlike Pitts, is not fool enough to let a "view" stand in his way. Mr. Fortune's dreams and visions all concern material prosperity. To his dismay, Mary Fortune joins the rest of the family in their protest against the sale of "the lawn." Mr. Fortune ignores the others, but he tries to win Mary Fortune's approval or at least dispel her displeasure by buying her a boat. For he thinks that "with grown people, a road led either to heaven or hell, but with children there were always stops along the way where their attention could be turned with a trifle." However, he fails to know his own "unmistakable likeness." When Mary Fortune rebels to the end and throws bottles at him in Tilman's general store as Tilman is signing the deed of sale, the old man decides to teach her a lesson. If her father could beat her for no reason (her father's fists are described as "two dark quartz stones"), then Fortune should beat her for her misconduct. But when he attempts to do this, she kicks and bites and pounds the old man with her "rocklike" fists until he is pinned beneath her, and she announces triumphantly her father's revenge: "You been whipped by me, and I'm PURE Pitts." This insult, coming from his "own image," gives the dying man a surge of strength, and he reverses their positions and bangs the child's head down on the rock beneath it three times. He staggers a few feet away and falls to face his own death, which approaches in the form of a giant lake that engulfs him.

One scene in the story brings together pragmatic and symbolic views of reality by showing the woods as the grandfather sees it from his bedroom window. He has just tried to ingratiate himself with Mary Fortune, who is sitting on the porch swing looking at the woods "as if it were a person that she preferred to him." When he reaches his bedroom he looks across the road "to assure himself again that there was nothing over there to see." Several times he looks, and every time he sees the same thing: "woods—not a mountain, not a waterfall, not any kind of planted bush or flower, just woods." But the third time he rises to look, the woods are charged with sunset:

... The gaunt trunks appeared to be raised in a pool of red light that gushed from the almost hidden sun setting behind them. The old man stared for some time, as if for a prolonged instant he were caught up out of the rattle of everything that led to the future and were held there in the midst of an uncomfortable mystery that he had not apprehended before. He saw it, in his hallucination, as if someone were wounded behind the woods and the trees were bathed in blood.

He recoils from this "unpleasant vision," this unappreciated hierophany. But it has some effect on him. He spends the evening "pointing out to himself the advantages for the future of having an establishment like Tilman's so near." At least he feels compelled to marshal reasons for his action which will outweigh the splendor of that view of the woods.

Balancing a view of the woods as a symbol of hope for the Pitts family is the bulldozer,[28] the "huge yellow monster" which, for Mark Fortune, symbolizes progress. As the story opens, he and Mary Fortune are watching it smooth out the hole which will be the site of the new fishing club; at the story's end, it is the last object which presents itself to the dying man's vision, as it sits to one side of him, "gorging itself on clay." It seems clear that Mark Fortune's materialistic idea of progress determines his view of reality. He, too, is "gorging" himself on clay, selling off his lots that border the newly created lake to "every Tom, Dick and Harry, every dog and his brother" who will pay the price. This story illustrates well that the symbolic value which O'Connor gave to certain objects in no way detracts from the reality which they possess. Rather, that reality is doubled by its symbolic extension.[29] The story brings into conflict pragmatic and symbolic views of reality and depicts this conflict by an art which combines both views. So the conflict between the child and her grandfather becomes a conflict between a pine woods and a bulldozer and ultimately a conflict between spiritual vision and material progress.

In the two stories just discussed, a significant epiphany occurs, in which reality becomes more than it is while remaining what it is; it manifests the holiness intrinsic to the natural world. An interesting contrast to this spiritual view of reality is presented in one of Flannery O'Connor's earliest stories, the one entitled "The Capture." In it, a young protagonist assigns a spiritual value to a material object (which is quite different from apprehending an object's spiritual value) and learns, to his bewilderment, his error. Ruller, age eleven, chases a wounded turkey through the woods, almost catches him, and then the wily bird eludes him. Ruller knows that his older brother has "gone bad," and he thinks the same thing is happening to him, as, in anger and disappointment, he says every blasphemous expression he has ever heard. Just when he thinks he is truly "bad," he sees the turkey again, right in a position for him to capture. He feels that God has put it in his path to "save" him. As he walks proudly home with the turkey slung over his shoulder, he knows that he is special; God wanted to keep him from evil, and He used the turkey to do so. In a burst of gratitude, he prays that he will see a beggar, so he can give away his hoarded dime. He does. Striding in full confidence of his importance to God, he is almost home when three country boys calmly take the turkey away from him. Confused and anxious, he runs toward home with the feeling that "Something Awful" is pursuing him.

Although this story does not possess the depth and complexity of O'Connor's more mature works, it penetrates convincingly into the mind of the boy to show a child's penchant for ordering reality according to his limited view of life. Through the child's error it reveals a greater truth: that God works through reality according to his own designs, not man's. Written for O'Connor's M.F.A. thesis under the title "The Turkey," the story was subsequently revised and entitled "The Capture" for publication in *Mademoiselle*.[30] A study of the revision shows that even as O'Connor was depicting a false view of the sacrality of the world, she was learning how to capture reality accurately in words. The turkey may be a symbol of God's pleasure or displeasure for the boy, but it is described as a living, wounded, frightened bird. In this single-character story, O'Connor penetrates a child's mind with sensitivity and skill; this treatment marks the beginning of her varied explorations of a child's apprehension of reality.

More complex are the views of earthly reality which the characters exhibit in "A Circle in the Fire." Structurally, this story is unique in the O'Connor canon, because the central figure, a twelve-year-old girl, does not become part of the conflict until the story's end. Although her viewpoint dominates the narration, she remains aloof from the action until the final scene. The conflict involves her mother, Mrs. Cope, a self-satisfied rural matron who sees her farm as her hard-won property, and three young boys who visit her, for whom the farm is heaven. Despite her farm life, Mrs. Cope fears the natural world because she intuitively feels that there is something uncanny behind it with which she cannot "cope." This general uneasiness converges in one large worry: "Mrs. Cope was always worrying about fires in her woods." The richness of reality lies heavy upon her: "she looked around at her rich pastures and hills heavy with timber and shook her head as if it might all be a burden she was trying to shake off her back." Not only plenitude weighs heavy; beauty makes her uneasy and moves her to fear. She looks at the sun—"swollen and flame-colored and hung in a net of ragged cloud as if it might burn through any second and fall into the woods"—and she shivers and catches both arms to her sides and thanks God "in a mournful marveling tone." She speaks a great deal of God and of thankfulness; she recounts a litany of blessings to the unlistening child in a "stricken voice." But she relies wholly on herself. The visitation of the boys takes place in the autumn, and the seasonal change has its effect on Mrs. Cope: "Even a small change in the weather made Mrs. Cope thankful, but when the season changed she seemed almost frightened at her good fortune in escaping whatever it was that pursued her."

The key to her fear of reality, her dread of fire, and her feeling of being pursued may be found in the biblical symbolism which O'Connor made her own—a symbolism which represents God as a consuming fire. In *A Study of Hebrew Thought,* Tresmontant says:

Fire in the Bible is the sign of God's love, His jealousy, and His wrath. "Yhwh your God is a devouring fire, a jealous God" (Deut. 4:24). It is fire which purifies, destroying the imperfect, perfecting the gold. . . .

Fire is an ambiguous power, both kind and awful. So too the love of God, the delight of the already purified saint, is a torment to any man who experiences it without communing with it. (Pp. 56–57)

In natural terms, this story communicates the supernatural reality of the pursuing love of God. Mrs. Cope experiences it mysteriously, without "communing with it." Only when control of reality is taken out of her hands, when the boys set fire to the woods, is she dimly aware of her true relationship to "her" property.

In her interaction with others, Mrs. Cope exhibits her characteristic mental orientation: she bends reality to her own wishes. She "handles" her hired woman, Mrs. Pritchard, by constantly remaking her according to her own image. When Mrs. Pritchard starts her calamitous stories, Mrs. Cope always changes the subject, though even the child notices that this merely puts Mrs. Pritchard in a bad humor. When the hired woman sees signs and omens in life's happenings, Mrs. Cope calmly exposes them as "figments of imagination." When Mrs. Pritchard takes a realistic view of such events as the arrival of the three boys at the farm, Mrs. Cope imposes her autocratic view. Her will orders the life around her. It takes her a long time to realize that she is powerless with the boys, three intruders who have been drawn to the farm by "the middle one"—Powell—and his memories of a life very different from life in the Atlanta "development" where the boys now live. Powell had lived on the farm when his father had worked there, and the memory of the woods, the fields, and the horses draws him, with his two friends, back. This hunger for "another world" is foreign to Mrs. Cope; she is unable to recognize it. When the smallest boy tells her that Powell wants to come here when he dies, Mrs. Cope looks blank, then blushes, then looks pained because she realizes that the boys are hungry. Even after they spurn her crackers, she can only muse that they *looked* hungry. When the boys tell of Powell's reliving his days on the farm during a tenement baseball game, and declaring, "Goddam, it was a horse down there name Gene and if I had him here I'd bust this concrete to hell riding him," Mrs. Cope reacts to his language and not to the reality of his longing. "I'm sure Powell doesn't use words like that, do you, Powell?" she asks. Even when she learns from his companions that Powell "ain't ever satisfied with where he's at except this place here" Mrs. Cope cannot recognize a longing for a dimly remembered paradisaic world, even though that same longing, disguised, pursues her.

Mrs. Cope's daughter, designated simply "the child," is listener and watcher for most of the story. A "pale fat girl of twelve with a frowning squint and a large mouth full of silver bands," she watches from windows, listens from stairwells, and grows painfully in the understanding of reality. Her mother tells her to stay away from the boys, and, later, seeing her dressed in overalls and an old man's hat, she lets the child know what a disappointment she is to her. The mother does not realize that her satiric question, "When are you going to grow up?" is being answered before her eyes. The child does not know who she is. That she does not identify with the two women in the story is evident after she sticks her head out of the window and makes a face and an explosive noise at the three boys. At the large boy's response—"Jesus. Another woman."—she withdraws abruptly, "squinting fiercely as if she had been slapped in the face and couldn't see who had done it." After that, she is completely hostile to the boys. The following day, rebelling against the femininity thrust upon her, she dresses as a boy, carries two guns, and strides into the woods to her fantasy world. The pines become the boys, and she murmurs, "I'm going to get you one by one and beat you black and blue." A clinging thorn vine becomes Mrs. Cope, and she reiterates the words she has just spoken to her mother: "Leave me be." When she comes upon the three boys bathing in the cow trough, her aggressiveness melts away and she is "prickle-skinned." Hidden, she watches them cavort in the water and then run around the field to dry, the sun glinting "their long wet bodies." She watches them lie panting on the grass, "their ribs moving up and down." She watches them start the fire which will rise "unchecked inside the granite line of trees."

Then the experiences of the past two days—her overhearing the adults' conversation about the woman who had conceived and borne a baby while living in an iron lung, her being called "woman" by the boy, her sight of the three naked boys, and her silent watching while the first match was struck—all converge into "some new unplaced misery that she had never felt before." When she can finally run for help, she can only scream the least imminent of her new discoveries, "Mama, Mama, they're going to build a parking lot here."

Approaching the terror-stricken Mrs. Cope, the child sees her "new misery" reflected in her mother's face, "but on her mother it looked old and it looked as if it might have belonged to anybody, a Negro or a European or to Powell himself." It is the misery which is the underside of joy and part of the burden and glory of humanity. It has its source in the essential incompleteness of life and its surcease in a view of reality which includes its infinite extensions. Mrs. Cope grasps the real and fears what is beyond her grasp; Mrs. Pritchard sees reality in its direst aspect; the boys seek quintessential reality in its symbol and destroy what they cannot have. The child, just entering into an understanding of the reality of her own nature, must forge her own path. She will be forced to name the "unplaced misery" which has invaded her, or be doomed to bear her mother's vague apprehension.[31]

In "The River," perhaps the best-known of the O'Connor child-protagonist stories, reality is presented according to Eliade's distinction between the sacred and the profane: all depends on the eye of the perceiver, and the roots of the eye are in the heart. The child, self-named "Bevel," moves from a profane world in which everything is a joke to a sacred world in which he "counts." From dawn, when his baby-sitter, Mrs. Connin, takes him from his parents' apartment, until late evening when she brings him back, he moves in a world of human concern and divine direction. It is not all pleasant. The woman's three sons trick him into letting a huge shoat out of the pigpen, and he screams in terror as the gray, wet, sour face pushes into his. But nothing is a joke; all is real. As real as the warmth of the woman holding him on her lap while he eats breakfast is the story she reads to him, "The Life of Jesus Christ for Readers Under Twelve." He learns that a carpenter named Jesus Christ made him, and he realizes the carpenter's power when he sees a picture of him "driving a crowd of pigs out of a man." They were real pigs, "gray and sour-looking," like the one which had just terrified him. By the time he arrives at the river the child is completely at home in the milieu of the sacred. Only when he is lifted onto the preacher's shoulder and becomes the center of attention does he shake off the aura of the sacred. Grinning, he "rolled his eyes in a comical way and thrust his face forward, close to the preacher's. 'My name is Bevvvuuuuul,' he said in loud deep voice and let the tip of his tongue slide across his mouth." But he realizes that his conduct is out of place immediately when the only one who laughs is the scoffer, Mr. Paradise. Looking at the preacher's face, the child believes again in the reality of this sacred world.

But Bevel cannot deal with symbolism. His child-mind is uncomplex; either all is a joke or all is real. His response to the preacher's invitation to "be washed in the river of suffering . . . and to go by the deep river of life" is a total "yes" as he thinks, "I won't go back to the apartment then, I'll go under the river." But strangely, he does go back to the apartment, to a world of cigarette butts and strange adults and loneliness. When he awakens in that apartment the next morning, he looks for his "Jesus" book, but it is gone. Deprived of that tangible link with the other world he has discovered, he seems about to lapse back into his everyday world as he dumps ash trays on the floor and explores the refrigerator. Then something absolutely unexpected and absolutely right happens—in the manner of the Greek peripety—to turn the story in its final direction. After wandering around the apartment aimlessly, the child lies down on the floor and studies his feet which he holds up in the air. "His shoes were still damp and he began to think about the river." One watches the world of the sacred absorb his consciousness as "very slowly, his expression changed as if he were gradually seeing appear what he didn't know he'd been looking for."

The last scene, in which Bevel returns to the river to find the kingdom of Christ, shows the action of evil in the milieu of the sacred. Lest the two worlds of the story seem completely dichotomous, the evil presence of Mr. Paradise shadows the backwoods activities. Bevel first hears of him when Mrs. Connin tells him that the shoat which frightened him "favors Mr. Paradise that has the gas station." The child's immediate response is, "I don't want to see him." From the picture in the Bible story book and his own experience, Bevel associates evil with pigs. During the sermon at the river, each time Bevel's attention is drawn to "the huge old man who sat like a humped stone on the bumper of a long ancient gray automobile," he reacts by drawing closer to Mrs. Connin or the preacher. At the story's close, it is the sight of this old man "like a giant pig bounding after him, shaking a red and white club" (actually a giant peppermint stick to lure

the child) which makes him "plunge under" for the final time.[32]
Bevel is intuitively repelled by evil and drawn toward the sacred.
Bevel's parents represent extreme secularism; the preacher
represents the extreme of the sacred. Between them stands Mrs.
Connin, part of both worlds as she stands at the apartment door
looking like "a speckled skeleton in a long pea-green coat and
felt helmet." One notes in her words and actions a common-sense
approach to the sacred. On examining the abstract watercolor
framed on the wall of the Ashfield apartment, her first reaction
is, "I wouldn't have paid for that; I would have drew it myself."
Later, thinking about it, she knows that she "wouldn't have drew
it." Here is a completely characteristic decision, as she moves
from a "secular" evaluation of the cost of the painting to a
"sacred" appraisal of its value. She accepts both visible and
invisible reality. With an exasperated "you pervide," she furn-
ishes a handkerchief and cleans the little boy's nose because it
needs cleaning; with a long look of amazement at his ignorance,
she tells the boy who Jesus is because he needs to know his
Saviour. Although extremely practical, she never loses her spiritual perspective. For example, before Mr. Ashfield manages to
shut the door on her and his little son, she asks for "his and my
carfare," as "it'll be twict we have to ride the car," and she
counts the money which the sleep-fogged father hands her. At
the story's end, she returns the boy, newly baptized, to the apartment where his parents are having a party and announces that
the preacher has prayed for the child's mother to be healed. This
announcement is greeted with derision, and the father murmurs,
"Healing by prayer is mighty inexpensive," as he holds out her
pay. Once again, the unexpected but absolutely right action
occurs:

> Mrs. Connin stood a second, staring into the room, with a
> skeleton's appearance of seeing everything. Then, without tak-
> ing the money, she turned and shut the door behind her.

Her repudiation of mammon recalls Christ's command to his
apostles to wipe the dust from their feet on the thresholds of those
homes which do not accept them.
Several times the language of the story is "double," having
both a sacred and a secular meaning. Mr. Ashfield's first words

to the baby-sitter—"Well then for Christ's sake fix him"—refer to the child's awkward position in his coat, but they contain an infinite extension of meaning. When the child asks Mrs. Connin if the preacher will "heal" him and she inquires, "What you got?" his answer, "I'm hungry," has both physical and spiritual connotations. The child's musing as he proceeds toward the river—"You found out more when you left where you lived"—suggests the paradigmatic idea of wisdom in exile. The little boy's frolicking as he walks toward his baptism—"he began to make wild leaps and pull forward on her hand as if he wanted to dash off and snatch the sun"—has evident symbolic value, as does his entering "the shadows of a wood," and "looking from side to side as if he were entering a strange country." The visitor in the apartment at the close of the story comments that the book Bevel has brought home is "valuable," meaning that it is "a collector's item"; Bevel, too, knew that it was valuable when he hid it in the inner lining of his coat. These two appraisals indicate—almost too overtly—the secular and the sacred worlds which this story contrasts.

The same penetration of spiritual reality which Bevel unconsciously showed is evident in the child who realizes what it means to be "A Temple of the Holy Ghost." In this story, Flannery O'Connor deals for the first time with a distinctly Catholic theological reality as her child-protagonist probes the mystery of Christ in the Eucharist and in man. Juxtaposing a carnival and a chapel, a freak and the Blessed Sacrament, O'Connor fuses most disparate elements into a singular unity. And the matrix of unity is the mind of a child. In Robert Fitzgerald's introduction to *Everything That Rises Must Converge*, he quotes O'Connor's comment on a discussion of the Eucharistic Symbol: "If it were only a symbol, I'd say to hell with it."[33] That expression of conviction is matched in intensity in "A Temple of the Holy Ghost" by the young girl's appreciation of the spiritual reality of the Eucharist.

All of life presents itself for contemplation to "the child's" searching mind. Her thoughts, in the company of others or in her bedroom, where "she let the darkness collect [to] make the room smaller and more private," are the "long, long thoughts" of youth. With an expression, "fierce and dreamy both," on her face, she is listener and observer. But once in the story she is moved to wrath, provoked by what she considers a desecration of spiritual reality. Her mother has brought her two cousins, age fourteen, from their convent school to spend the weekend. The girls immediately doff their school uniforms and dress in red skirts and loud blouses. They parade in front of the mirror, giggle, gossip about boys, and ignore the child—two years younger. The mother invites two neighborhood boys to come to dinner and take the girls to the fair. The boys arrive with harmonica and guitar, and as they are both preparing to become Church of God preachers, they sing hymns, crooning them as love songs to the two girls. The girls respond by singing the "Tantum Ergo," an ancient Latin hymn of praise to the Holy Eucharist. Dumbfounded, the boys gape; then one ventures, "That must be Jew singing." The child, who has been hiding in the bushes watching the scene on the porch, is driven to fury. "You big dumb Church of God ox," she roars. That the boys would sing hymns as love songs was bad enough; that the girls would sing the most sacred Catholic hymn as entertainment was worse. But the boy's thinking this ancient expression of belief in the Eucharistic presence of Christ to be "Jew singing" is error beyond endurance. The child can only be grateful that she doesn't belong to the Church of God.

Her reaction to this irreverence is predictable because, earlier in the story when the two visitors jokingly call each other "Temple One" and "Temple Two," one sees that spiritual realities *are* realities to the child. Amid sobs of laughter, the two girls tell the mother that one of the nuns had told them to resist "ungentlemanly" advances of any young man by saying, "Stop, sir! I am a Temple of the Holy Ghost!" The child silently considers this idea and can find nothing funny about it; in fact, she is "pleased with the phrase. It made her feel as if somebody had given her a present." That the thought lingers in the child's mind is evident when, later, she and her mother are discussing their boarder, Miss Kirby, who is almost friendless and has little to recommend her. The child muses that, although "it's all over her head," even she is a Temple of the Holy Ghost. Through the story her mind fingers the phrase and grasps its actuality.

Sacred and secular reality are imaginatively combined when

the child muses about being a saint. This is a very real ambition for her; it is "the occupation that included everything you could know." She dreams of being a martyr, because she could be a saint only "if they killed her quick." Her dreams of martyrdom mingle with remembrances of last year's carnival as she imagines herself, in circus tights, facing a cageful of lions who fall at her feet, converted. Mixed incongruously with romantic ideas of martyrdom is a conception of true prayer. The child intuits the distinction between "hanging by her chin on the side of the bed, empty-minded," and being moved by sorrow or beauty or loss to fill her mind with God. Through the child's imaginative wanderings, one can see that the world is "whole" to her; all of reality has spiritual extensions.

Two exposition scenes, one imaginary and one real, combine sacred and secular reality and form the center of the story. When the girls come home from the fair, they tell the child about seeing a freak who was both man and woman. This freak went from the men's side of the tent to the women's side, exposing himself and saying such things as "God made me thisaway. . . . I ain't disputing His way. . . . I got to make the best of it." The child does not understand how someone could be both man and woman without two heads, but she tries to think it out. Her mind wanders, and she mentally transforms the circus tent into a church. In her mind there gradually evolves a litany which combines the freak's words with the concept of being "a Temple of the Holy Ghost." She visualizes the audience of country people, with their solemn church-faces and hears them shout "Amen" after each statement and clap their hands in rhythm. Lingering on the edge of sleep, she combines the sacred and secular, church and circus, saint and freak, and from her musings emerges a singular idea of the dignity of man. The second exposition scene takes place in the convent chapel. The child and her mother take the girls back to school and are invited to come to the chapel for Benediction of the Holy Eucharist. Although the child sluggishly follows the nun to the chapel, after she hears the first few lines of the "Tantum Ergo" she realizes that she is in the Eucharistic presence of God. But as the priest elevates the Host for the blessing, her mind is on the freak, and he is saying, "I don't dispute hit. This is the way He wanted me to be." In a distorted yet true and childlike way, this scene encompasses both the mystery of the Eucharist—God under the form of bread—and the miracle of man—"I am a Temple of the Holy Ghost." A complex symbolism of light connects sacred and secular reality. After the girls have left for the fair, the child goes to her room to think. She looks out the window at the "speckled sky where a long finger of light was revolving up and around and away, searching the air as if it were hunting for the lost sun. It was the beacon light from the fair"—the secular, searching for the sacred. On the drive to the convent, the child leans her head out the car window, and, when the wind blows her hair like a veil over her eyes, she is able to "look directly into the ivory sun which was framed in the middle of the blue afternoon." This "ivory circle" image returns with spiritual overtones when the priest raises "the monstrance with the Host shining ivory-colored in the center of it." The story closes with a final image which connects the fair, the sun, and the Host: "The sun was a huge red ball like an elevated Host drenched in blood and when it sank out of sight it left a line in the sky like a red clay road hanging over the trees." It is the "red clay road"—the bloody, earthy path that touches all of reality—which will be the child's only way to the sanctity she desires.

Below the surface of these stories Flannery O'Connor explores the "symbolic theology" which is "coextensive with creation." This idea is taken from Edith Stein, a writer who seems to have impressed O'Connor, for reasons which will be evident. A German-Jewish philosopher interested chiefly in phenomenology, Edith Stein studied under and became an assistant to Edmund Husserl. Searching for truth by turning from idealistic philosophy to the world of objects, or phenomena, Edith Stein finally found truth in Catholicism. After her conversion, she became a Carmelite nun and continued her philosophical work in the Carmel at Cologne until the Nazi persecution of the Jews forced her into exile in the Dutch Carmel at Echt. There she was captured by the Nazis and gassed at Auschwitz in 1942. That her extraordinary life impressed Flannery O'Connor seems evident from O'Connor's closing sentence of a review of Edith Stein's *The Science of the Cross* which she wrote for the October 1, 1960, issue of the Georgia diocesan *Bulletin*. In it, O'Connor said:

It is a moving book but less for what is in it [a presentation of the life and doctrine of St. John of the Cross] than for Edith Stein's own background—for the modern crucifixion that the reader knows was waiting for her as she wrote the book.

One can see similarities between the German-Jewish philosopher and the Irish Catholic writer, the most striking of which is their conviction that attention to visible reality—to phenomena —would lead them to truth. This attention to "what is" led Edith Stein to move from agnosticism to Catholicism and Flannery O'Connor to develop a writing style which probed reality relentlessly. In her copy of *The Writings of Edith Stein*, O'Connor marked passages in the essay on "The Knowledge of God" which indicate her interest in Edith Stein's discussion of the way in which God reveals the spiritual through the material. Miss Stein asserts that the world itself is the basis for natural theology; it "points beyond itself to Him who mysteriously reveals Himself through it." It is the basis for symbolic language, which not only expresses real or assumed knowledge, but also—and O'Connor underlined this sentence—induces "knowledge of something not yet known." This leads Miss Stein to call God "the first and original theologian," because, in His creation, He reveals Himself through a "symbolic theology." Edith Stein develops this idea by showing that it is the task of human theologians to interpret natural revelation, "translating it into human language so that they can lead others to God through symbolic theology."[34] Earlier in this chapter, attention was called to Flannery O'Connor's use of the phrase "vocation of spirit." This phrase expresses her desire to do what Edith Stein describes. Without ever leaving the realm of fiction, she writes "symbolic theology." Especially in these child-stories, she immerses her protagonist in a world of phenomena, and portrays the character's awareness of the numinous quality of that world.

CHAPTER VI

The Tattooed Christ:

a prophet's view of reality

"The poet is traditionally a blind
man, but the Christian poet, and
storyteller as well, is like the blind
man whom Christ touched, who
looked then and saw men as if
they were trees, but walking. This
is the beginning of vision, and it
is an invitation to deeper and
stranger visions that we shall have
to learn to accept if we want to
realize a truly Christian literature." F.O'C.

Shortly after Flannery O'Connor's death on August 3, 1964, *Esprit*, a literary magazine of the University of Scranton, published a memorial edition in her honor. This magazine had received the "interest, encouragement and guidance"[1] of Flannery O'Connor over a period of eight years. The edition contained tributes by important literary figures and student analyses of O'Connor's fiction. One of the most moving tributes was telephoned to the staff from her Washington home by Katherine Anne Porter, who was ill at the time. Entitled "Gracious Greatness," the tribute reads in part:

> Now and again there hovers on the margin of the future a presence that one feels as imminent—if I may use stylish vocabulary. She came up among us like a presence, a carrier of a gift not to be disputed but welcomed. She lived among us like a presence and went away early, leaving her harvest perhaps not yet altogether gathered.

This description of an imminent presence hovering on the margin of the future is one artist's recognition of the prophet in another. Miss Porter continued her tribute by reminiscing about her two meetings with Flannery; she related an anecdote which shows how few realized the "presence" among them. She tells of hearing the following conversation at a party at the O'Connor home:

> . . . Someone mentioned Flannery's name and another—a neighbor, mind you, who had probably been around there all her life—said: "Who is Flannery O'Connor? I keep hearing about her." The other one said "Oh you know! Why, that's Regina Cline's daughter; that little girl who writes."[2]

Unobtrusive was the presence of a prophet in Milledgeville, but the prophet's voice was heard clearly in her lectures, and the prophet's call for a return to reality rings through her fiction.

O'Connor's interest in Old Testament prophets is evident in the number of books about them in her library. Chief among these is Bruce Vawter's *The Conscience of Israel*, which O'Connor reviewed for the Georgia diocesan *Bulletin* in March, 1962. In her review, O'Connor stresses Vawter's achievement in giving his readers an enlightened—as opposed to a traditional—view of the prophets. She says:

Twentieth-century Biblical criticism has returned the prophets to their genuine mission, which was not to innovate, but to recall the people to truths they were already well aware of but chose to ignore. . . . Father Vawter restores [the prophets] to their exotic Oriental culture where they were seen by their contemporaries as inspired men in communication with "that otherness that men have always associated with the divine."

Vawter describes the prophets as inspired men who had a deep conviction, expressed in Scripture pictorially by the story of each one's call, that they were the instruments of the Lord to bring his recalcitrant people to an understanding of the error of their ways. He stresses the idea that the prophets were often unwilling, initially, to undertake the work of the Lord. Only when they were convinced that divine power would compensate for their weakness did they undertake the Lord's mission. Vawter depicts the prophets as outcasts from their own people because they would not condone the waywardness they saw about them. Usually they announced a message of doom. Yet they were acknowledged as inspired men, and admired for their fearlessness.[3] From the number of her marginal markings, it seems evident that O'Connor was impressed by Vawter's conception of the prophetic role.

Another volume which O'Connor marked, Eric Voegelin's *Israel and Revelation*,[4] deals with the prophets from a philosophical point of view that complements Vawter's religious view. Voegelin sees the prophets as men inspired by God to keep the Israelites from "parochialism"—from believing that the transcendent God was their God alone. According to Voegelin, the revelation of God to Israel constituted a new form of order—the order of history—but this form was not dependent upon the stability of Israel as a nation. The prophet's task was to keep the people of Israel attuned to the continual revelation of God, even when their nation was destroyed and they were dispersed into exile. Voegelin summarizes the role of the prophet in this statement, which O'Connor marked:

The prophets were faced with the task of reformulating the problem of history in such a manner that the empirical Israel of their time could disappear from the scene without destroying by its disappearance the order of history as created by revelation (p. 460).

Voegelin explains that the prophets—especially Isaias and Jeremias—wrought a new understanding of order: "The order of society in history is reconstituted in fact through the men who challenge the disorder of the surrounding society with the order they experience as living in themselves" (p. 483). In other words, the prophet's "placement" in God establishes an order in his soul which gives him a firm basis from which to challenge the disorder he sees about him. Eventually he will lead men to a more perfect order. O'Connor marked this summary passage:

The insight that existence under God means love, humility, and righteousness of action rather than legality of conduct was the great achievement of the prophets in the history of Israelite order (p. 440).

One further idea of Voegelin's seems to have been important in O'Connor's characterization of the prophets in her fiction. In *The World of the Polis,* the second volume of his *Order and History,* Voegelin points up a parallel between Israel and Greece. Both nations experienced the "leap in being, the epochal event that breaks the compactness of the early cosmological myth and establishes the order of man in his immediacy under God" (p. 6). Each nation articulated this "leap in being" in a different way, thus creating the two ordering principles of religion and philosophy. Voegelin discusses in detail this "leap in being," this movement toward a transcendental source of order. It is a vital movement which rejects the closed world of the myth even as it opens up a new spiritual order of being. Voegelin stresses the responsibility which this contact with a spiritual world puts upon each person. O'Connor marked this central passage:

The leap in being entails the obligations to communicate and to listen. Revelation and response are not a man's private affair; for the revelation comes to one man for all men, and in his response he is the representative of all mankind. And since the response is representative it endows the recipient of revelation, in relation to his fellow men, with the authority of the prophet.[5]

From Voegelin's treatment of the prophet there emerges the idea of a person whose soul is attuned to the order of God, whether or not this order prevails about him. The hallmarks of this order are love, humility, and good works. By virtue of his calling, the prophet has an obligation to all men. Vawter's study of the prophets stresses the personal element. The prophets are recipients of a call from God. Through direct or indirect means, He leads them to see—even dimly—the life He has destined for them. They are free to accept or reject this destiny. If they accept it, they find strength and consolation in the Lord, even though their call may lead to a life of great hardship. The prophets are men of their times, often weak and not anxious to be that "center of order" the Lord desires.

O'Connor had at least one other "sourcebook" for her concept of the prophet. In a letter to Sister Bernetta Quinn, dated January, 1960, she says:

I have been reading what St. Thomas has to say in the *De Veritate* on prophecy. He says prophecy depends on the imaginative and not the moral faculty. It's a matter of seeing. Those who, like Tarwater, see, will see what they have no desire to see and the vision will be the purifying fire. I think I am not done with prophets.[6]

Further on in the same letter, she adds: "the idea of anyone's having a vocation to be a prophet doesn't commend itself to [man's] sense of the fitness of things in the twentieth century" (p. 183). In O'Connor's library I found the book she had been reading—*Truth*, Vol. II, a translation of Questions 10 to 20 of St. Thomas Aquinas's *De Veritate*. Indicative of her creative mind is the one point—the place of the imagination in prophecy— which O'Connor drew from this dry, scholastic discussion of prophecy, couched in the Thomistic mode of a question, followed by sections headed Difficulties, To the Contrary, Reply, Answers to Difficulties, Answers to Contrary Difficulties. Thomas's discussion concerns the prophetic mode and not the prophet as person.[7] When O'Connor wrote this letter to Sister Bernetta, she had finished her most expansive treatment of the prophet in *The Violent Bear It Away*. That she was "not done with prophets" is evident from her writing of "Revelation," published shortly before her death, and "Parker's Back," published posthumously. In each of these stories prophecy becomes—ever more imaginatively—"a matter of seeing."

Basic to an understanding of the vocation of a prophet—actually, any vocation embarked upon with a sense of destiny—is the Hebrew concept of the freedom of man. In the historical form of order, God's dealings with His people form a sacred history which orders men's lives by illuminating present events in the light of paradigmatic events in the past and at the same time directing all toward a final historical point in the future. Within this framework, each man has his destined role, under the providence of God. Because they are writing to reach a primitive mentality, the biblical writers depict man's understanding of his destiny in dramatic ways—Jacob's stealing his brother's birthright or Paul's being thrown from his horse. But this is not God's usual way of communicating with men. He speaks through the circumstances of man's life. In order to discern God's will, man opens his heart and mind to the reality of life around him, for in the mystery which that reality embraces he will see divine direction. Then he is free to accept or reject that direction.

In the last story O'Connor wrote, "Parker's Back," she explores the mystery of divine direction. Unlikely candidate for God's election though he is, O. E. Parker is "chosen," and the story illuminates the communication of that choice and the effect that it has on his life. God leads Parker to understand his destiny through a strange combination of circumstances: his attraction to tattoos and his marriage to a woman who abhors them. This story achieves a goal set by a statement which O'Connor marked in her copy of Emmanuel Mounier's *The Character of Man*: "To draw mystery into the light of day, without losing its strength and fascination, is the highest achievement either of art or of thought."[8] The "light of day" is the absolute credibility of this story; the "mystery" is God's way with man.

A "peculiar unease" which settles in Parker when he is fourteen years old is the first indication of God's designs upon him.

At a fair he sees a man tattooed from head to foot; when the man flexes his muscles, the pattern of men and beasts and flowers on his skin appears to have a subtle motion of its own. After this vision fills his eyes, Parker is never the same; the "unease" in him can be satisfied only by tattoos, which he gets, one after the other, all over his body, for the next fourteen years. But the "unease" remains. Each tattoo dispels it for a time, but always it returns. He longs to see on his own body the "moving arabesque of color" that fills his imagination, but when he examines himself in a mirror, he sees only "something haphazard and blotched." It seems as if his desire can never be satisfied, for, when the story opens, he has only one body-space left, and that a place he cannot see—his back. When his discontent is at its height, he meets his future wife.

Another unlikely instrument of God's providence, Sarah Ruth Cates is destined to lead Parker to the goal of his quest. After Parker leaves the navy, he starts to sell fruit to country people living on back roads in the rural South. He meets Sarah Ruth when his truck breaks down near her house. He attracts her attention by shouting blasphemies when he pretends to have smashed his hand in the car motor. Daughter of a fundamentalist preacher, she responds to his language by swatting him with a broom. He courts her, marries her, and stays with her after she becomes pregnant, although all his actions are incomprehensible to himself: while he is courting her he swears each day that he will not return; after he has "made up his mind . . . to have nothing further to do with her," he marries her; although she is "ugly and pregnant and no cook," he stays with her. "He was puzzled and ashamed of himself." But their courtship and marriage are completely reasonable from Sarah Ruth's point of view. She bears his courting because he brings fruit every time he calls; she becomes really interested in him when she learns that his initials, O. E., stand for Obadiah Elihue, two significant Old Testament names (the first a minor prophet; the second a comforter of Job). She evidently marries him to "save" him. After marriage, she spends her time telling him "what the judgement seat of God would be like for him if he didn't change his ways." Parker's decision to have a religious picture tattooed on his back to "bring Sarah Ruth to heel" is mysterious in view of her complete scorn for his tattoos: "except in total darkness she preferred Parker dressed and with his sleeves rolled down." Her beating him with a broom when he shows her the tattoo on his back is completely plausible. Nurtured in fundamentalist doctrine, she can only cry out "Idolatry" when Parker tells her that the face tattooed on his back is the face of God.

One can see in Parker's openness to life's mystery and in Sarah Ruth's certainty about life the difference between the many who are "called" and the few who are "chosen." Trusting exclusively in a literal interpretation of Scripture, Sarah Ruth follows the narrow path to salvation which excludes any other means of apprehending God. Her eyes, "grey and sharp like the points of two ice picks," reveal her determined character. Parker's mind bends toward mystery. Since the time he was initially drawn to the mystery of moving color on the body of the tattooed man, he has been responsive to the inner promptings of his spirit, even if he does not understand them. From that time, his life has had a mysterious orientation; "it was as if a blind boy had been turned so gently in a different direction that he did not know his destination had been changed." This openness to mystery is reflected in his eyes, "which were the same pale slate-color as the ocean and reflected the immense spaces around him as if they were a microcosm of the mysterious sea." Parker, aware of mystery, is open to the power of grace. Confronted with mystery, Sarah Ruth closes her heart. After raising welts on the face of the Christ tattooed on her husband's back and driving him out of the house, she looks out of the window at him sobbing against a tree, and "her eyes hardened still more." Parker had thought that his wife would like his tattoo because "she can't say she don't like the looks of God." But his wife has a narrow conception of Divinity. With her enraged assertion that "God don't look like that! . . . He don't *look*. . . . He's a spirit. No man shall see his face," she cuts herself off from grace.

The lesser mysteries of Parker's attraction to tattoos and to his wife coalesce in a greater one which leads to his choice of a tattoo to please her: the face of a Byzantine Christ "with all-demanding eyes." While baling hay in a field "cleared save for one enormous old tree standing in the middle of it," Parker's attention is concentrated on a design for his back. He crashes into the tree and is hurled from the tractor before it bursts into flames.

> The first thing Parker saw were his shoes, quickly being eaten
> by the fire; one was caught under the tractor, the other was
> some distance away, burning by itself. He was not in them.
> He could feel the hot breath of the burning tree on his face.
> He scrambled backwards, still sitting, his eyes cavernous, and
> if he had known how to cross himself he would have done it.

One who is familiar with biblical symbolism will recognize the
signs of God's call to Moses to be his spokesman: the burning
bush and the baring of the feet. Parker does not hear the voice
of God as Moses did; he knows only "that there had been a great
change in his life, a leap forward [Voegelin's "leap in being"]
into a worse unknown, and that there was nothing he could do
about it." He races to the city to the tattoo artist's shop and flips
through the pages of a religious art book, past the "up-t-date"
pictures of Christ until "on one of the pages a pair of eyes
glanced at him swiftly."

> Parker sped on, then stopped. His heart too appeared to cut
> off; there was absolute silence. It said as plainly as if silence
> were a language itself, GO BACK.

Attracted by the eyes of Christ, under whose gaze he felt "as
transparent as the wing of a fly," Parker has that Byzantine face
tattooed in brilliant blocks of color on his back. Having done
this, he knows that "the eyes that were now forever on his back
were eyes to be obeyed."

Flannery O'Connor revivifies the scriptural dictum that a
prophet is not accepted in his own country when she describes
the reception of the Christ-bearing Parker at a favorite haunt of
his, a pool hall, where he is thrown out bodily, and in his own
home, where he is beaten. Although often scorned by those to
whom he gives witness, a prophet *knows* that he is chosen by
God. Using familiar symbols, O'Connor depicts this "knowledge"
of the prophet before the final scene of his suffering. Parker
returns to his home just before dawn, but his wife refuses to
admit him. She keeps asking who is there and will not accept
O. E. for an answer. Just as Parker turns from the door, dawn
breaks: "a tree of light burst over the skyline." He falls back

against the door "as if he had been pinned there by a lance." Turning back to the door, he bends down to the keyhole and whispers, "Obadiah," and "all at once he felt the light pouring through him, turning his spider web soul into a perfect arabesque of colors, a garden of trees and birds and beasts." Through "feeling," the prophet is confirmed in faith.

In the character of Parker, this story explores the imaginative faculty on which, according to St. Thomas, prophecy depends. It also exhibits O'Connor's imaginative power, which could transform the following disparate sources into an intricately wrought artifact. One of O'Connor's essays indicates that Parker's mysterious movement toward an unknown goal was suggested by her own experience. In her essay, "The King of the Birds," she states that she has "no short or reasonable answer" to the question of why she raises peacocks. As a child she had collected chickens and was always in search of an odd or unusual specimen. This collection became "a passion, a quest." Even though, as an adult, she had pheasants and quail and turkeys and geese and ducks as well as various types of hens, she said she "felt a lack." She was finally led "by instinct, not knowledge," to raising peacocks. As she stated it, "My quest, whatever it was actually for, ended with peacocks."[9] The peacock became a prime joy in her life—and a perfect symbol for her fiction. In her story, "The Displaced Person," she pictures the peacock standing "as if he had just come down from some sun-drenched height to be a vision for them all." Her mysterious attraction to strange birds that led finally to her acquisition of peacocks seems analogous to Parker's mysterious attraction to tattoos that finally led to his total absorption in Christ.

Other sources in O'Connor's library appear to be connected with the conception of this story. The idea for the great metaphor in this story may have been inspired by a book in her library about the art of tattooing. Entitled *Memoirs of a Tattooist—George Burchett*,[10] it describes intricate ways of tattooing and contains many photographs of tattoos. In it is a picture of a man clothed only in a loincloth, whose body is completely covered with garish tattoos. One can almost see what Parker saw—"a moving arabesque of color." In the story, utter silence is used as a sign of God's direction. This metaphor may have been suggested by the sentence which O'Connor marked in Karl Barth's *Evangelical Theology*: "It is a terrible thing when God keeps silence, and by keeping silence, speaks."[11] The description of Parker as a boy—"heavy and earnest, as ordinary as a loaf of bread," his undistinguished career in the navy, and his work as a merchant, "selling the fruits of the earth," all link him with Jung's "silent folk of the land." In *Modern Man in Search of a Soul*, Jung speaks of innovations never coming from above, but always from below, from the simple people of the earth. O'Connor underlined this passage:

> And it is just people of the lower social levels who follow the unconscious forces of the psyche; it is the much-derided, silent folk of the land—those who are less infected with academic prejudices than great celebrities are wont to be. All these people, looked at from above, present mostly a dreary or laughable comedy; and yet they are as impressively simple as those Galileans who were once called blessed.[12]

This story tells of a simple person who follows instinctively the promptings of his spirit. After Parker is thrown out of the pool hall, the narrator muses that "throughout his life, grumbling and sometimes cursing, often afraid, once in rapture, Parker had obeyed whatever instinct of this kind had come to him." This story seems to be an imaginative elaboration of Jung's theory.

Searing illness may have been the catalyst which effected the transmutation of these various sources into a work of fiction. Caroline Gordon tells of seeing Flannery working on "Parker's Back" during her last illness. Miss Gordon writes:

> I had the privilege of visiting Flannery O'Connor in a hospital a few weeks before her death. She told me that the doctor had forbidden her to do any work. He said that it was all right to write a little fiction, though, she added with a grin and drew a notebook out from under her pillow. She kept it there, she told me, and was trying to finish a story which she hoped to include in the volume which we both knew would be published posthumously.[13]

It seems strangely fitting that the story of a man led by mysterious ways to incarnate the Redeemer on his own body should be the final story of an author led by equally mysterious ways to make Redemption a reality in her fiction.

The story, "Revelation," introduces a new element into O'Connor's presentation of the prophet in her fiction. In this story, the prophet is conceived as one through whom God speaks, as through a mouthpiece. Mary Grace, a fat Wellesley student with acne and obvious emotional problems, becomes a prophet of salvation for Ruby Turpin, a middle-aged, complacent matron. The circumstances leading up to the prophet's revelation, which takes place in a doctor's waiting room, establish just enough motivation for the girl's revelatory statement to Mrs. Turpin and contain just enough mystery to make Mrs. Turpin know that she cannot dismiss the girl's words as the raving of a mad woman. Crowded together in the waiting room are nine people. As Mrs. Turpin looks around her, she silently groups her companions by social class and concludes that she and her husband Claud and the "pleasant lady" sitting opposite her are socially superior to all the others. These two women carry on a banal conversation about their weight, the weather, the "sunburst" clock on the wall, the difficulties of farming without adequate help, and the problem of the "niggers." Every once in a while a "white-trash woman" tries to "get a leg in" on the conversation, and Mrs. Turpin barely gives her "the edge of her attention." But when Mrs. Turpin mentions that she and Claud have, among other things, "a few hogs" on their farm, the white-trash woman becomes indignant:

> "One thang I don't want," the white-trash woman said, wiping her mouth with the back of her hand. "Hogs. Nasty stinking things, a-gruntin and a-rootin all over the place."

Mrs. Turpin insists that their hogs live in a pig parlor and implies that they are cleaner than the woman's little boy who is slouched next to her. But the woman persists in her view of hogs as hogs, no matter how swept and garnished the "parlor" they live in. During the conversation it becomes obvious to Mrs. Turpin that the surly Wellesley girl is irritated by their talk, perhaps because it distracts her from reading *Human Development*. Strangely she directs her irritation solely at Mrs. Turpin, "as if she had some very special reason for disliking her." This puzzles Mrs. Turpin, and forces her to analyze the girl's look closely:

> She [Mary Grace] was looking at her as if she had known and disliked her all her life—all of Mrs. Turpin's life, it seemed too, not just all the girl's life. Why, girl, I don't even know you, Mrs. Turpin said silently.

Forcing her attention away from the girl, Mrs. Turpin plunges into the conversation again, and when it reaches a discussion of her own good disposition, she cries out in thanksgiving for the *status quo,* "Oh thank you Jesus, Jesus, thank you!" Immediately the girl hurls her book at Mrs. Turpin, leaps across the coffee table, and tries to strangle her.

Mrs. Turpin's reaction points directly toward the affirmative ending of the story. She recognizes the prophet:

> She leaned forward until she was looking directly into the fierce brilliant eyes. There was no doubt in her mind that the girl did know her, knew her in some intense and personal way, beyond time and place and condition. "What you got to say to me?" she asked hoarsely and held her breath, waiting, as for a revelation.

Mary Grace's (the single name "Grace" would have been overly suggestive) message is psychologically linked with the previous conversation which had annoyed her, and yet it is the one statement capable of arousing Mrs. Turpin. The girl whispers, "Go back to hell where you came from, you old wart hog."

The prophet speaks. Her auditor hears her message and recognizes its supernatural origin. The rest of the story explores Mrs. Turpin's reaction to this message, a reaction which parallels that of many biblical figures who heard the prophets' declaration: "Thus saith the Lord." The reaction moves from denial to questioning to understanding. All afternoon Mrs. Turpin denies to herself the meaning of the message. But at sunset, the Negroes sitting on her husband's truck echo in their own idiom her evaluation of herself: "You the sweetest lady I know"; "Stout as she can be and sweet. Jesus satisfied with her!" In recognizing the emptiness of their praise she recognizes the falseness of her own self-evaluation. But a mighty question arises in her mind and she marches to the pig parlor with "the look of a woman going single-handed, weaponless, into battle." The location of the pig parlor is carefully described; rising on a little knoll, it is surrounded at a distance by trees. The setting is both a place where natural echoes form and the traditional O'Connor area of spiritual confrontation. While she hoses down the hogs, Mrs. Turpin voices the question on her mind: *Why me?* There were other people in the room worse than she to whom God could have spoken. By all her standards of virtue she was far ahead of the others. Becoming enraged at the obvious injustice of the revelation, she roars at the Almighty: "Who do you think you are?" and, while "the color of everything, field and crimson sky, burned for a moment with a transparent intensity," the echo returns to her clearly "like an answer from beyond the wood."

The echo of this question is a comment on Mrs. Turpin's entire life. She habitually passes judgment on others: "Who do you think you are?" To lull herself asleep, she ranks people in social classes instead of counting sheep: "Who do you think you are?" By hearing aloud the question which her thoughts and actions would implicitly evoke, she is led into gazing into the pigpen "as if through the very heart of mystery." There she sees hogs which are still hogs, even though they are hosed and housed in a pig parlor. They are still animals which, if given the opportunity, will return to "a-gruntin and a-rootin and a-groanin." Intrinsic to them is their animal nature, and, to Mrs. Turpin, gazing down on them, "they appeared to pant with a secret life." She remains looking at them, penetrating the reality of them, "as if she were absorbing some abysmal life—giving knowledge"—the knowledge of who she is. This knowledge translates itself into vision, as she sees in the sky "a vast swinging bridge extending upward from the earth through a field of living fire." In the procession of souls on the bridge she sees respectable people like herself and Claud at the end of the line, behind the "niggers" and "white-trash" and freaks and lunatics, and she realizes that, as the respectable move toward heaven, even their virtues are being burned away. Natural virtue does as much for fallen men as parlor treatment does for pigs: it does not change their intrinsic nature. Only one thing can change man: his participation in the grace of Redemption.

One may wonder—why this prophet? why this revelation? According to her own lights, Ruby Turpin was a righteous woman, filled with gratitude to God for making her as she was. Why such a jolt from on high? A passage which O'Connor marked in Claude Tresmontant's *A Study of Hebrew Thought* suggests an answer:

> History reveals God's method to us. Suffering is an element of it. But suffering in itself does not purify. It has too often and unthinkingly been said that it does. No, suffering and failure are an intervention of God meant to prevent man from *settling* in a condition that is not his vocation, which is beatitude.[14]

Because Ruby Turpin's vocation is beatitude, she is not allowed to "settle" for mere benevolence. A prophet is sent to her, and she receives the word of God.

Climactic in impact is O'Connor's imaginative portrayal, in *The Violent Bear It Away*, of the prophet's role. She uses the biblical paradigm of the call of a prophet to explore the mystery of man's freedom to accept or reject his destiny under God. That the figure of the last of the prophets, John the Baptist, overshadows the story, is indicated by the epigraph: "From the days of John the Baptist until now, the kingdom of heaven suffers violence, and the violent bear it away" (Matt. 11:12). The young protagonist, Francis Marion Tarwater, has been educated by his great-uncle to believe that the Lord has chosen him to be a prophet. Old Mason Tarwater, himself a prophet of the Lord, has been dead for half a day when the novel opens, and the boy begins at once to question the truth of the old man's teaching. In a defiant gesture, he attempts to burn his great-uncle's body instead of burying it, and he leaves the backwoods farm to seek out his only other "connection," his uncle Rayber, an atheistic schoolteacher. The novel depicts his struggle between the influences of his great-uncle and of Rayber, who tries to win the boy to his rationalistic mode of thinking. The pawn in the struggle is Bishop, Rayber's idiot son. Tarwater's great-uncle had told him that his first task would be to baptize Bishop, a task which the old man had been unable to perform. The boy simultaneously repudiates the task as being beneath the dignity of a prophet and knows that it is truly a commission of the Lord, on which his destiny rests.

Beneath the overt struggle between two contrary influences is the more intangible wrestling of young Tarwater with the Lord, a wrestling which has its locus in the boy's perception of reality. Tarwater has his own notion of the way the Lord should communicate with him; slowly he realizes that God speaks to man through the created world. He believes that he can take complete control of his life by "doing"; he learns, through his involuntary baptism of Bishop, his subjection to rape by a homosexual, and his discovery that someone else has buried old Mason, that "being done unto" is also an essential part of life. These realizations are often expressed in the humorous juxtaposition of Tarwater's "great expectations" and actual occurrences. For example, early in the story, Tarwater muses over old Mason's conviction that the Lord had chosen him, the old man's protégé, to carry on his work as a prophet:

> The Lord may send you off, he thought. There was a complete stillness over everything and the boy felt his heart begin to swell. He held his breath as if he were about to hear a voice from on high. After a few moments he heard a hen scratching beneath him under the porch.

This conflict between the way Tarwater expects the Lord to deal with him and the way God traditionally deals with his people— through the created world—centers in man's openness to reality, a theme which the entire novel explores. Tarwater instinctively feels the pull of reality but he divorces it from the providence of God:

> [Tarwater] tried . . . to keep his vision located on an even level, to see no more than what was in front of his face and to let his eyes stop at the surface of that. It was as if he were afraid that if he let his eye rest for an instant longer than was needed to place something . . . the thing would suddenly stand before him, strange and terrifying, demanding that he name it and name it justly and be judged for the name he gave it. He did all he could to avoid this threatened intimacy with creation. When the Lord's call came, he wished it to be a voice from out of a clear and empty sky, the trumpet of the Lord God Almighty, untouched by any fleshly hand or breath.

It takes violence to convince Tarwater that the Lord speaks in human voices and by human actions.

Even though he is dead when the novel opens, old Mason's presence permeates the novel. He is pictured as the boy remembers him and as Rayber recalls him. His prime quality is the freedom of his life, which derives from his absolute faith in his call from the Lord and his readiness to do his work. He "waits on the Lord" in freedom, and when the Lord has no commission for him, he goes about his "bidnis" of bootlegging liquor, farming, and raising up a prophet to follow him, the young Tarwater. He had rescued the child Tarwater from Rayber, baptized him, and taught him—as young Tarwater later recalls it—"Figures, Reading, Writing, and History begining with Adam expelled from the Garden and going on down through the presidents to Herbert Hoover and on in speculation toward the Second Coming and the Day of Judgement." He often reminds Tarwater that his life would have been very different if he—the old man—had not carried out the Lord's command to save Tarwater from his uncle Rayber. He tells the child, "Because I acted, you sit here in freedom, you sit here a rich man, knowing the Truth, in the freedom of the Lord Jesus Christ." Tarwater initially fails to understand the meaning of "freedom in the Lord." For instance, when his great-uncle takes him to the city on legal business, Tarwater is scandalized that the old man ignores what Tarwater thinks is the evident evil around him. When the prophet fails to thunder out denunciations of the city, Tarwater demands: "What kind of a prophet are you?" The old man tells him "mildly" that he is in town on business and dismisses his protests with "And I know what times I'm called and what times I ain't." He is truly free in the Lord.

The great horror of the old man's life, which he continually recounts to the boy, is his bondage in the home of Rayber. He had lived with the schoolteacher for three years, hoping to convert him, but he found that the schoolteacher's interest in him was strictly scientific: the teacher was gathering material about compulsive obsession for a paper later published in a learned journal. From Mason's point of view, the schoolteacher was trying to get the old man "inside his head"—to reduce him to a series of statistics. Mason delights in telling the boy how he

freed himself and returned later to free Tarwater. The boy intuitively recognizes his great-uncle's freedom, even in his voice,
which, as he tells the tale, would "run away from him as if it
were the freest part of his free self, and were straining ahead of
his heavy body to be off." But the boy is not willing to accept
the source of the freedom. When his uncle rejoices that they are
both free, "not inside anybody's head," Tarwater can almost
"smell his freedom, pine-scented, coming out of the woods." But
when the old man continues, "You were born into bondage and
baptized into freedom, into the death of the Lord, into the death
of the Lord Jesus Christ," the child would feel "a sullenness
creeping over him, a slow warm rising resentment that this freedom had to be connected with Jesus and that Jesus had to be the
Lord." This desire to attain his great-uncle's freedom, yet unwillingness to attain it in the Lord's way, is the central conflict in
the novel—a conflict which is wholly interior.

Rayber exhibits a clinical kind of freedom. After Old Mason's
death, Tarwater goes to Rayber to test out the upbringing which
the old man had given him by matching it against Rayber's
rationalism. But it is an uneven conflict, for the seeds of the old
man's teaching are deep in both of them. As a child, Rayber had
been taken from his home by the old man, baptized, and in-
structed in the ways of the Lord. After four days, Rayber's
father, a salesman and "prophet" of life insurance, came to claim
him, but in that time Mason had given Rayber an understanding
of a new life in God that he could never forget. The brief dialogue between Mason and young Rayber as they watch the boy's
father coming across the field to take him home points to the
life-in-Christ which baptism effects:

> "He's going to take me back with him," [Rayber] said.
> "Back with him where?" his uncle growled. "He ain't got
> any place to take you back to."
> "He can't take me back with him?"
> "Not where you were before."
> "He can't take me back to town?"
> "I never said nothing about town," his uncle said.

Even after he had learned to distrust and then repudiate the old
man's doctrine, Rayber could never return to where he was

before. He could only effect a compromise. To screen spiritual reality out of his mind, he asserted rigid ascetic discipline over himself. "He did not look at anything too long." One central scene in the novel shows Rayber breaking this resolution. Ironically, it also shows the only instance of Tarwater's being open to his uncle Rayber's influence. Yet neither suspects the secret thoughts of the other. Tarwater slips out of the house one night to attend a revival service featuring the "Carmodys for Christ," and Rayber surreptitiously follows him. The boy enters the pentecostal tabernacle to hear Lucette, the child missionary, preach, and Rayber peers through a window to watch Tarwater's reaction. But Rayber's attention is drawn instead to the stage, where the Carmodys talk about their missionary life and introduce their daughter, Lucette. The child's words force Rayber's mind back to his own childhood, to his deep absorption in spiritual reality, and to his repudiation of it. He sees Lucette as a child captive as he had been, "cursed with believing" that the spiritual world is a real world. He longs to save her as he saved himself and hopes to save Tarwater. As his heart goes out to her in pity and love, his eyes speak to her a message of "salvation." She reads that message according to her view of reality and calls out, "I see a damned soul before my eyes." Rayber quickly drops from sight, and obliterates her words by turning off his hearing aid, but her last words—words which Tarwater must also hear—are "Be saved in the Lord's fire or perish in your own." Rayber's reaction to his own weakness is one of loathing for Tarwater, who has implicated him in this self-betrayal, and of a nameless fury, which "seemed to be stirring from buried depths that had lain quiet for years and to be working upward, closer and closer toward the slender roots of his peace." Tarwater also has a strong reaction to the child's message that one must "know" Christ now by accepting his will, which is "plain as the winter," if one is to know him when he comes in glory. He bursts forth from the tabernacle, "his face strangely mobile as if successive layers of shock were settling on it to form a new expression." Everything about Tarwater indicates that he is ready to capitulate to Rayber's way of controlling spiritual reality by circumscribing his life. He raises his arm to greet Rayber; his attitude betokens "relief amounting to rescue"; his eyes are "submissive." He walks slightly behind Rayber (through the previous days, he was always a pace ahead of Rayber as they explored the city), and when they arrive home, he lingers at the door of Rayber's room "as if waiting for an invitation to enter." But Rayber misses all these signs; deafness and fury dull his perception. The next morning it is too late; "Tarwater's face had hardened again." Both Rayber and Tarwater reject the influence of the child missionary, whose message is grace for one and temptation for the other.

Those portions of the novel that detail Rayber's efforts to win Tarwater to his atheistic rationalism show clearly Rayber's own inner struggle. The external conflict between uncle and nephew masks a more subtle interior conflict. Rayber buys the boy new clothes; Tarwater refuses to wear them. Rayber takes him all over the city to show him what the world offers; Tarwater remains unimpressed. Rayber tries to find out his academic ability by giving him a disguised test; Tarwater sees through the subterfuge immediately and spits out, "And I ain't taking no test." The scene in the park moves from this overt conflict to each character's inner one: Rayber wrestles with the uncontrollable feeling of love for his idiot son which overcomes his rationalism at times, and Tarwater battles the Lord's summons to him to baptize Bishop. The three pause in the park, and Rayber takes Bishop on his lap to tie his shoes. After the shoes are tied, he holds him there and "without warning his hated love gripped him and held him in a vise." Then Christ's paradigmatic agony in the garden is re-enacted:

> [Rayber's] forehead became beady with sweat; he looked as if he might have been nailed to the bench. He knew that if he could once conquer this pain, face it and with a supreme effort of his will refuse to feel it, he would be a free man. He held Bishop rigidly. Although the child started the pain, he also limited it. . . .

Seeing only Rayber's tenderness and being unaware of his agony, Tarwater jeers at his care of the idiot, and they continue their walk through the park. Tarwater's own re-enactment of that same paradigmatic agony occurs when he watches Bishop climb into a shallow pool at the base of a park fountain and knows that the hour has come for him to baptize the boy. Unwilling to do what he considers a useless act—he thinks it would be as much use to baptize a dog—Tarwater nevertheless moves toward the child to baptize him. At the final instant, Rayber realizes his intent and snatches the child out of the pool. It becomes clear to Rayber then that Bishop is the key to Tarwater's future, even as the child is the center of his own life. He realizes that old Mason has commissioned Tarwater to baptize Bishop as a symbol of the boy's acceptance of God's will in his life. An idiot child, one whom Rayber designates as "an X, signifying the general hideousness of fate," is the matrix of both their destinies.

Tarwater's decision to embrace the life which God has destined for him is hastened by violence, both the violence which he perpetrates in drowning Bishop and the homosexual violence which is done to him. In none of Flannery O'Connor's fiction is her belief in the power of violence to return one to reality more forcefully demonstrated. In the drowning of Bishop and the rape of Tarwater by a stranger, she makes concrete the spiritual power of violence which, in both these instances, brings good out of evil. Emmanuel Mounier explains philosophically the power of violence in a chapter on confrontation in his book, *Personalism*. O'Connor marked these lines, which follow an allusion to Jacob's wrestling with the angel to gain his blessing:

> It is difficult, even in philosophizing, to manage the language of love with discretion, especially in the presence of sensitive souls who feel an invincible repugnance against allowing any place or any value to use of force. What do they understand of Gandhi's cry, "I would run the risk of violence a thousand times rather than permit the emasculation of a whole race." Love is a struggle; life is a struggle against death; spiritual life is a struggle against the inertia of matter and the sloth of the body. The person attains self-consciousness, not through some ecstacy, but by force of mortal combat; and force is one of its principal attributes. Not the brute force of mere power and aggression, in which man forsakes his own action and imitates the behaviour of matter; but human force, which is at once internal and efficacious, spiritual and manifest.[15]

In the margin of these lines, O'Connor wrote, "the violent bear it away." Tarwater comes to his own "self-consciousness" as, standing in the lake at Cherokee, he holds the struggling Bishop under the water; it is this "self-consciousness" which compels him (in the deep, spiritual—as opposed to clinical—meaning of that verb) to "spill into the water" the words of baptism. But even after this experience Tarwater is still unsure of himself and of his mission. His doubt and insecurity become evident as he tells the truck driver who gives him a lift what he has just done. The boy demeans the efficacy of the baptism and insists that he acted directly against the Lord's command by drowning Bishop. "I had to prove that I wasn't no prophet and I proved it." He thinks the words of baptism were merely an accident. Psychologically this explanation is convincing to Tarwater because he believes himself to be a "doer." Throughout the novel he taunts Rayber, the reasoner, with the assertion, "I can act. I can make things happen." By his murderous act, he has indicated his "no" to the Lord's command; this act outweighs any religious words. But through the sadistic assault of the violet-eyed stranger on him the young boy learns that he cannot control his destiny single-handedly. He learns that being acted upon, as well as acting, is an intrinsic part of living. His passivity in the violent evil that is perpetrated on him renders that evil no less real, just as his willing only subconsciously the words of baptism in no way negates their reality. Like the Misfit, Tarwater attempts to make his decision for or against the Lord "without homage." The rape recalls him to the reality of his creaturehood.

Even though the novel illuminates the value of violence in making man face reality, the final sign of the Lord's seal upon Tarwater is the sign of love. The first sentence of the novel reads: "Francis Marion Tarwater's uncle had been dead for only half a day when the boy got too drunk to finish digging his grave and a Negro named Buford Munson, who had come to get a jug filled, had to finish it and drag the body from the breakfast table where it was still sitting and bury it in a decent and Christian way, with the sign of its Saviour at the head of the grave and enough dirt on top to keep the dogs from digging it up." The novel is so constructed that Tarwater believes throughout that he has burned his uncle's body. He thinks he has given this definite sign of his rebellion against the designs of the Lord which the old man had communicated to him. He also believes that his great-uncle's claim to be a prophet has been weakened by the fact that he was not buried in a manner befitting a prophet; the boy had "done" his first "no" by burning him instead of burying him. When Tarwater returns to Powderhead to live out his denial, he expects to find old Mason's ashes scattered to the winds, "the sign of the broken covenant." Instead, he finds "a newly mounded grave," with a rough cross at its head, and he knows that the Lord's covenant with Mason is still intact because of the selfless concern of an old Negro. Even though violence has prepared him to know and accept his destiny, it is love which convinces him. As he stares down at the cross on the grave, his hands open "stiffly as if he were dropping something he had been clutching all his life." And when the commission of God rings in his ear, it is not the "speed of justice" that he is commanded to preach, as was his great-uncle; Tarwater is appointed to warn God's people of "the terrible speed of mercy." The merciful act of Buford Munson, rather than "wheels of fire in the eyes of unearthly beasts," is for Tarwater the definitive sign of his election.

Rayber's struggle between the "freedom" he has attained by denying everything which his intellect cannot grasp and the freedom of the sons of God to which he has been called has an ambiguous end. One can read this conflict in his eyes, which had "a peculiar look—like something human trapped in a switch box." Rayber's dependence on eyeglasses and on his hearing aid (the old man had shot him in the ear when he attempted to reclaim Tarwater) suggests the technological screen between himself and the world around him. Rayber expresses his idea of freedom when he says about the child Tarwater: "This one is going to be brought up to expect exactly what he can do for himself. He's going to be his own saviour. He's going to be free." The schoolteacher's hard-won freedom is subject to only one irrational influence—his love for his idiot child, Bishop. With no warning, at times a strong sense of benevolent love would come "rushing from some inexplicable part of himself" and overwhelm him. Anything, "anything he looked at too long," could bring it on, and the only way he could contain its powerful surge was to center this irrational love in Bishop. O'Connor communicates this idea by showing Bishop to be symbolically a part of Rayber's person. When Tarwater comes to Rayber's home, he sees the idiot child standing behind his father, and he knows "with a terrible certainty sunk in despair that he was expected to baptize the child he saw and begin the life his great-uncle had prepared him for." He shouts his protest, "Git!" to the child, who, frightened, clings to his father. Rayber takes the child on his shoulder, and, in Tarwater's eyes, they become one:

> The boy had a vision of the schoolteacher and his child as inseparably joined. The schoolteacher's face was red and pained. The child might have been a deformed part of himself that had been accidentally revealed.

This unity is communicated from Rayber's point of view when, later in the story, Bishop leans against his father's side, and, "absently, Rayber put his hand on the little boy's ear and rubbed it gingerly, his fingers tingling as if they touched the sensitive scar of some old wound." If the child is symbolic of one part of Rayber's nature, the affective part, it is significant that he is an idiot, for the entire story communicates the belief that love is not subject to reason; it reaches beyond reason to supernatural faith. Rayber's conflict between living a full life and living a strictly rational life comes to a climax when, at Cherokee Lodge, a run-down lake resort, he hears Bishop's cry and knows that Tarwater is drowning the boy. Long before, when he had attempted to drown the boy himself, he had reasoned out his position. If he did not have Bishop on whom to focus his "terrifying love," then he would be forced to communicate it to everyone; then "the whole world would become his idiot child." The only alternative to that would be to "resist feeling anything at all, thinking anything at all"; to "anesthetize his life." However, when Bishop is drowned, he has no choice. He stands "waiting for the raging pain . . . to begin, so that he could ignore it," but it does not come. He feels nothing. The affective part of his nature is irrevocably lost when Bishop dies. Tarwater, the prophet who was destined to "burn [his] eyes clean," has done just that. The fire is over. Life is over. If, as he had imagined, "to feel nothing was peace," he has a lifetime of that "peace" ahead of him. The novel leaves him "collapsed" in that deadening knowledge.

Just as O'Connor "makes visible" the inner tension in Rayber by externalizing one area of his divided self in Bishop, so also she gives the conflict in Tarwater a sensible—although invisible —symbolic form. Tarwater's call to embrace his destiny is a hunger in him that cannot be satisfied by food; it is a silence which surrounds and settles upon him; it is an invisible country, the borders of which he is constantly encountering. By her symbolic use of hunger, silence, and spiritual terrain, Flannery O'Connor explores the great mystery of man's life: the mystery of human freedom. Against Rayber's clinical analysis of Tarwater's "obsessive compulsion" are arraigned symbolic expressions of man's knowledge of his destiny. The three symbols are woven throughout the narrative. Mysterious hunger grips the boy as he leaves Powderhead; implacable silence surrounds him as he stands at Rayber's door; when he steps over his uncle's threshold, a country he does not wish to enter lies ahead of every step. As the novel progresses, the symbols unite. His hunger grows until it becomes "an insistent silent force inside him, a silence akin to the silence outside." That silence outside is "a strange waiting silence. It seemed to lie all around him like an invisible country whose borders he was always on the edge of." When he attempts to satisfy his hunger by eating ravenously, the food seems to sink "like a leaden column inside him and to be pushed back at the same time by the hunger it had intruded upon." After he attempts to break the silence by the thunder of his *doing* "no," he sees in the depths of a well two "silent serene eyes," the eyes of Bishop, gazing implacably at him. After Tarwater embraces the destiny which alone can free him, the three symbols of his vocation unite to confirm his faith in his destiny:

He felt his hunger no longer as a pain but as a tide. He felt it rising in himself through time and darkness, rising through the centuries, and he knew that it rose in a line of men whose lives were chosen to sustain it, who would wander in the world, strangers from that violent country where the silence is never broken except to shout the truth.

Similarly, Flannery O'Connor gives symbolic expression in *The Violent Bear It Away* to the activities of the devil—himself a believer in violence. Speaking of the role that the devil plays in her fiction, she said:

From my own experience in trying to make stories "work," I have discovered that what is needed is an action that is totally unexpected, yet totally believable, and I have found that, for me, this is always an action which indicates that grace has been offered. And frequently it is an action in which the devil has been the unwilling instrument of grace. This is not a piece of knowledge that I consciously put into my stories; it is a discovery that I get out of them.

I have found, in short, from reading my own writing, that my subject in fiction is the action of grace in territory held largely by the devil.[16]

The devil in the story is the "stranger," sometimes called "friend," who carries on a mental dialogue with Tarwater. The philosophical basis of the voice of the "stranger" may well be this passage which O'Connor marked in Emmanuel Mounier's *The Character of Man*:

When we say that thought is dialogue, we mean this quite strictly. We never think alone. The unspoken thought is a dialogue with someone who questions, contradicts, or spurs one on. This inner debate, however complicated and prolonged—it may last a lifetime—is quite different from rumination, which is a wandering around the same spot. Even if immobilized by crises from time to time, the inner dialogue moves towards an aim. It is, in spite of its interiorization, realistic thought. Its coherence is made of social encounters and solid experience. It has the same pattern as the elementary behaviour of thought, which is both *conversation* and *meditation*. (P. 252)

Written on a card in this book in O'Connor's hand is this sentence: "Rayber's thought has ceased to be dialogue—no voice answers him; no voice questions." Rayber has completely stifled the questioning part of his nature. In contrast, Tarwater's thought is a continual dialogue with an inner voice, sometimes "stranger," sometimes "friend." Three times in the novel the devil speaks to Tarwater from a source outside his own mind, using a human voice. It is a traditional teaching of Christian theology that temptations to evil come from three sources: the world (persons and things external to man), the flesh (man's innate frailty), and the devil (Satan).[17] This novel suggests that these three are one.

After Tarwater realized that his great-uncle was dead, he calmly finishes his breakfast, and then speaks disrespectfully to the corpse in a voice which "sounded like a stranger's voice, as if the death had changed him instead of his great-uncle." Typical of the devil's method, the stranger's first counsel is to do good. While Tarwater thinks about moving a fence before he buries the old man, the stranger's "disagreeable" voice tells him to "bury him first and get it over with." But soon the stranger begins to insinuate that the boy's uncle wouldn't go to this bother, that Tarwater is a fool to believe the old man's teaching, that the Lord is not at all concerned about his prophet-elect. When the stranger suggests that there are two directions which the boy must choose between, Tarwater mutters "Jesus or the devil." The stranger contradicts him:

No no no, the stranger said, there ain't no such thing as a devil. I can tell you from my own self-experience. I know that for a fact. It ain't Jesus or the devil. It's Jesus or *you*.

Flannery O'Connor once quoted Baudelaire's statement that Satan's cleverest wile is to convince people that he doesn't exist.[18] In this sequence the devil carefully leads Tarwater to think of his rebellion against the Lord's command as self-assertion, as freedom: Jesus or you. During the dialogue, the stranger takes shape in Tarwater's mind. His face was "sharp and friendly and wise, shadowed under a stiff broad-brimmed panama hat that obscured the color of his eyes." Tarwater began to feel that he was "just now meeting himself." With the soft words, "Moderation never hurt no one," the stranger approved of Tarwater's drinking his great-uncle's corn liquor. Once the boy was drunk, he did not hear the voice of the stranger, but set about on his own to burn the shack with his great-uncle in it.

Throughout the novel, the stranger speaks with Tarwater until, at the end, the boy expels him with a burning torch. Three times in the story he takes flesh and becomes a person whom Tarwater encounters; a thread of description identifies him with the voice in Tarwater's mind. Meeks, the copper-flue salesman who gives Tarwater a ride to the city, instructs him in the wisdom of the world. Work hard and love your neighbor for whatever you can get out of him are Meeks's two great commandments. That he personifies the devil is suggested by his sharp face and broad-brimmed stiff gray hat, and his being referred to as "the stranger." In the park scene later in the novel, after Tarwater has almost yielded to his desire to baptize Bishop, he walks deep into the woods and sits on a bench near a man "of a generally gray appearance." A description of the man indicates a physical link with Meeks:

"Be like me, young fellow," the stranger said, "don't let no jackasses tell you what to do." He was grinning wisely and his eyes held a malevolent promise of unwanted friendship. His voice sounded familiar but his appearance was as unpleasant as a stain.

The homosexual who offers Tarwater a ride, drugs him, and rapes him is the devil in his most chilling guise. A "pale, lean, old-looking young man with deep hollows under his cheekbones," he wore a "lavender shirt and a thin black suit and a panama hat." After the shock of this attack, Tarwater shudders "convulsively" when he perceives the stranger's voice in his mind again. He is standing at a forked tree, looking down at Powderhead, when he senses the evil one. "The presence was as pervasive as an odor, a warm sweet body of air encircling him, a violet shadow hanging around his shoulders." The boy makes a torch and lights the brush until he has made "a rising wall of fire between him and the grinning presence. He glared through the flames and his spirits rose as he saw that his adversary would soon be consumed in a roaring blaze." The burning out of evil which occurs physically in this scene occurs spiritually in the last scene, as Tarwater gazes down on the grave of the old prophet. The Negro, Buford, watches the boy's "strange spent face":

> The skin across it tightened . . . and the eyes, lifting beyond the grave, appeared to see something coming in the distance. Buford turned his head. The darkening field behind him stretched downward toward the woods. When he looked back again, the boy's vision seemed to pierce the very air. The Negro trembled and felt suddenly a pressure on him too great to bear. He sensed it as a burning in the atmosphere. His nostrils twitched.

The Negro's sensitiveness to spiritual reality allows him to recognize what he sensed as "a burning in the atmosphere," the final interior purification of the prophet-elect. Old Tarwater had described his own purification to the boy in terms of fire. As a neophyte prophet, the old man had announced the world's destruction by fire, unaware that the destruction of his own pride would have to come first. It seemed that his prophecy was being fulfilled when "one morning, he saw to his joy a finger of fire coming out of [the sun] and before he could turn, before he could shout, the finger had touched him and the destruction he had been waiting for had fallen into his own brain and his own body. His own blood had been burned dry and not the blood of the world."

The stranger's inability to read Tarwater's mind (an actual limitation of the devil's power, according to theologians) is made clear in one scene which is presented twice in the novel. The episode in the park in which Tarwater, inspired, goes forward to baptize Bishop and Rayber snatches him from the pool has a different meaning for each participant. The first time the scene is presented, only Tarwater's actions are described, and Rayber concludes from these that the boy has a compulsion to baptize Bishop which nothing but some shock can eliminate. The same scene is represented, later, in Tarwater's mind. The stranger had been pressing on him the need of a definite sign from God, and Tarwater, after his unsettling experience at the pentecostal tabernacle, demands a sign from the Lord. The next day he feels the presence of mystery as he enters the park, and the burst of sunlight on the child in the pool draws him irresist-

ibly to the pool's edge to baptize Bishop. After Rayber snatches
the child from the water, Tarwater leans over the pool and stares
at his own silent, starved eyes.

I wasn't going to baptize him, he said, flinging the silent words
at the silent face. I'd drown him first.

Drown him then, the face appeared to say. That this suggestion comes straight from his own heart is made clear when the
voice of the evil spirit comments that the sun falling on a dimwit
is not an acceptable sign. The stranger is unaware of the new
temptation which has entered Tarwater's heart. After Tarwater
manifests this new possibility, the stranger furthers the temptation: "water is made for more than one thing. . . . Don't you
have to do something at last, one thing to prove you ain't going
to do another?"

Tarwater's freedom of choice in dealing with Bishop is drama-
tized on the stairway of the Cherokee Lodge soon after Rayber
brings the two boys to the lake resort. The proprietress chides
Tarwater for his callous treatment of Bishop in a tone which
indicates that she believes the child is a holy being. This is a
new idea for Tarwater; he has considered Bishop an animal, even
likening him to a hog. Because he judges Bishop to be worthless,
he scoffs at the Lord's command to baptize him. The intimation
that the child could have some intrinsic worth causes Tarwater
to look directly at Bishop for the first time.

He seemed to see the little boy and nothing else, no air around
him, no room, no nothing, as if his gaze had slipped and fallen
into the center of the child's eyes and was still falling down
and down and down.

Bishop precedes him to the stairway, and, halfway up, he turns,
squats, and puts his feet up for Tarwater to tie his shoes. The
boy bends and ties them. In the entire novel this is his only act
of kindness to another. The woman calls to Tarwater as he
finishes this task. "His eyes as they turned and looked down at
her were the color of the lake just before dark when the last
daylight has faded and the moon has not risen yet, and for an
instant she thought she saw something fleeing across the surface
of them, a lost light that came from nowhere and vanished into

nothing." His eyes reveal that he has discerned another way of reconciling his prophetic destiny and his "absurd" initial task of baptizing an idiot: to view Bishop as a human being worthy of human love and divine attention. He rejects this alternative and can then look steadily at Bishop because he has decided to drown him. In the design of the novel it is fitting that both Rayber, who considers Bishop a horrible mistake of nature, and Tarwater, who considers him unworthy of a prophet's attention, are overwhelmed with love for the child when each performs the humble service of tying his shoes.

Through Rayber's dream, Flannery O'Connor presents symbolically the theme of the novel. After his evening of following Tarwater through the city streets and alleys to the pentecostal tabernacle, Rayber dreams that he is chasing Tarwater "through an interminable alley that twisted suddenly back on itself and reversed the roles of pursuer and pursued." In the dream, the boy overtakes him, gives him a thunderous blow on the head, and disappears. Besides foreshadowing the end of the novel, this dream suggests that Rayber realizes that old Mason's teaching is pursuing him again in the person of young Tarwater. Rayber was fourteen when he deliberately closed his eyes to the life of the spirit which his uncle had shown him and returned to Powderhead to shout his denial to the old man. Tarwater is fourteen, and Rayber knows that he is facing the same decision. Rayber's struggle is not only to convince the boy to choose *his* way; it is also to remain convinced of the wisdom of his choice. The old man is present again to Rayber in the person of the boy whom he had raised. At various times, Rayber shows by a barely perceptible physical movement that a longing "like an undertow in his blood [is] dragging him backwards to what he knew to be madness." The novel demonstrates his freedom to resist this "undertow," just as it demonstrates Tarwater's freedom to accept it.

Basic to the validity of the central conflict is the question of Tarwater's freedom. Rayber's strictly clinical diagnosis of Tarwater's conflict might suggest that the boy is not truly free to reject his vocation. In a letter to Winifred McCarthy, O'Connor answers such an objection:

Tarwater is certainly free and meant to be; if he appears to have a compulsion to be a prophet, I can only insist that in this compulsion there is the mystery of God's will for him, and that it is not a compulsion in the clinical sense.[18]

In the novel, O'Connor suggests this mystery of God's will through the metaphor of blood. In a strange amalgam of mystery and reason, Rayber formulates the problem:

> The affliction was in the family. It lay hidden in the line of blood that touched them, flowing from some ancient source, some desert prophet or pole-sitter, until, its power unabated, it appeared in the old man and him, and, he surmised, in the boy. Those it touched were condemned to fight it constantly or be ruled by it. The old man had been ruled by it. He, at the cost of a full life, staved it off. What the boy would do hung in the balance.

These two all-or-nothing positions mark extreme reactions to spiritual reality. But through these extremes, Flannery O'Connor depicts intensity of belief in a manner which accords with her talent. In a letter to a friend, she explains why backwoods prophets are key characters in her fiction:

> ... I can write about Protestant believers better than Catholic believers—because they express their belief in diverse kinds of dramatic action which is obvious enough for me to catch. I can't write about anything subtle. Another thing, a prophet is a man apart. He is not typical of a group. Old Tarwater is not typical of the Southern Baptist, or the Southern Methodist. Essentially he's a crypto-Catholic. When you leave a man alone with his Bible and the Holy Ghost inspires him, he's going to be a Catholic one way or another, even though he knows nothing about the visible Church. His kind of Christianity may not be socially desirable but it will be real in the sight of God.[19]

Both the actuality of Christian belief and the truth of man's freedom to accept or reject such belief are illuminated starkly in this tale of prophets and their descendants.

The final story explored in this study demonstrates, perhaps better than any of the other works, that O'Connor is herself a

prophet of reality. In "The Displaced Person," one sees evidence
of the kind of prophecy that O'Connor attributed to the novelist:

> The writer's gaze has to extend beyond the surface, beyond
> mere problems, until it touches the realm of mystery which is
> the concern of prophets. True prophecy in the novelist's case
> is a matter of seeing near things with their extensions of mean-
> ing and thus of seeing far things close up.[20]

The "near" situation which this story explores is the disruption of
normal farm and social life which a displaced person from Po-
land, Mr. Guizac, causes at Mrs. McIntyre's farm. Mechanically
inclined, hard-working, and thrifty, he brings such new prosperity to the farm that Mrs. McIntyre exclaims with gratitude,
"That man is my salvation!" But he displays a single-mindedness
in the work which must be done; he does not adjust to the lazy,
thieving ways of the Negroes nor condone the slovenly habits of
the white dairyman, Mr. Shortley. He does not speak the language of his new country nor understand its social customs.
Eventually the prosperity which he brings to the farm has its own
price: the Shortleys leave to keep from being fired; Mrs. Shortley
dies from a heart attack caused by their sudden departure; and
the Negroes become sullen. Mrs. McIntyre herself turns against
the Pole when she learns that he has promised his sixteen-year-old
cousin in marriage to Sulk, a half-witted Negro, if Sulk pays half
of her fare from the refugee camp in which she has been living.
When she discovers this arrangement, Mrs. McIntyre is convinced
that the man whom she termed a "miracle" has turned into a
"monster." From that time on, her perspective changes. Mr.
Guizac's virtues become faults. She wants desperately to get rid
of him, but lacks the courage to fire him. On a chill autumn
day, she and Mr. Shortley and Sulk watch the displaced person
as he lies on the ground fixing a machine; they fail to warn him
that the brake on a nearby tractor has slipped, and the three,
with a look "that froze them in collusion forever," watch the
tractor crush him to death.

Such is the "near" situation. That it will have "extensions of
meaning" is indicated by the description of the peacock which
opens the story. The peacock's tail, "glittering green-gold and

blue in the sunlight . . . flowed out on either side like a floating train and his head on the long blue reed-like neck was drawn back as if his attention were fixed in the distance on something no one else could see." Throughout the story the displaced person suggests the divine displacement, the Incarnation; and the peacock suggests the glory of spiritual reality. In a perceptive analysis of this story, Robert Fitzgerald says of the peacock: "An unpredictable splendor, a map of the universe, doted upon by the priest, barely seen by everyone else: this is a metaphor, surely, for God's order and God's grace."[21] One is tempted to make a direct analogy between the story and its significance, but Flannery O'Connor does not write allegory. She calls herself "a realist of distances," and she displays that realism here. In its extended meaning, "The Displaced Person" suggests man's alienation from his true country—the supernatural realm; symbolically the story unites the historical coming of Christ in his humanity and his final coming in glory at the end of time.

This union is suggested in a scene in which the priest who arranged for the Guizac family to come to America is listening to Mrs. McIntyre's complaints about the displaced person. Just as the unpleasant conversation is ending, the priest sees the peacock. Gazing at the "tiers of small pregnant suns float[ing] in a green-gold haze," the priest murmurs, "Christ will come like that," as he envisions the glory of Christ's coming at the end of time. Then, seconds later, he murmurs, "the Transfiguration," recalling the scriptural account of Christ's being transfigured in glory once during his earthly life. While his mind is filled with Christ's glorification, Mrs. McIntyre has been defending her intention to dismiss Mr. Guizac. As the cock lowers his tail, she repeats her previous sentence about the displaced person: "He didn't have to come in the first place." Still caught up in his own thoughts, the priest's mind moves from the glory of Christ's divinity to the grace of his humanity, and he replies, "He came to redeem us."

There are two prophets in this story, which pits the laws of the countryside against the precepts of the "true country," and each prophet is overtaken suddenly by death. Mrs. Shortley, the "giant wife of the countryside," suffers a fatal heart attack; Mr. Guizac is, in effect, murdered by his employer and her two farm hands. The first, goaded by fear and ignorance, makes herself into a prophet; the second, living in trust and innocence, becomes an unwitting prophet. Mrs. Shortley, who dies in the first part of this tripartite story, becomes Mr. Guizac's chief foe. She truly believes he is diabolical because she cannot countenance what she cannot understand. As soon as she sees him bow from the waist and kiss Mrs. McIntyre's hand, she distrusts him. In her thoughts, she connects him with the "Europe" which the newsreels have shown her: a mysterious "devil's experiment station" typified by "a small room piled high with bodies of dead naked people all in a heap, their arms and legs tangled together, a head thrust in here, a head there, a foot, a knee, a part that should have been covered up sticking out, a hand raised clutching nothing." Looking with unseeing eyes at the peacock in the tree in front of her, its tail like "a map of the universe,"[22] she experiences an "inner vision" of millions of D.P.'s replacing all the Negro farm hands. She is afraid of all foreigners, "people who were all eyes and no understanding," people whose religion had not been reformed. In fact, this "unreformed" religion becomes the basis of her fear. She pictures the priest as an emissary of the devil, perhaps the devil himself. Fear of the unknown drives her to her Bible. "She pored over the Apocalypse and began to quote from the Prophets" and before long she has a vision, born of ignorance. (The description of her exertion while climbing a steep incline to drive home the cows indicates that her "vision" is actually a minor heart attack.) With her eyes closed she sees a blood-red figure with spinning white wheels, and she hears a voice say, "Prophesy." In a comic parody of the warnings of the Old Testament prophets, she cries in a loud voice, "The children of wicked nations will be butchered. Legs where arms should be, foot to face, ear in palm of hand. Who will remain whole? Who will remain whole? Who?" This prophecy is related to her final heart attack. As the Shortleys drive away from the farm, her vision seems to reverse itself, as if she is "looking inside" herself. She grasps her husband's elbow and her daughter's foot "as if she were trying to fit the two extra limbs onto herself." Her eyes, forced closed during her "vision," are open in death "to contemplate for the first time the tremendous frontiers of her true country."

A false prophet wedded to the countryside, Mrs. Shortley finds her "true country" in death; a true prophet whose life is conformed to spiritual reality, Mr. Guizac abides in his true country. The displaced person does not prophesy; in fact, he hardly speaks in the story. Yet he is a true prophet, one of the men "who challenge the disorder of the surrounding society with the order they experience as living in themselves," to use Voegelin's definition. Mr. Guizac evokes the hostility of the people around him because he orders his life to a reality which they cannot grasp. As Mrs. McIntyre says, "He's upset the balance around here." Only at his death does Mrs. McIntyre realize that the center of balance might not be herself. She watches the figures bending over Mr. Guizac's body—the priest, his wife, and his two children. She hears the priest murmur words that she doesn't understand and sees him put something into the crushed man's mouth. Dimly aware of an invisible reality, she "felt she was in some foreign country where the people bent over the body were natives, and she watched like a stranger while the dead man was carried away in the ambulance."

The "extensions of meaning" in this story include most of Flannery O'Connor's ideas about man's relationship to reality which the preceding chapters have explored. Both Mrs. Shortley and her husband falsify their own natures. Mrs. Shortley becomes a false prophet because she fears the mysterious reality which the displaced person has introduced into her secure world; her husband makes himself an arm of the Lord to avenge his wife's death, for which he blames the displaced person. Mrs. McIntyre is so concerned over the prosperity of her farm that she alienates herself from any other reality. As far as she is concerned, "Christ is just another D.P." She listens to the priest's talk about "when God sent his Only Begotten Son" with impatience, and finally interrupts with the statement, "I want to talk to you about something serious." The death of the displaced person has a historical and social significance as deep as its religious one. The death-dealing conflict between the European "old world" with its unreformed religion and quaint social customs and the new, brash, pragmatic American world is epitomized in the death of Mr. Guizac at the hands of a resentful white farm laborer, a sullen Negro, and a fear-filled landowner, all of whom share an intuition that the foreigner is likely to displace them. Father Flynn is childlike in his attention to reality. For him, its numinous quality is immediately evident. As soon as he arrives at the farm, he is entranced by the glory of the peacock, even with its splendid tail folded. The old priest "crept forward on tiptoe and looked down on the bird's back where the polished gold and green design began." Whenever he visits the farm he seems to have two objects in mind: to speak of spiritual reality to Mrs. McIntyre, and to see it in the natural world around him. Mrs. Shortley notices that he goes about "picking up feathers off the ground." One time, finding "two peacock feathers and four or five turkey feathers and an old brown hen feather," he "took them off with him like a bouquet"—a reminder of the grandeur with which the world is charged. Mr. Guizac, more a "presence" than an actor in the story, is a prophet who carries with him the aura of his native country, Christianity. In "The Displaced Person," one thus sees in microcosm all of Flannery O'Connor's main themes.

That this one story contains so many O'Connor themes is both a sign of Flannery's artistry and an indication of the unity of her vision of natural and supernatural reality. She explored these same themes, concentrating on one and then another, in all her fiction. From a comment in a letter to a friend, written late in her short life, she seems to have realized that she had developed these themes as extensively as she could. With her clear gaze turned toward herself, she wrote to Sister Mariella Gable, "I've been writing for eighteen years and I've reached the point where I can't do again what I know I can do well, and the larger things that I need to do now, I doubt my capacity for doing."[23] Fourteen months later she was dead.

John Ciardi has said that a man is finally defined by what he gives his attention to. During her years of writing, Flannery O'Connor gave her attention to the visible world around her, and the spiritual life that permeates it. She said once that writing was a terrible experience (adding, cryptically, "You never know if you will finish it or it will finish you").[24] "Terrible," too, is the fiction which she wrote. Her stories cause terror or fear; they are dreadful; they elicit awe; they are extreme in degree; they are intense, severe, excessive. Only art could make such fiction beautiful; only reality could sustain such intense art. Only an artist penetrated with Christianity could use such extreme means to evoke from reality its full measure of splendor.

Notes

Chapter I

1"The Nature and Aim of Fiction," in Flannery O'Connor, *Mystery and Manners*, Occasional Prose, sel. and ed. Sally and Robert Fitzgerald (New York: Farrar, Straus and Giroux, 1969), p. 79.

2"The Fiction Writer and His Country," *Mystery and Manners*, p. 32.

3"Writing Short Stories," *Mystery and Manners*, p. 91.

4C. Ross Mullins, "Flannery O'Connor: An Interview," *Jubilee*, XI (June, 1963), 33.

5"Peabodite Reveals Strange Hobby," *Peabody Palladium* [Peabody High School Newspaper, Milledgeville, Ga.], Dec. 16, 1941.

6"The King of the Birds," *Mystery and Manners*, p. 4.

7Margaret Inman Meaders, "Flannery O'Connor: 'Literary Witch'," *The Colorado Quarterly*, X (Spring, 1962), 378.

8"Novelist and Believer," *Mystery and Manners*, p. 167.

9Frank Daniel, "Flannery O'Connor Shapes Own Capital," *Atlanta Journal and Constitution*, July 22, 1962.

10*Mystery and Manners*, p. 34.

11Betsy Lochridge, "An Afternoon with Flannery O'Connor," *Atlanta Journal and Constitution*, Nov. 1, 1959, p. 40.

12"This discovery of being bound through the senses to a particular society and a particular history, to particular sounds and a particular idiom is for the writer, wherever he may be, the beginning of a recognition that first puts his work in real, human perspective for him. He begins to learn that the imagination is not free, but bound." Flannery O'Connor, "The Role of the Catholic Novelist," *Greyfriar* [Siena College, Loudonville, N. Y.], VII (1964), 7.

13"The Novelist and Free Will," *Fresco* [University of Detroit] I (Winter, 1961), 100–101.

14"The Catholic Novelist in the Protestant South," *Mystery and Manners*, p. 193.

15(Cambridge: Harvard University Press, 1935), pp. 156–57.

16(New York: Vintage Books, 1956), p. 195.

17(New York: Pelican Books, n. d.), p. 45.

18*Georgia Education Association Journal* (March, 1960).

19"Catholic Novelists and Their Readers," *Mystery and Manners*, p. 182.

20James F. Farnham, "The Grotesque in Flannery O'Connor," *America*, CV (May 13, 1961), 277.

21"The Catholic Novelist in the Protestant South," *Mystery and Manners*, p. 204.

22(New York: Harcourt, Brace, 1933), p. 169.

23Meaders, "Flannery O'Connor," p. 385.

24Lochridge, "Afternoon with O'Connor," p. 40.

25(New York: Farrar, Straus and Giroux, 1965), p. viii.

26Tr. J. F. Scanlan (New York: Charles Scribner's Sons, 1949), p. 54.

27Quoted by James A. Tate in an unpublished essay, "A Reminiscence," in the Flannery O'Connor collection at Georgia State College, Milledgeville.

28"A belief in fixed dogma cannot fix what goes on in life or blind the believer to it. It will, of course, add a dimension to the writer's observation which many cannot, in conscience, acknowledge exists, but as long as what they *can* acknowledge is present in the work, they cannot claim that any freedom has been denied the artist. A dimension taken away is one thing, a dimension added is another; and what the Catholic writer and reader will have to remember is that the reality of the added dimension will be judged in a work of fiction by the truthfulness and wholeness of the natural events presented." "The Church and the Fiction Writer," *Mystery and Manners*, p. 150.

29"The Role of the Catholic Novelist," p. 12.

30Letter to Sister M. Kathleen Feeley, S.S.N.D., Mar. 28, 1969.

31*Christian Letters to a Post-Christian World* (Grand Rapids: William B. Eerdmans Publishing Co., 1969) pp. 79–80.

32"The King of the Birds," *Mystery and Manners*, pp. 14–15.

Chapter II

1"The Nature and Aim of Fiction," in Flannery O'Connor, *Mystery and Manners*, ed. Sally and Robert Fitzgerald (New York: Farrar, Straus and Giroux, 1969), p. 81.

2*Mystery and Manners*, p. 10.

3"Flannery O'Connor: An Interview," *Jubilee*, XI (June, 1963), 35.

4Unpublished letter to Paul Currey Steele, August 5, 1955.

5*Mystery and Manners*, p. 65.

6"Catholic Novelists and their Readers," *Mystery and Manners*, pp. 177–78.

7"The Nature and Aim of Fiction," *Mystery and Manners*, pp. 82–83.

8The book which the mother picked up from Hulga's bedroom is Martin Heidegger's *Existence and Being*. Flannery O'Connor had this book in her library, with the passage which is quoted in the story marked in pencil. The book is signed and dated 1954; the story was first published in 1955.

9"All during the story 'Good Country People' the wooden leg is growing in importance. And thus when the Bible salesman steals it, he is stealing a great deal more than the wooden leg." F. O'C. in "An Interview with Flannery O'Connor," *Censer* [College of St. Teresa, Winona, Minnesota], (Fall, 1960), p. 30.

10Title of Granville Hicks's review of *Everything That Rises Must Converge*, in *Saturday Review*, LXVIII (May 29, 1965), 23.

11Tr. Rosemary Sheed (New York: Sheed and Ward, 1958), p. 18.

12*Flannery O'Connor* [Pamphlets on American Writers, No. 54] (Minneapolis: University of Minnesota Press, 1966), p. 17.

13*Mystery and Manners*, pp. 41–42.

14*Patterns in Comparative Religion*, p. 14.

15"Playhouse of the Stars" presented it March 1, 1957, with Gene Kelly as Shiftet, Agnes Moorehead as the mother, and Janice Rule as Lucynell.

16"Writing Short Stories," *Mystery and Manners*, p. 95.

17Robert Donner, "She Writes Powerful Fiction," *Sign*, XL (March, 1961), 48.

18"Motley Special: An Interview with Flannery O'Connor," *Motley* [Spring Hill College, Mobile, Alabama], (Spring, 1959), p. 30.

19Caroline Gordon told me that Flannery was a marvelous student. When Miss Gordon advised her to read something, she read it, and knew intuitively why the suggestion was made. Other students, Miss Gordon commented, think that, when you tell them to read Flaubert, you want them to come back and tell you what is wrong with his writing.

20*Mystery and Manners*, p. 35.

21"The practical Christian, as distinguished from the academic, will find that the finale of this story allows for and implies the action of redemptive grace working for and in the three chief characters: eternal peace for the poor, bungling mother; salvation by way of protection for the congenitally deprived 'slut'; redemption through projected suffering for Thomas, the ease-enslaved son, who will never again know the comforts of home." Sister Bertrande Meyers, "Four Stories of Flannery O'Connor," *Thought*, XXXVII (Autumn, 1962), 419.

22(New York: Sheed and Ward, 1959), p. 27.

23"The Grotesque in Southern Fiction," *Mystery and Manners*, p. 43.

24*Ibid*, pp. 48–49.

25Tr. Michael Francis Gibson (New York: Desclée Company, 1960), pp. 17–18.

26(New York: Doubleday Anchor Book, n.d.), p. 41.

27Letter to Sister Kathleen Feeley, June 22, 1969.

28"Writing Short Stories," *Mystery and Manners*, p. 88.

29"In the act of writing, one sees that the way a thing is made controls and is inseparable from the whole meaning of it. The form of a story gives it meaning which any other form would change. . . ." "The Teaching of

Literature," *Mystery and Manners*, p. 129.

30"Interview with Flannery O'Connor," p. 4.

31(New York: Harcourt, Brace, 1933), p. 122.

32Tr. Grover Foley (New York: Holt, Rinehart and Winston, 1963), p. 152.

33Although Stanley Edgar Hyman asserts that "the Church is wickedly satirized in a scatterbrained and irascible old priest, blind in one eye and deaf in one ear" [*Flannery O'Connor*, p. 27] it seems more likely that the two priests, each with different limitations, exemplify the power of the Spirit to work through imperfect human agents, as it is their influence which prepares Asbury for spiritual regeneration.

34(Westminster, Md.: The Newman Press, 1955), p. 56.

35Unpublished manuscript, "A Reminiscence," in the F. O'C. collection in the library of Georgia State College at Milledgeville.

36Unpublished manuscript of speech, Georgia State College for Women, Jan. 7, 1960.

37This story is one of the author's two earliest ones. (The other, "The Capture," which appeared in *Mademoiselle*, XXVIII [November, 1948] is one of O'Connor's M.F.A. thesis stories, slightly revised.) That she considered including it in what she knew would be a posthumous collection is evident from a paper which I found in one of her books, listing the first six stories in the order in which they appear in *Everything That Rises Must Converge*, and as the seventh, "The Partridge Festival." This list may have been made about 1962, before Miss O'Connor had written "Revelation," "Parker's Back," and "Judgement Day," which subsequently became the last three stories in the collection.

Leon Driskell makes a good case, in "Parker's Back vs. The Partridge Festival: Flannery O'Connor's Critical Choice" [*The Georgia Review*, XXI (Winter, 1967), 476–490] for O'Connor's excluding this story because its bleak doctrinal insistence upon carnality would have marred the thematic pattern of the collection. However, I interpret the story differently, and can see no intrinsic reason for its omission.

38Tr. A. V. Littledale (Baltimore, Md.: Helicon Press, 1959), p. 16.

Chapter III

1Ed. Anton Pegis (New York: Random House, 1948), p. xxiv.

2(New York: Vintage Books, 1945), Vol. II, p. 4.

3Gerard E. Sherry, "An Interview with Flannery O'Connor," *The Critic*, XXI (June/July, 1963), 29.

4(Baton Rouge: Louisiana State University Press, 1956), p. 273.

5(New York: Meridian Books, 1960), p. 123.

6"Novelist and Believer," in Flannery O'Connor, *Mystery and Manners*, ed. Sally and Robert Fitzgerald (New York: Farrar, Straus and Giroux, 1969), pp. 159–161.

7"The Peeler," *Partisan Review*, XVI (December, 1949), 1197.

8"On Her Own Work," *Mystery and Manners,* p. 116.

9Letter to William Sessions in *The Added Dimension,* ed. Melvin J. Friedman and Lewis A. Lawson (New York: Fordham University Press, 1966), p. 223.

10(New York: Doubleday Anchor Book, n. d.), p. x.

11"Introduction to Second Edition of *Wise Blood," Mystery and Manners,* p. 114.

12"The Grotesque in Southern Fiction," *Mystery and Manners,* pp. 45–46.

13Introduction to *Everything That Rises Must Converge* (New York: Farrar, Straus and Giroux, 1965), p. xxviii.

14"On Her Own Work," *Mystery and Manners,* p. 112.

15Trans. Richard and Clara Winston (New York: Pantheon Books, 1963), p. 65.

16(New York: Harper and Row, 1957), p. 36.

Chapter IV

1C. Ross Mullins, "Flannery O'Connor: An Interview," *Jubilee,* XI (June, 1963), 35.

2Georgia State College for Women, Milledgeville, Fall, 1943, pp. 5–7, 18.

3"Introduction to *A Memoir of Mary Ann,"* in Flannery O'Connor, *Mystery and Manners,* ed. Sally and Robert Fitzgerald (New York: Farrar, Straus and Giroux, 1969).

4*Mystery and Manners,* pp. 208–209.

5(New York: Prentice-Hall, 1947), p. 110.

6"Writing Short Stories," *Mystery and Manners,* p. 104.

7Katherine Fugin, Faye Rivard and Margaret Sieh, "An Interview with Flannery O'Connor," *The Censer* [College of St. Teresa, Winona, Minnesota], (Fall, 1960), p. 30.

8Jean Marie Kann, O.S.F., "Everything That Rises Must Converge," *The Catholic World,* CXCVI (December, 1966), 157.

9"The Regional Writer," *Mystery and Manners,* p. 59.

10"Iowa City is a nice, colorless place and was quite a relief to me after 20 years of the South—I felt the absence of tension almost at once." Unpublished letter to Paul Curry Steele dated July 6, 1955.

11"The Catholic Novelist in the Protestant South," *Mystery and Manners,* p. 209.

12"Whenever I'm asked why Southern writers particularly have a penchant for writing about freaks, I say it is because we are still able to recognize one."

"I hate to think that in twenty years Southern writers too may be writing about men in gray-flannel suits and may have lost their ability to see that these gentlemen are even greater freaks than what we are writing about now." "The Grotesque in Southern Fiction," *Mystery and Manners,* p. 44 and p. 50.

13(New York: Vintage Books, 1945), Vol. II, p. 134.

14Among them are the following: Schokel's *Understanding Biblical Research,* Rowley's *Old Testament and Modern Study,* Wright's *The Bible and the Ancient Near East,* Heaney's *Faith, Reason and the Gospels,* Knox's *St.* Paul's Gospel, Van Zeller's *The Outspoken Ones,* Gelin's *Key Concepts of the Old Testament,* Guillet's *Themes of the Bible,* Danielou's *The Dead Sea Scrolls and Primitive Christianity,* McKenzie's *The Two-Edged Sword,* Daniel-Rops' *What Is the Bible,* Levie's *The Bible: Word of God in Words of Men,* and Vawter's *The Conscience of Israel.*

15(Baton Rouge: Louisiana State University Press, 1956), p. 4.

16*Mystery and Manners,* pp. 202, 203.

17"Who has a cultural education now?" was Flannery O'Connor's response to the question of why contemporary writers use so few classical allusions. Fugin, *et al.,* "Interview with O'Connor." Caroline Gordon commented that she could tell when she read Flannery's first work *(Wise Blood)* that the writer had not been educated in the classics.

18(New York: Vintage Books, 1956), p. 205.

19"The image of the South, in all its complexity, is so powerful in us [Southern writers] that it is a force which has to be encountered and engaged. The writer must wrestle with it, like Jacob with the angel, until he has extracted a blessing." "The Catholic Novelist in the Protestant South," *Mystery and Manners,* p. 198.

20Quoted in "Flannery O'Connor, A Realist of Distances," *The Added Dimension,* ed. Melvin J. Friedman and Lewis A. Lawson (New York: Fordham University Press, 1977), p. 176.

21Mullins, "Flannery O'Connor," p. 33.

22"Industrialization is what changes the culture of the South, not integration." Gerard E. Sherry, "An Interview with Flannery O'Connor," *The Critic,* XXI (June/July, 1963), 31.

23"Manners are the next best thing to Christian charity. I don't know how much pure unadulterated Christian charity can be mustered in the South, but I have confidence that the manners of both races will show through in the long run." *Ibid.*

24"Catholic Novelists and their Readers," *Mystery and Manners,* p. 175.

25(New York: Sheed and Ward, 1957), p. 40.

Chapter V

1Flannery O'Connor, *Mystery and Manners,* ed. Sally and Robert Fitzgerald (New York: Farrar, Straus and Giroux, 1969), p. 6.

2*Ibid.,* p. 80.

3(Westminster, Md.: The Newman Press, 1955), p. 38.

4Tr. Michael Francis Gibson (New York: Desclée Company, 1960), pp. 51–53.

5"On Her Own Work," *Mystery and Manners,* p. 109.

6Tr. Willard R. Trask (New York: Harper and Row, 1961), pp. 11–12.

7*A Study of Hebrew Thought,* p. 51.

8Jean Marie Kann, O.S.F., "Everything That Rises Must Converge," *The Catholic World,* CXCVI (December, 1966), 159.

9For Mr. Zuber's column, she reviewed Teilhard's *The Divine Milieu* in
1961 and *Letters From a Traveller* in 1963, Nicholas Corte's *Pierre Teilhard
de Chardin* in 1960, and Oliver Rabut's *Teilhard de Chardin* in 1961.

10(Baltimore: Helicon Press, 1959), p. 67.

11"The Church and the Fiction Writer," *Mystery and Manners*, p. 148.

12*American Scholar*, XXX (Fall, 1961), 618.

13Claude Tresmontant, *Pierre Teilhard de Chardin*, p. 43.

14(New York: Harcourt, Brace, 1933), p. 61.

15Tresmontant, *Pierre Teilhard de Chardin*, p. 44.

16"On Her Own Work," *Mystery and Manners*, p. 113.

17Tresmontant, *Pierre Teilhard de Chardin*, p. 84.

18*The Bulletin* [Georgia diocesan weekly], February 4, 1961, p. 6.

19*Ibid.*, December 23, 1961, p. 6.

20*Mystery and Manners*, pp. 204–208.

21Tresmontant, *Pierre Teilhard de Chardin*, p. 86.

22*Mystery and Manners*, p. 157.

23"The Nature and Aim of Fiction," *Mystery and Manners*, p. 84.

24Between the story's periodical publication and its inclusion in her first
collection, Flannery added the clause "even his face lightened" to the final
sentence about Nelson to emphasize his interior enlightenment.

25Quoted by Celestine Sibley in an obituary in the *Atlanta Constitution*,
August 6, 1964, p. 5.

26Quoted by Gilbert H. Muller, "The City of Woe: Flannery O'Connor's
Dantean Vision," *The Georgia Review*, XXIII (Summer, 1969), 206.

27"The Teaching of Literature," *Mystery and Manners*, pp. 131–32.

28One of the books on Flannery O'Connor's "Southern history" shelf is
C. Vann Woodward's *The Burden of Southern History*. Speaking of the industrialization of the South, Woodward says: "The symbol of innovation is
inescapable. The roar and groan and dust of it greet one on the outskirts
of every Southern town. That symbol is the bulldozer" (Baton Rouge:
Louisiana State University Press, 1960), p. 6.

29In Erich Heller's *The Disinherited Mind*, Flannery marked the following
passage which summarizes the relationship between the real and the symbolic: "An allegory, being the imaginary representation of something abstract,
is, as it were, doubly unreal; whereas the symbol, in being what it represents,
possesses a double reality" (New York: Farrar, Straus and Cudahy, 1957),
p. 210.

30*Mademoiselle*, XVIII (November, 1948), 148–49.

31The last sentence of the story employs a biblical symbolism which is
strangely unsatisfying. As the child becomes conscious of her mother's misery,
she "could just catch in the distance a few wild high shrieks of joy as if the
prophets were dancing in the fiery furnace in the circle the angel had
cleared for them." The allusion, which the title supports, recalls the incident
in the Book of Daniel when the three young men were thrown into a fiery
furnace for refusing to worship an idol, and an angel preserved them from
the flames and led them forth unharmed. Only one incident in the story

supports the allusion. When the caretaker tells the boys that Mrs. Cope owns the woods, the little one, disparaging such an idol, replies, "Man, Gawd owns them woods and her too." The boys, as do their prototypes, recognize God's sovereignty. But the allusion is not sufficiently prepared for, and the language at the story's end is not elevated enough to carry its weight of connotation. Furthermore, in this incident, fire is not God's method of purification but Nebuchadnezzar's method of punishment. Therefore, the allusion fails to enrich the story. However, the artifact possesses intrinsic richness in its exploration of modes of apprehending reality.

32Asked during a student interview whether grace leads Bevel to drown himself, Flannery replied, "Bevel hasn't reached the age of reason; therefore he can't commit suicide." Katherine Fugin, Faye Rivard and Margaret Sieh, "An Interview with Flannery O'Connor," *The Censer* [College of St. Teresa, Winona, Minnesota], (Fall, 1960), p. 28. Actually the story demonstrates the words of Pascal—"the heart has reasons that the reason knows not of."

33(New York: Farrar, Straus and Giroux, 1965), p. xiii.

34Tr. and ed. Hilda Graef (Westminster, Md.: The Newman Press, 1956), pp. 77, 78.

Chapter VI

1"Forward," *Esprit*, VIII (Winter, 1964), 2.

2*Ibid.*, p. 52.

3*The Conscience of Israel* (New York: Sheed and Ward, 1961), *passim*.

4(Baton Rouge: Louisiana State University Press, 1956).

5Voegelin, *The World of the Polis*, p. 6.

6Quoted in *The Added Dimension*, ed. Melvin J. Friedman and Lewis A. Lawson (New York: Fordham University Press, 1977), p. 167.

7Tr. James V. McGlynn, S.J. (Chicago: Henry Regnery Co., 1953), pp. 62–87.

8Tr. Cynthia Rowland (New York: Harper and Brothers, 1956), p. 246.

9Flannery O'Connor, *Mystery and Manners*, ed. Robert and Sally Fitzgerald (New York: Farrar, Straus and Giroux, 1969), p. 4.

10Compiled and edited by Peter Leighton (London: Oldbourne Press, n.d.)

11*Evangelical Theology: An Introduction*, tr. Grover Foley (New York: Holt, Rinehart and Winston, 1963), p. 136.

12(New York: Harcourt, Brace, 1933), p. 211.

13"An American Girl," in *The Added Dimension*, p. 135.

14Tr. Michael Francis Gibson (New York: Desclée Company, 1960), p. 153.

15(New York: Grove Press, 1952), p. 49.

16"On Her Own Work," *Mystery and Manners*, p. 118.

17"It is ironical that in these most evil times we should need fresh evidence of the existence of Satan, but such is the case. According to Baudelaire, the devil's greatest wile is to persuade us he does not exist. The Christian drama is meaningless without Satan, but only recently there has been considerable publicity about a dispute among Anglicans over whether the devil should be allowed to remain in their catechism. Such is the trend of the times." From

Flannery O'Connor's review of *Evidence of Satan in the Modern World* by Leon Christiani in *The Bulletin*, March 2, 1962.

[18]Quoted in "On Her Own Work," *Mystery and Manners*, p. 116.

[19]Letter to Sister Mariella Gable, O.S.B. in *Esprit*, VIII (Winter, 1964), 26–27.

[20]Quoted in "Flannery O'Connor: 'Literary Witch'," by Margaret Meaders, *Colorado Quarterly*, X (Spring, 1962), 384.

[21]"The Countryside and the True Country," *Sewanee Review*, LXX (Summer, 1962), 388.

[22]In Voegelin's *Israel and Revelation*, p. 320, the robe of the high priest is described, using quotations from Philo's *Vita Mosis*: "In its colors and ornaments the robe was 'a copy and imitation' of the universe, so that its wearer would be 'transformed from a man into the nature of the world,' that he would become an 'abbreviated cosmos.'" In the margin, O'Connor wrote: "the peacock."

[23]*Esprit*, VIII, 27.

[24]Quoted in an obituary, "Baldwin Author Claimed by Death," *Macon Telegraph*, August 4, 1964, p. 2.

Bibliography

PRIMARY SOURCES

O'Connor, Flannery. *American Scholar*, XXX (Fall, 1961), 618. Review of *The Phenomenon of Man* by Teilhard de Chardin.

————. *The Bulletin* [Georgia diocesan weekly], March 17, 1962. Review of *The Conscience of Israel* by Bruce Vawter.

————. *The Bulletin*, n.d. Review of *The Critic*, a Catholic review of Books and the Arts.

————. *The Bulletin*, Feb. 4, 1961. Review of *The Divine Milieu* by Teilhard de Chardin.

————. *The Bulletin*, March 2, 1962. Review of *Evidence of Satan in the Modern World* by Leon Christiani.

————. *The Bulletin*, Oct. 1, 1960. Review of *The Science of the Cross* by Edith Stein.

————. *The Bulletin*, Dec. 23, 1961. Review of *Teilhard de Chardin* by Oliver Rabut, O.P.

————. "The Capture," *Mademoiselle*, XXVIII (November, 1948), 148–49+.

————. *Everything That Rises Must Converge*. New York: Farrar, Straus and Giroux, 1965.

————. "Excuse Us While We Don't Apologize," *The Corinthian* [Georgia State College for Women, Milledgeville], 1945, p. 4.

————. "The Geranium." Unpublished M.F.A. thesis, University of Iowa, 1947.

————. *A Good Man Is Hard To Find*. New York: New American Library, 1956.

————. "Home of the Brave," *The Corinthian* [Georgia State College for Women, Milledgeville], Fall, 1943, pp. 5–7, 18.

————. *Mystery and Manners*, Occasional Prose, sel. and ed. Sally and Robert Fitzgerald. New York: Farrar, Straus and Giroux, 1969.

————. "The Novelist and Free Will," *Fresco* [University of Detroit], I (Winter, 1961), 100–101.

————. Original typescript of an untitled talk delivered on January 7, 1960, at Georgia State College for Women, Milledgeville.

————. "The Partridge Festival," *The Critic*, XIX (February/March, 1961), 20–23, 82–85.

————. "The Peeler," *Partisan Review*, XVI (December, 1949), 1189–1206.

————. "The Role of the Catholic Novelist," *Greyfriar* [Siena College, Loudonville, N. Y.], VII (1964), 5–12.

————. *The Southern Cross* [Savannah diocesan weekly], April 27, 1963. Review of *Letters from a Traveler* by Teilhard de Chardin.

————. *The Violent Bear It Away*. New York: New American Library, 1961.

————. *Wise Blood*. New York: Farrar, Straus and Cudahy, 1962.

SOURCE BOOKS IN FLANNERY O'CONNOR'S LIBRARY

Augustine, Saint. *Nine Sermons on the Psalms*, tr. Edmund Hill. New York: P. J. Kenedy and Sons, 1959.

Babbitt, Irving. *Rousseau and Romanticism*. New York: World Publishing Company, 1965.

Barth, Karl. *Evangelical Theology: An Introduction*, tr. Grover Foley. New York: Holt, Rinehart and Winston, 1963.

Bergson, Henri. *The World of Dreams*. New York: The Philosophical Library, 1958.

Bouyer, Louis. *The Spirit and Forms of Protestantism*, tr. A. V. Littledale. Westminster, Md.: Newman Press, 1957.

Buber, Martin. *Eclipse of God*. New York: Harper and Row, 1957.

Burchett, George. *Memoirs of a Tattooist*, ed. Peter Leighton. London: Oldbourne Press, n.d.

Carritt, E. F. (ed.). *Philosophies of Beauty*. New York: Oxford University Press, 1931.

Cecil, David. *Early Victorian Novelists*. New York: Pelican Books, n.d.

Chaine, Joseph. *God's Heralds*, tr. Brenden McGrath. New York: Joseph F. Wagner, Inc., 1954.

Chase, Richard. *The American Novel and Its Tradition*. Garden City, N. Y.: Doubleday, 1957.

Corte, Nicholas, pseud. *Pierre Teilhard de Chardin: His Life and Spirit*. New York: Macmillan Co., 1960.

Eliade, Mircea. *Patterns in Comparative Religion*, tr. Rosemary Sheed. New York: Sheed and Ward, 1958.

—————. *The Sacred and the Profane*, tr. Willard R. Trask. New York: Harper and Row, 1961.

Foerster, Norman. *Image of America*. Indiana: University of Notre Dame Press, 1962.

Foerster, Norman, *et al. Literary Scholarship*. Chapel Hill: University of North Carolina Press, 1941.

Freud, Sigmund. *Basic Writings*, tr. and ed. with an introduction by A. A. Brill. New York: Modern Library, 1938.

Gelin, Albert. *The Key Concepts of the Old Testament*, tr. George Lamb. New York: Paulist Press, 1963.

Guardini, Romano. *The Conversion of St. Augustine*, tr. Elinor Briefs. Westminster: The Newman Press, 1960.

Guitton, Jean. *The Modernity of Saint Augustine*, tr. A. V. Littledale. Baltimore, Md.: Helicon Press, 1959.

Heller, Erich. *The Disinherited Mind*. New York: Farrar, Straus and Cudahy, 1952.

Hostie, Raymond, S.J. *Religion and the Psychology of Jung*, tr. G. R. Lamb. New York: Sheed and Ward, 1957.

Hügel, Friedrich von. *Letters to a Niece*, ed. with an introduction by Gwendolen Greene. Chicago: Henry Regnery Company, 1955.

James, Henry. *The American Scene*. New York: Scribner, 1946.

—————. *Daumier: Caricaturist*. Emmaus, Pa.: Rodale Press, 1954.

—————. *The Future of the Novel*. New York: Vintage Books, 1956.

—————. *Hawthorne*. New York: Doubleday Dolphin Books, n.d.

—————. *Notebooks*, ed. F. O. Matthiessen and Kenneth B. Murdock. New York: George Braziller, Inc., 1955.

Jung, Carl G. *Modern Man in Search of a Soul*. New York: Harvest Books, Harcourt, Brace and World, 1933.

Kirk, Russell. *Beyond the Dreams of Avarice*. Chicago: Henry Regnery Company, 1956.

Lawler, Justus George. *The Christian Imagination*. Westminster, Md.: The Newman Press, 1955.

Levie, Jean, S.J. *The Bible, Word of God in Words of Men*. New York: P. J. Kenedy and Sons, 1961.

Lubac, Henri de, S.J. *Further Paradoxes*, tr. Ernest Beaumont. Westminster, Md.: The Newman Press, 1958.

Lynch, William F., S.J. *Christ and Apollo*. New York: Sheed and Ward, 1960.

————. *The Image Industries.* New York: Sheed and Ward, 1959.

Maritain, Jacques. *Art and Scholasticism with Other Essays,* tr. J. F. Scanlan. New York: Charles Scribner's Sons, 1949.

————. *Creative Intuition in Art and Poetry.* New York: Meridian Books, Inc., 1960.

Meseguer, Pedro, S.J. *The Secret of Dreams.* Westminster, Md.: The Newman Press, 1960.

Mounier, Emmanuel. *The Character of Man,* tr. Cynthia Rowland. New York: Harper and Brothers, 1956.

————. *Personalism,* tr. Philip Mairet. New York: Grove Press, 1952.

Newman, John Henry. *Grammar of Assent.* Garden City, New York: Doubleday and Co., 1955.

Pieper, Josef. *Belief and Faith,* tr. Richard and Clara Winston. New York: Pantheon Books, 1963.

Rabut, Oliver, O.P. *Teilhard de Chardin.* New York: Sheed and Ward, 1961.

Raven, Charles E. *Teilhard de Chardin, Scientist and Seer.* New York: Harper and Row, 1962.

Santayana, George. *Three Philosophical Poets.* Cambridge: Harvard University Press, 1945.

Stein, Edith. *Writings,* tr. with an introduction by Hilda Graef. Westminster, Md.: The Newman Press, 1956.

Tate, Allen (ed.). *A Southern Vanguard.* New York: Prentice-Hall, Inc., 1947.

Teilhard de Chardin, Pierre. *The Divine Milieu.* New York: Harper and Brothers, 1960.

Thomas Aquinas, Saint. *Introduction,* ed. with an introduction by Anton C. Pegis. New York: Random House, 1948.

————. *Truth,* Vol. II, tr. James V. McGlynn, S.J. Chicago: Henry Regnery Co., 1953.

Tocqueville, Alexis de. *Democracy in America,* Vol. II. New York: Vintage Books, 1945.

Tresmontant, Claude. *Pierre Teilhard de Chardin: His Thought.* Baltimore, Md.: Helicon Press, 1959.

————. *A Study of Hebrew Thought,* tr. Michael Francis Gibson. New York: Desclée Company, 1960.

Van Doren, Mark. *Nathaniel Hawthorne.* New York: Compass Books, Viking Press, n.d.

Vawter, Bruce. *The Conscience of Israel.* New York: Sheed and Ward, 1961.

Voegelin, Eric. *Order and History:* Vol. I *Israel and Revelation;* Vol.

II *The World of the Polis*; Vol. III *Plato and Aristotle.* Baton Rouge: Louisiana State University Press, 1956.

ADDITIONAL SOURCES

Alice, Sister Mary, O.P. "My Mentor, Flannery O'Connor," *Saturday Review*, XLVIII (May 29, 1965), 24–25.

"Baldwin Author Claimed by Death," *Macon Telegraph*, Aug. 4, 1964, pp. 1–2.

Boman, Thorleif. *Hebrew Thought Compared with Greek.* Philadelphia: The Westminster Press, 1960.

Daniel, Frank. "Flannery O'Connor Shapes Own Capital," *Atlanta Journal and Constitution*, July 22, 1962.

Donner, Robert. "She Writes Powerful Fiction," *The Sign*, XL (March, 1961), 46–48.

Drake, Robert. *Flannery O'Connor.* Grand Rapids, Michigan: William B. Eerdmans Publishing Co., 1966.

Driskell, Leon. "Parker's Back vs. The Partridge Festival: Flannery O'Connor's Critical Choice," *The Georgia Review*, XXI (Winter, 1967), 476–490.

————. and Joan T. Brittain. *The Eternal Crossroads: The Art of Flannery O'Connor.* Lexington: University of Kentucky Press, 1971.

Esprit, VIII (Winter, 1964) [University of Scranton, Scranton, Pa.]. Memorial edition.

Faricy, Robert L., S.J. Letter to Sister M. Kathleen Feeley, SSND, March 28, 1969.

Farnham, James F. "The Grotesque in Flannery O'Connor," *America*, CV (May 13, 1961), 277–81.

Fiedler, Leslie. *Love and Death in the American Novel.* New York: Criterion Books, 1960.

Fitzgerald, Robert. "The Countryside and the True Country," *Sewanee Review*, LXX (Summer, 1962), 380–94.

Friedman, Melvin J. and Lewis A. Lawson (eds.). *The Added Dimension: The Art and Mind of Flannery O'Connor.* New York: Fordham University Press, 1966.

Fugin, Katherine, Faye Rivard and Margaret Sieh. "An Interview with Flannery O'Connor," *The Censer* [College of St. Teresa, Winona, Minn.], (Fall, 1960), pp. 28–30.

Georgia Education Association Journal, March, 1960, n.p.

Gossett, Louise Y. *Violence in Recent Southern Fiction.* Durham, N. C.: Duke University Press, 1965.

Hendin, Josephine. *The World of Flannery O'Connor*. Bloomington: Indiana University Press, 1970.

Hicks, Granville. "A Cold, Hard Look at Humankind," *Saturday Review*, XLVIII (May 29, 1965), 23–24.

Hyman, Stanley Edgar. *Flannery O'Connor* [Pamphlets on American Writers No. 54]. Minneapolis: University of Minnesota Press, 1966.

Kann, Jean Marie, O.S.F. "Everything That Rises Must Converge," *The Catholic World*, CXCVI (December, 1966), 154–159.

Lochridge, Betsy. "An Afternoon with Flannery O'Connor," *Atlanta Journal and Constitution* (Nov. 1, 1959), pp. 38–40.

Martin, Carter W. *The True Country: Themes in the Fiction of Flannery O'Connor*. Nashville, Tenn.: Vanderbilt University Press, 1969.

Meaders, Margaret. "Flannery O'Connor: 'Literary Witch,' " *Colorado Quarterly*, X (Spring, 1962), 377–86.

Meyers, Sister Bertrand, D.C. "Four Stories of Flannery O'Connor," *Thought*, XXXVII (Autumn, 1962), 410–26.

"Motley Special: An Interview with Flannery O'Connor," *Motley* [Spring Hill College, Mobile, Alabama], (Spring, 1959), pp. 29–31.

Muller, Gilbert H. "The City of Woe: Flannery O'Connor's Dantean Vision," *The Georgia Review*, XXIII (Summer, 1969), 206–213.

Mullins, C. Ross. "Flannery O'Connor: An Interview," *Jubilee*, XI (June, 1963), 32–35.

"Peabodite Reveals Strange Hobby," *Peabody Palladium* [Peabody High School Newspaper, Milledgeville, Ga.], December 16, 1941.

Reiter, Robert (ed.). *Flannery O'Connor*. St. Louis: B. Herder Co., n.d.

Sayers, Dorothy L. *Christian Letters to a Post-Christian World*. Grand Rapids: William B. Eerdmans Publishing Co., 1969.

Sherry, Gerard. "An Interview with Flannery O'Connor," *The Critic*, XXI (June/July, 1963), 29–31.

Sibley, Celestine. Obituary of Flannery O'Connor, *Atlanta Constitution*, August 6, 1964, p. 5.

Stern, Richard. "Flannery O'Connor: A Remembrance and Some Letters," *Shenandoah*, XVI (Winter, 1965), 5–10.

Tate, James O. "A Reminiscence." An unpublished essay in the library of the Georgia State College at Milledgeville.

Turner, Margaret. "Visit to Flannery O'Connor Proves a Novel Experience," *Atlanta Journal and Constitution* (May 29, 1960), p. 2G.

Woodward, C. Vann. *The Burden of Southern History*. Baton Rouge: Louisiana State University Press, 1960.

Zuber, Leo J. Letter to Sister M. Kathleen Feeley, SSND, June 22, 1969.

Index